RACING POST
ANNUAL 2020

Racing Post Floor 7, The Podium, South Bank Tower Estate, 30 Stamford Street, London, SE1 9LS. 0203 034 8900
Irish Racing Post The Capel Building, Mary's Abbey, Dublin 7. 01 828 7450

Editor Nick Pulford
Art editor David Dew
Cover design Samantha Creedon
Chief photographers Edward Whitaker, Patrick McCann
Other photography Dan Abraham, Tom Bolwell & Mattia Reiniger/ Great British Racing, Connors, Mark Cranham, Getty, John Grossick, Caroline Norris, PA, Tracy Roberts
Picture artworking David Cramphorn, Liam Hill, Stefan Searle, Shane Tetley
Graphics Stefan Searle
Feature writers Richard Birch, Scott Burton, David Carr, Graham Dench, Andrew Dietz, Richard Forristal, Jonathan Harding, David Jennings, Lee Mottershead, Tony O'Hehir, Lewis Porteous, Nick Pulford, John Randall, Brian Sheerin, Alan Sweetman, Peter Thomas, Joe Tuffin, Robbie Wilders

Advertisement Sales
Racing Post: Floor 7, The Podium, South Bank Tower Estate, 30 Stamford Street, London, SE1 9LS. 0203 034 8900. Charlie Allen, charlie.allen@racingpost.com

Archant Dialogue
Advertising Sales
Gary Millone, 01603 772463, gary.millone@archantdialogue.co.uk
Advertising Production Manager
Kay Brown, 01603 772522, kay.brown@archantdialogue.co.uk
Prospect House, Rouen Road, Norwich NR1 1RE. 01603 772554
archantdialogue.co.uk

Distribution/availability
01933 304858 help@racingpost.com

Published by Racing Post Books
27 Kingfisher Court, Hambridge Road, Newbury, Berkshire RG14 5SJ

ISBN 978-1-83950-018-3 [UK]
ISBN 978-1-83950-019-0 [Ireland]

Printed in Great Britain by Buxton Press. Every effort has been made to fulfil requirements with regard to copyright material. The author and publisher will be glad to rectify any omissions at the earliest opportunity.

racingpost.com/shop

THIS year's Racing Post Annual cover salutes the group of people who had us on the edge of ou[r seats,] had us laughing, crying, cheering, biting our nails, trembling with excitement, willing them on to great triumphs.

Those emotions are not unusual in racing. We are blessed to follow a sport where spine-tingling moments are never far away. They are the moments that make us feel we are part of something special.

But the fantastic power of our superheroes was that they took those moments beyond racing in 2019; they made the wider public feel the magic too. In their deeds, but also their words, these exceptional people showed everyone how great racing can be.

One dictionary says a superhero has supernormal powers – defined as "beyond what is normal; in greater number, amount etc than the normal".

Frankie Dettori and Ruby Walsh, two of our cover stars, built their careers on going beyond the normal, burning so deep into our consciousness that they are known by their first names.

But if we say other names from 2019, we will all remember the days when Bryony, Hayley and Rachael illuminated our sport so brightly. And there was also Khadijah, who lit up Goodwood with a beaming smile and a historic first when she rode a race in a hijab – and won.

It was not just racing's people who took the sport beyond the normal. Enable and Tiger Roll, two more of our cover stars from an incredible year on the track, also burst out of racing's bubble with their mighty feats. They could achieve even more in 2020.

We are lucky to have them. Every single one of them.

Nick Pulford

Nick Pulford
Editor

CONTENTS

BIG STORIES

FINAL FURLONG

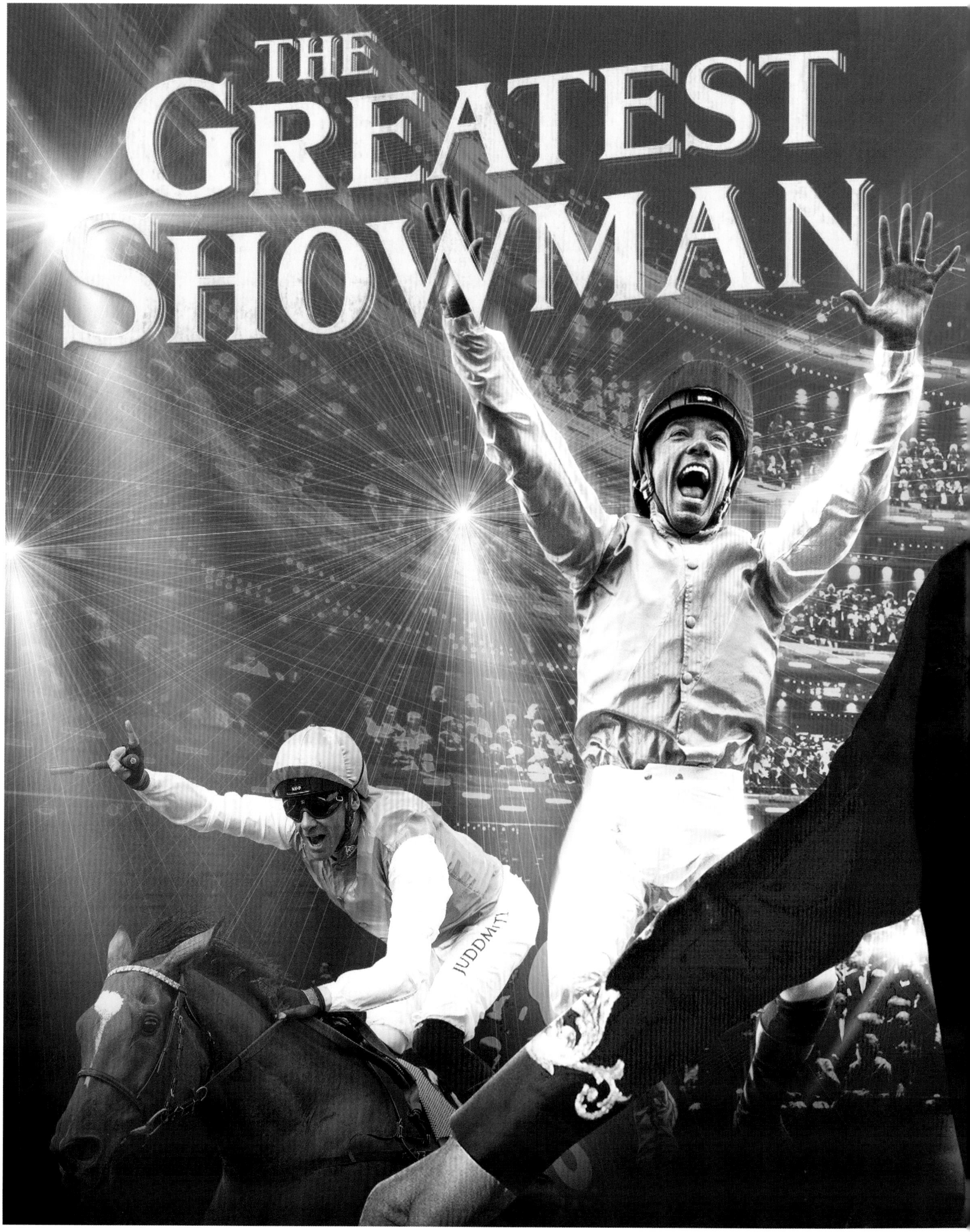

THE GREATEST SHOWMAN

Frankie Dettori, for so long racing's brightest star, took centre stage again in an incredibly successful season

By Lee Mottershead

THERE is no one bigger in the world of horseracing than Frankie Dettori. In 2019 there was no one better. As a 48-year-old veteran of his sport, he enjoyed the most successful season of a career that is now well over three decades old. Group 1 races were mopped up at unprecedented speed but with characteristic flair and brilliance. Not that long ago we feared he was finished. He probably feared the same. We were all wrong, for not since Leonardo da Vinci has an Italian enjoyed a finer renaissance.

The equine work of art with which Dettori will now always be most associated is Enable. He has never spoken about a horse like he spoke about her, nor does he believe he has ever ridden a better thoroughbred. His love for the wondermare shone through in words and deeds. From the moment attention switched from jumping to the Flat, the year's narrative was a one-way road to Enable's bid for Arc history, yet she was far from the only treasured partner in Dettori's campaign. There was supreme stayer Stradivarius, crack miler Too Darn Hot and a clutch of fillies and mares who, while not

▸▸ *Continues page 6*

quite in Enable's class, proved more than good enough to claim yet more top-flight glory for their rider.

The leading ladies, along with Stradivarius and Too Darn Hot, were trained by John Gosden, the man who saved Dettori by appointing him stable jockey during a telephone conversation late in 2014 that began with Gosden saying: "Hello matey, I've got a plan."

He had a plan that saved Dettori once before, albeit in not quite such dramatic circumstances, after the Sardinian burned his bridges with Luca Cumani in 1993. Gosden stepped in and offered him the job of riding his Sheikh Mohammed-owned horses. In 2019, with much water having flowed under many bridges, Dettori was successful for Gosden in a Group race wearing what used to be the sheikh's maroon and white silks – now attached to Sheikha Al Jalila Racing – aboard Fanny Logan. That was further evidence of the rapprochement between the Godolphin founder and his former Godolphin rider. "He is a great jockey," said Sheikh Mohammed in the Royal Ascot's winner's circle. At Ascot this year, as at Ascot in so many previous years, Dettori was greater than all his rivals.

****

THE first Group 1 of the year came at Epsom on May's final day when Dettori drove Anapurna to a neck success in the Oaks. On that occasion she was the Gosden stable's second string, returned at 8-1 in a market led by the trainer's Mehdaayih, whose owners stuck with Rab Havlin, her winning rider in three previous starts. Havlin endured a torrid time in the Classic, repeatedly finding himself short of room. Dettori encountered no such trouble. That afternoon at Epsom, and on numerous other afternoons to come, he was on the right horse, in the right place at the right time.

For Dettori there is no more important place than Ascot, especially over those five days in June when it stages the most famous Flat festival in the world. On its second afternoon he got off the mark for the meeting aboard Raffle Prize, whose Queen Mary Stakes victory came in the colours of Sheikh Mohammed's son Sheikh Hamdan. The race prizes were presented by Dame Darcey Bussell, who received one of Dettori's extravagant embraces on the presentation podium. For Sheikh Mohammed there was a respectful handshake but there were also smiles. "He was very pleased," Dettori said. So was winning trainer Mark Johnston, who dished out abundant praise when speaking to ITV's Oli Bell. "I was with you at the Highclere Ascot preview the other day," he told Bell. "You introduced Frankie Dettori as the greatest jockey with the exception of Lester Piggott. With no disrespect to Lester, is he [Frankie] not just the greatest jockey?"

He was great again later that Wednesday afternoon when joining forces with Sir Michael Stoute to win the Prince of Wales's Stakes aboard Crystal Ocean. It was the race in which Enable had at one point looked set to make her reappearance,

▲ First of many: Frankie Dettori starts the Group 1 ball rolling with Oaks victory for John Gosden on Anapurna

only for the point of return to be pushed back to the Coral-Eclipse.

"As soon as I knew Enable wasn't running I rang Michael's office the same morning," Dettori said. "I didn't get a yes that morning – but I got one in the afternoon!"

It had turned into a wonderful Wednesday for Dettori, yet he had been anything but chirpy earlier in the day, as his long-time manager Peter Burrell revealed on what turned into an unforgettable Thursday. "He was very grumpy," Burrell said. "For an hour and a half he wouldn't speak to me. We came as close to having a row as at any stage in 31 years. I can tell you the reason why it happened as well. He so wants it here."

It was not the first time Burrell had

▸▸ *Continues page 8*

OMAHA BEACH
VINO ROSSO
MAXIMUS MISCHIEF
COAL FRONT
MITOLE

seen Dettori grumpy. Dettori gets like that and Dettori would be the first to admit it. He would, in many ways, provide fascinating raw material for a psychological study, a feeling only strengthened by the comments of Gosden when interviewed for a Racing Post profile of Dettori later in the year.

"The first thing you have to realise is he is highly intelligent and extraordinarily instinctive, both with people and horses," Gosden said. "He's a very emotional person but he's good at disguising and hiding it. Like a lot of very talented people he hits highs and he hits lows. There have been very great performers who walked off stage and were immediately very different. Sometimes those people can withdraw a little into themselves. Frankie is no exception."

Yet he is exceptional, which he showed on day three of Royal Ascot, rattling off the first four winners. The third Group 1 of 2019 was landed on Stradivarius in the Gold Cup. The fourth, and Dettori's seventh winner of the meeting, was secured on the Martyn Meade-trained Advertise in Friday's Commonwealth Cup. The Saturday yielded only losers, but the man of the meeting was still buzzing, as he showed when rushing over to Charlie Appleby and giving the Godolphin trainer a big hug following Blue Point's success in the Diamond Jubilee Stakes. "What a legend," Appleby said as Dettori departed. As things turned out, the legend's year was only really just starting.

On June 30 he collected the Grand Prix de Saint-Cloud aboard Coronet. That made it a Group 1-winning weekend. The next in the calendar was a double Group 1-winning weekend, with Enable kicking things off with a sparkling return at Sandown and Too Darn Hot scoring on Sunday in the Prix Jean Prat. Now the year's Group 1 count stood at seven. Star Catcher turned seven into eight in the Irish Oaks. Seven days later it was Enable's turn again.

The King George VI and Queen Elizabeth Stakes of 2019 was a race for the ages. One month earlier Dettori had helped to make sure Crystal Ocean won a belated first Group 1. On this occasion he helped to make sure he did not win a second.

Ascot catches Frankie fever again

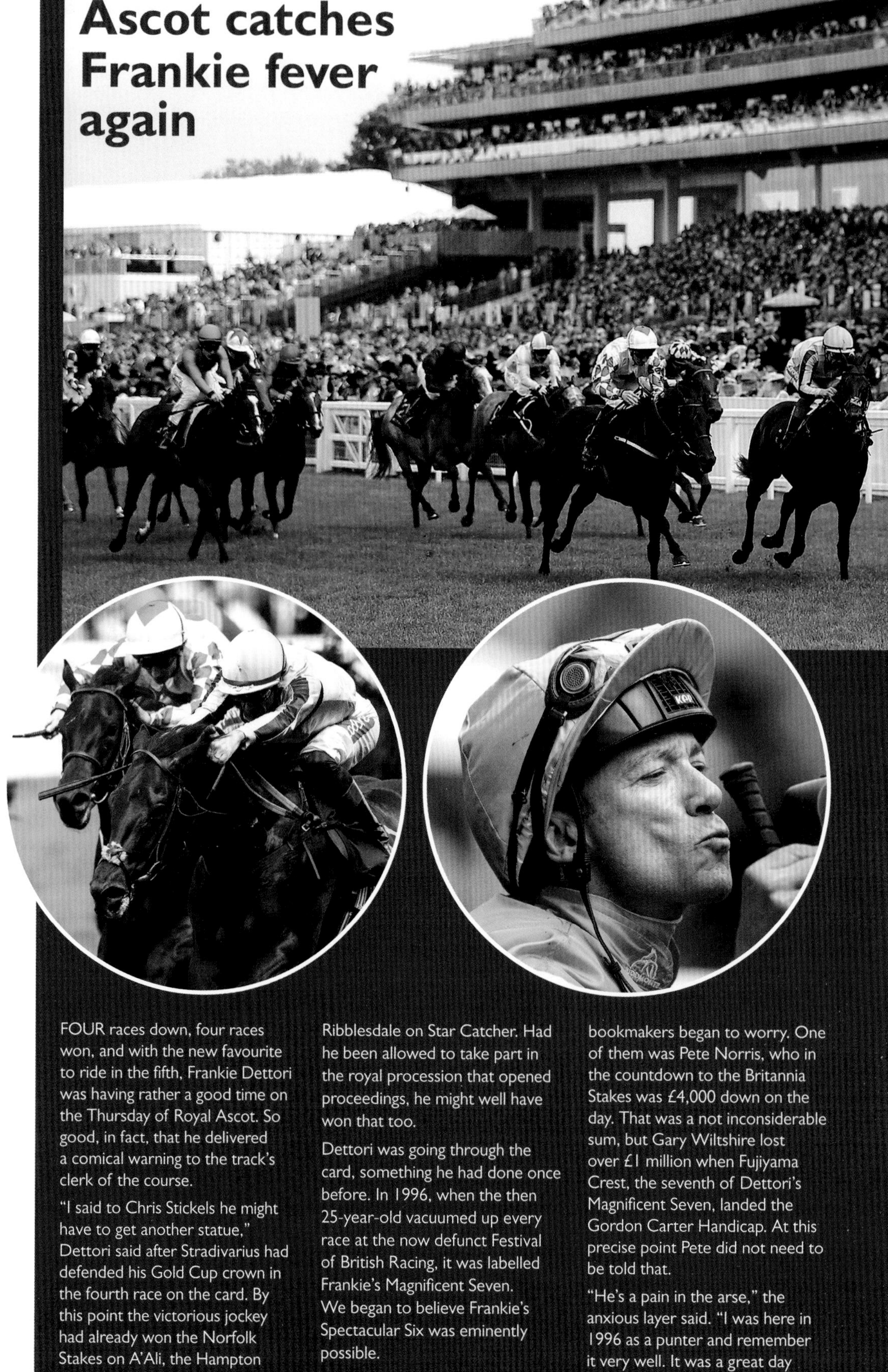

FOUR races down, four races won, and with the new favourite to ride in the fifth, Frankie Dettori was having rather a good time on the Thursday of Royal Ascot. So good, in fact, that he delivered a comical warning to the track's clerk of the course.

"I said to Chris Stickels he might have to get another statue," Dettori said after Stradivarius had defended his Gold Cup crown in the fourth race on the card. By this point the victorious jockey had already won the Norfolk Stakes on A'Ali, the Hampton Court on Sangarius and the Ribblesdale on Star Catcher. Had he been allowed to take part in the royal procession that opened proceedings, he might well have won that too.

Dettori was going through the card, something he had done once before. In 1996, when the then 25-year-old vacuumed up every race at the now defunct Festival of British Racing, it was labelled Frankie's Magnificent Seven. We began to believe Frankie's Spectacular Six was eminently possible.

As many of us began to believe, bookmakers began to worry. One of them was Pete Norris, who in the countdown to the Britannia Stakes was £4,000 down on the day. That was a not inconsiderable sum, but Gary Wiltshire lost over £1 million when Fujiyama Crest, the seventh of Dettori's Magnificent Seven, landed the Gordon Carter Handicap. At this precise point Pete did not need to be told that.

"He's a pain in the arse," the anxious layer said. "I was here in 1996 as a punter and remember it very well. It was a great day but this is a bit different. I'm on

▲ Fab four: Frankie Dettori lights up the third day of Royal Ascot with consecutive victories on (from left) A'Ali, Sangarius, Star Catcher and Stradivarius; below, the next day's front page of the Racing Post

the wrong side of the fence now. People are just backing him blind. They're coming over, asking what he's riding and then backing him. We could be going evens about this horse and they would still back him. They have no idea of value but they're still winning."

The horse in question was Turgenev. In the morning he had been available at 25-1 for the 28-runner Britannia. Come the off he was the 7-2 favourite. With two furlongs to run those odds seemed perfectly fair.

"And Frankie is leading!" shouted racecourse commentator Ian Bartlett as Turgenev surged clear. The grandstands erupted in excitement and the excitement lasted until a few strides from the line when Biometric did to Turgenev what Waldgeist subsequently did to Enable.

"It's one for the good guys," said bookmaker Dave Bow after a small but meaningful fist pump. On an extraordinary afternoon he had been saved from paying out a small fortune. For now, Ascot has also been saved from having to commission a second Dettori statue.

RACING POST

FANTASTIC FRANKIE

Dettori sets Royal Ascot alight as Gold Cup victory on Stradivarius caps an awesome foursome

In a pulsating piece of sporting theatre run at a furious gallop, Enable and Crystal Ocean slugged it out up Ascot's home straight. Crystal Ocean gave James Doyle everything he had. Enable gave Dettori that little bit more.

"What a race," said each of the two jockeys when asked for their thoughts. Dettori felt it evoked memories of the Grundy-Bustino showdown in 1975, although in the closing stages of this showdown it was obvious that Dettori, riding largely with hands and heels, was trying hard not to drain his willing ally. If she had anything left, Dettori did not. He was emotionally exhausted. The cold troubling him at the time was a factor. The race he had just ridden in was surely a bigger one.

The sneezing had stopped by the time Dettori was able to ease down Stradivarius in the final metres of the Goodwood Cup. Twenty-four hours later Too Darn Hot passed the same winning post in front to take the Sussex Stakes on what proved to be his final outing.

★★★★

DETTORI had locked away 11 Group 1 triumphs in the space of only 62 days, the last ten of them coming in just 43 days. To put the achievement in context, Ryan Moore has never won so many Group 1s in such a tight timescale, not even when in 2016 and 2017 he set and then equalled the record for a European-based Flat jockey of 22 Group/Grade 1 successes in one year.

Asked if he had ever experienced such a remarkable period, Dettori was adamant. "No!" he said. "It's not just any Group 1s. If you look at the list they are amazing, mammoth races, the King George, Eclipse and Gold Cup. They're proper Group 1s. I've had an amazing summer and long may it continue."

It continued, thanks hugely to Gosden. "Frankie was telling me the responsibility is too much," he said after the Sussex. "I told him: 'What's bad for you is sitting in that weighing room and not having a ride. Let me tell you, you're a showman and you love being here.'"

Dettori loved being at Deauville on August 4 when again teaming up with

▸▸ *Continues page 10*

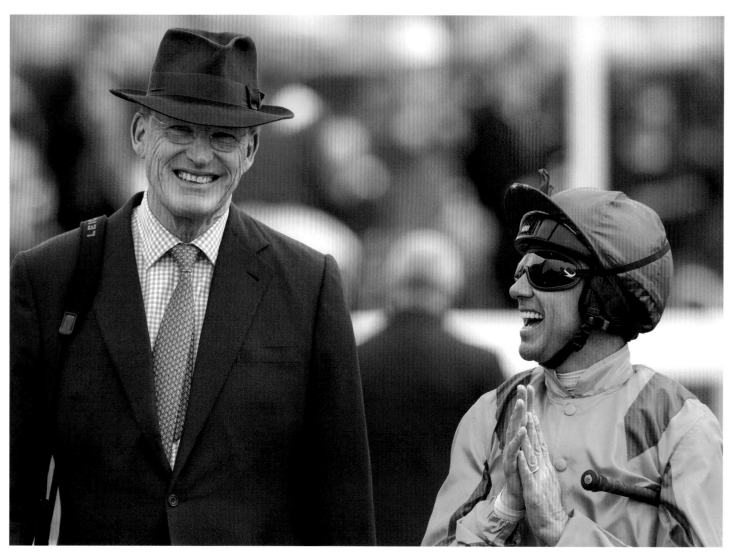

Advertise to pocket the Prix Maurice de Gheest, and on August 18, the day Coronet also doubled her Group 1 tally in the Prix Jean Romanet.

Two victories at the highest level is a fantastic achievement for a thoroughbred. Ten is extraordinary. Four days after Coronet's lucrative seaside excursion Enable went into Group 1 double figures in the Yorkshire Oaks, delighting the Knavesmire faithful and her adoring jockey, who was moved to tears by the experience, believing it was likely to be her final appearance on home soil.

In the handicap that preceded the Yorkshire Oaks, Dettori had been beaten a head into second. That was in the mind of the man with the Geordie accent who, as Enable's beau entered the paddock behind a security guard, shouted: "Forget about the last race, Frankie, forget about the last race." The man need not have worried. There had only ever been one race on Dettori's mind that day.

He won it, and after winning it he let his feelings show. "How embarrassing," he said. "I was crying out of happiness and because it's the last time we're going to see her in England." Just saying those words – which thankfully turned out to be wrong – left him choked once more. "Don't start me again," he said. "It was amazing – and what a reception."

It was indeed a fabulous reception. Dettori was afforded another when the red-hot St Leger favourite Logician became a Classic hero in the Enable colours of Khalid Abdullah. That was the 15th Group 1 of his jockey's year. With the scene switched from Doncaster to Longchamp 24 hours later, the 16th was brought up on Star Catcher in the Prix Vermeille. That equalled Dettori's personal best from 18 years earlier.

▲ Formidable team: Frankie Dettori and John Gosden cut a swathe through the European Group 1 season in 2019

▼ Dettori after another Group 1 success on Coronet in the Prix Jean Romanet at Deauville in August

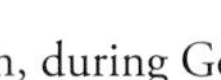

BACK then, during Godolphin's period of pomp, the season's highlight had been lifting the Arc on Sakhee. Dettori was desperate for his latest season's highlight to be lifting the Arc on Enable. For that reason he kept words to a minimum when, on Longchamp's Arc eve programme, his 17th Group 1 of 2019 was notched on Anapurna in the Prix de Royallieu. In Dettori's head all that day, just as it had been in his head all year long, was Enable's bid to become the first triple winner of Flat racing's most prestigious showpiece.

It was not to be, the pain made deeper by the fact the dream so very nearly came true. Prior to the contest that followed the Arc heartbreak, an amateur photographer took a picture of Gosden with his arm around the shoulders of Dettori. Both men had their heads down. Both bore

▸▸ *Continues page 12*

expressions that told the story better than words ever could. They looked devastated.

Dettori flew home and shed a tear, but when in the future he looks back on what happened to him in 2019, or more accurately what he helped to make happen, there will be smiles, not tears. After he locked away his 18th Group 1 of the year – and the 250th of his career – aboard Star Catcher on Qipco British Champions Day, there might even be some toasts.

Late in 2020 Dettori will turn 50. He has no intention of retiring before then, particularly following the glorious news that Enable will stay in training as a six-year-old. Given all he accomplished at 48, and the thrilling days that await him at 49, there is no reason why he should.

When Waldgeist galloped past Enable the sound was sucked out of Longchamp. Yet when Enable had paraded in front of the grandstands, and then again when the stalls crashed open, it was easy to hear the noise being made. It was a musical chant, one more associated these days with Jeremy Corbyn, but one that day devoted to racing's number-one name.

"Oh, Frankie Dettori," they sang. When you think about the man, his renaissance and annus mirabilis, "Oh, Frankie Dettori" just about sums it up.

Frankie's five most memorable wins of 2019

Crystal Ocean, Prince of Wales's Stakes, Royal Ascot, June 19
No horse deserved a Group 1 more than Sir Michael Stoute's stalwart, who duly had his day in 'the sun' when galvanised through the Ascot gloom on his one outing under Dettori

Stradivarius, Gold Cup, Royal Ascot, June 20
Caught in a pocket on the home turn, Stradivarius was moved into daylight two furlongs out and then asserted his brilliance to defend the stayers' crown

Enable, King George VI and Queen Elizabeth Qipco Stakes, Ascot, July 27
It was one of the great Flat duels, with Enable and Crystal Ocean scrapping furiously up the home straight, and at the end of the titanic struggle it was the mighty mare who prevailed by a neck

Too Darn Hot, Qatar Sussex Stakes, Goodwood, July 31
We never saw Too Darn Hot again but he left a fine impression on his farewell, swamping high-quality rivals for speed when asked to win his race

Logician, William Hill St Leger, Doncaster, September 14
The market expected and Frankel's son delivered, quickening smartly in the closing stages to give his jockey a sixth win in the Town Moor Classic

▲ Golden glow: from top, Frankie Dettori celebrates Stradivarius's Gold Cup repeat; all smiles after the St Leger; Too Darn Hot lands the Sussex Stakes; rain fails to dampen the mood following Crystal Ocean's Royal Ascot victory

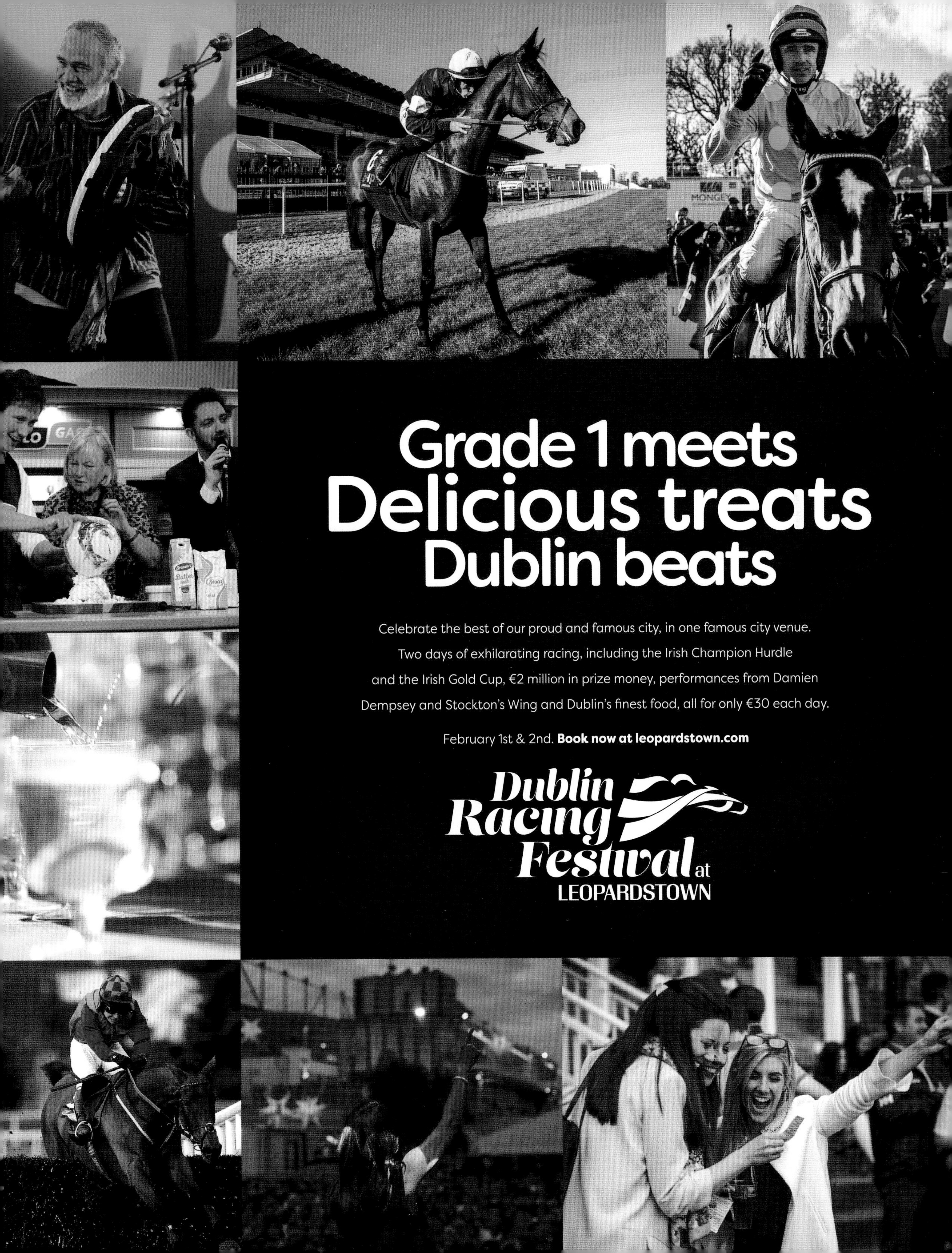
Grade 1 meets
Delicious treats
Dublin beats
Celebrate the best of our proud and famous city, in one famous city venue. Two days of exhilarating racing, including the Irish Champion Hurdle and the Irish Gold Cup, €2 million in prize money, performances from Damien Dempsey and Stockton's Wing and Dublin's finest food, all for only €30 each day.
February 1st & 2nd. Book now at leopardstown.com
Dublin Racing Festival at LEOPARDSTOWN

ECSTASY &AGONY

Enable and Frankie Dettori had a summer of love before autumn brought the pain of Arc defeat

By Peter Thomas

FOR those of us not in the first flush of youth – and these days that's a category that undeniably includes Frankie Dettori – it's less common than it used to be to find sporting moments that stir the senses, athletes who collide with our lives meaningfully enough to jolt the world just a little on its axis.

So when the seasoned Milanese declared of Enable – the latest in an exhilarating series of Group 1 performers that began in 1990 with Markofdistinction – "she's taken me places emotionally that I've never been before", we knew she must be the real thing.

The enduring 48-year-old even invoked the name of the great Brigadier Gerard – a horse who landed his 2,000 Guineas when Dettori was barely four months old – to emphasise the full breadth, depth and longevity of Enable's talent, at which point old-timers wondered if they should raise an objection on principle, then looked at her racing record and thought better of it.

Enable's astonishing run of Group 1 success ended when she was beaten into second in the Prix de l'Arc de Triomphe in October, but she has surely moved any racing man and woman with a measurable pulse throughout her three-year journey on the track, from Newcastle to Paris to Kentucky and back home again. Such is the honesty and ambition with which she has been campaigned by owner Khalid Abdullah and trainer John Gosden that she has reached out and touched a generation of racing fans, scarcely missing a target as her three seasons of top-level action have unfolded (not forgetting that Newcastle fillies' maiden win on her first run as a juvenile, for which she was mystifyingly allowed to go off 7-2 second favourite behind Dellaguista, who retired with a peak rating of 82).

That's the thing with Enable: for all her talent, she was no shining light in her early days and never a fizz-bang on the gallops, so a lot of what she had remained latent until she was asked to unleash it on the racecourse. Perhaps that's why, after two full seasons of high

▸▸ *Continues page 16*

achievement, we went into 2019 still with even higher expectations of what she might be capable of. She already had two Arcs under her saddle cloth, but she might manage three, we thought; those seven Group 1s could easily become ten, 11, even 12 at a push.

Connections had already served notice that they had no interest in hiding her considerable light under a bushel. If they were committing to another year on the racecourse – passing up the opportunity of a blue-blooded foal – there was no point doing it for the bare minimum of reward. Her owner didn't need the money, as far as we knew, but Enable's legacy was the carrot in her final season and we had a good idea where she was headed and when.

★★★★

NOT that all was plain sailing. A minor setback at home pushed back her reappearance date little by little until the Eclipse presented itself as a viable first option, even though it was over an inadequate mile and a quarter – the trip at which she had met her only defeat, behind a nippier stablemate, the Dettori-ridden Shutter Speed, at Newbury as a three-year-old.

Inevitably she started odds-on at Sandown and the inadequate distance proved no hindrance whatsoever as she was sent on two furlongs from home by Dettori and stayed on willingly to repel the bold challenge of Magical by a secure three-quarters of a length. The foundations had been laid, they looked sturdy enough to bear an ambitious final campaign and, with all the hard work done at home, the rest of the year seemed to slot into place of its own accord.

▼ Welcome back: Enable in front of her adoring public at Sandown following her seasonal debut in the Eclipse

▼ The Racing Post front page after Enable's successful return

RACING POST

TOO DARN HOT IN DEAUVILLE

WARREN GATLAND

A MESSAGE OF HOPE AFTER DARK TIMES

'She's special. I love her so much'

Dettori puts Enable top of his all-time list after awesome return in Eclipse

Pages 2-4

Next port of call was the King George VI and Queen Elizabeth Stakes, which in 2017 she had won in the kind of style that made the Ascot mud and rain look like a stroll in the park rather than a threat to her efficacy. That day she dismissed Ulysses by four and a half lengths; this time she was facing the live threat of Crystal Ocean, a Royal Ascot winner for Dettori the previous month and seemingly on the crest of a wave, and he served up to her perhaps the sternest test of her life. With a rating of 127, the Sir Michael Stoute-trained challenger was officially 2lb superior

▸▸ *Continues page 18*

Gosden keeps stars shining in glittering season

This was the year of Frankie Dettori, another year of Enable and Stradivarius, but behind them all it was the year of John Gosden too.

Gosden has become more accustomed to big-race victory in recent years and 2019 provided plenty more of that precious commodity. He was a powerful force all year, from Classics to the Cambridgeshire Handicap, and his handling of his biggest stars was as sure-footed as ever.

One example was the waiting game he played with Enable, whose return was held up in the spring until the trainer sensed she was ready to be unleashed in the Eclipse. "She's very competitive but that didn't really begin to show until the last 14 days, at which point suddenly the edge came back," he explained after the Eclipse. "Before that she was doing everything perfectly but the hunger wasn't there. She was just going through the motions. She wasn't concentrating but then she became fitter, quicker and sharper, just like a boxer. She suddenly went into the zone."

Gosden had 15 Group 1 successes in the European season, all of them in partnership with Dettori, and three were in Classics with Anapurna landing the Oaks at Epsom, Star Catcher taking the Irish version at the Curragh and Logician impressing in the St Leger at Doncaster. Too Darn Hot had been expected to be a Classic star but had a troubled spring before Gosden got him back to top form to land Group 1 wins in the Prix Jean Prat and Sussex Stakes.

On their incredibly successful partnership, Dettori said: "He's become a good mate as much as a father figure and in our working relationship we've always had great chemistry. It's got to the point where he has two jobs, to keep his horses happy and to keep me happy, but I work from the top and he works from the bottom and we work it out, and I'd say he's more patient than he was as a younger man. With another 20 years under his belt he's an even better trainer."

The proof is in the results.

to Enable but had to concede her 3lb, which promised a titanic tussle for the title of best middle-distance horse in the land. We were not to be disappointed.

Dettori, riding with the tactical genius of a senior statesman and the energy of a young pup, talked us through the race, with Norway setting a testing pace and Enable settled towards the rear. "I was drawn 13 of 13, the worst draw of the lot, and it was very obvious to me everybody was trying to keep me wide, so I had to go to Plan B – I didn't want to be as far back as I was but I didn't want to go six wide either.

"The first five horses didn't count and I figured all I had to look out for was Crystal Ocean, but unfortunately Pierre-Charles Boudot [on Waldgeist] had my spot and I had to sit and suffer behind him when really I wanted to be on the tail of James Doyle on my biggest rival.

"I know what the French horses are like, though. They've got one weapon, a one-furlong kick, so I knew Pierre was going to wait for the straight and I decided I'd kick earlier, get behind Crystal Ocean at the four. If you'd done that to an English horse, he'd have gone with you and kept you out, but he let me go as I knew he would, then I took his spot and it's game on, me and James.

"I asked her to go, kept the momentum going, and I thought I was going to go past him and put the race to bed, but he fought back and fought back again, and it was the hardest race I've been involved in. We locked horns and we both had to dig deep, but I only hit her once – after 30 years you do what your instincts tell you is best to keep your head in front. It really was just instinct – maybe I thought the ground was loose and she was giving me everything and just waving my stick was good enough to do the job, maybe another smack would have knocked her off balance.

"It was the right thing to do and she showed the kind of courage she'd maybe never had to show before. It was an amazing race and I never get tired of watching it. It showed what a great mare she is and how much British crowds love good horses. They clapped Crystal Ocean in, which says a lot."

Enable's best Group 1 run of each season

2017 Prix de l'Arc de Triomphe, Chantilly, October 1, Racing Post Rating 129
The 10-11 favourite gave the best performance of her life as she powered two and a half lengths clear of Cloth Of Stars, completing a six-race winning run that also included the King George

2018 Breeders' Cup Turf, Churchill Downs, November 3, RPR 124
Having won a second Arc in a tight finish at Longchamp, she made history as the first winner of that race to follow up at the Breeders' Cup, holding off Magical by three-quarters of a length

2019 Yorkshire Oaks, York, August 22, RPR 128
Her King George duel with Crystal Ocean was an epic, but just under four weeks later she was close to her peak in ratings terms, beating Magical by two and three-quarter lengths this time

For a moment the horse Gosden called "the people's mare" had looked under threat, but in the final desperate yards she dragged a little more from her locker and got the job done, not prettily but pretty damn well. With hindsight, perhaps we should have paid a little more attention to the proximity in third place of Waldgeist, but we weren't to know.

The next time we saw Enable on the racecourse, in the Yorkshire Oaks, the only thing being tested was Dettori's power of emotional restraint – a battle that was lost almost as soon as it began.

"I'm an emotional guy and I was choked up," he explained without the need for apology. It had been a bloodless victory on the Knavesmire, but the crowd turned it into a fond (albeit premature) farewell and when the rider realised the significance of the moment, he could barely contain himself.

"When Oli [Bell of ITV Racing] said this was the last time we'd see her in England, I thought 'oh ****, maybe it's true'. I couldn't get the words out. Every time I tried to say something I felt I was going to cry, tears of happiness for all we've achieved together.

"There's been a lot of circus around her but rightly so. We've got to make a fuss about these horses because they don't come round very often and she's the best in the world."

▲ Her majesty: from top, Enable reigns in the 2017 Arc, the 2018 Breeders' Cup Turf and the 2019 Yorkshire Oaks

▼ How the Racing Post reported Enable's King George and York wins

RACING POST
EPIC ENABLE

RACING POST
QUEEN IN THE NORTH
York hails sensational Enable
THE MAIN PERFORMANCE
AND NOT PLAYING SECOND FIDDLE

****

IN TRUTH, we have been lucky that Dettori was the man paired with perhaps the best racemare we have seen in a lifetime. In different hands, she could have turned out to be a great racehorse with a high BHA rating and a cupboard full of silverware, but in the effusive Italian's hands she has metamorphosed into a precious jewel in racing's crown, a worldwide superstar with the ability to transcend national boundaries, unite the uninitiated and the

▸▸ *Continues page 20*

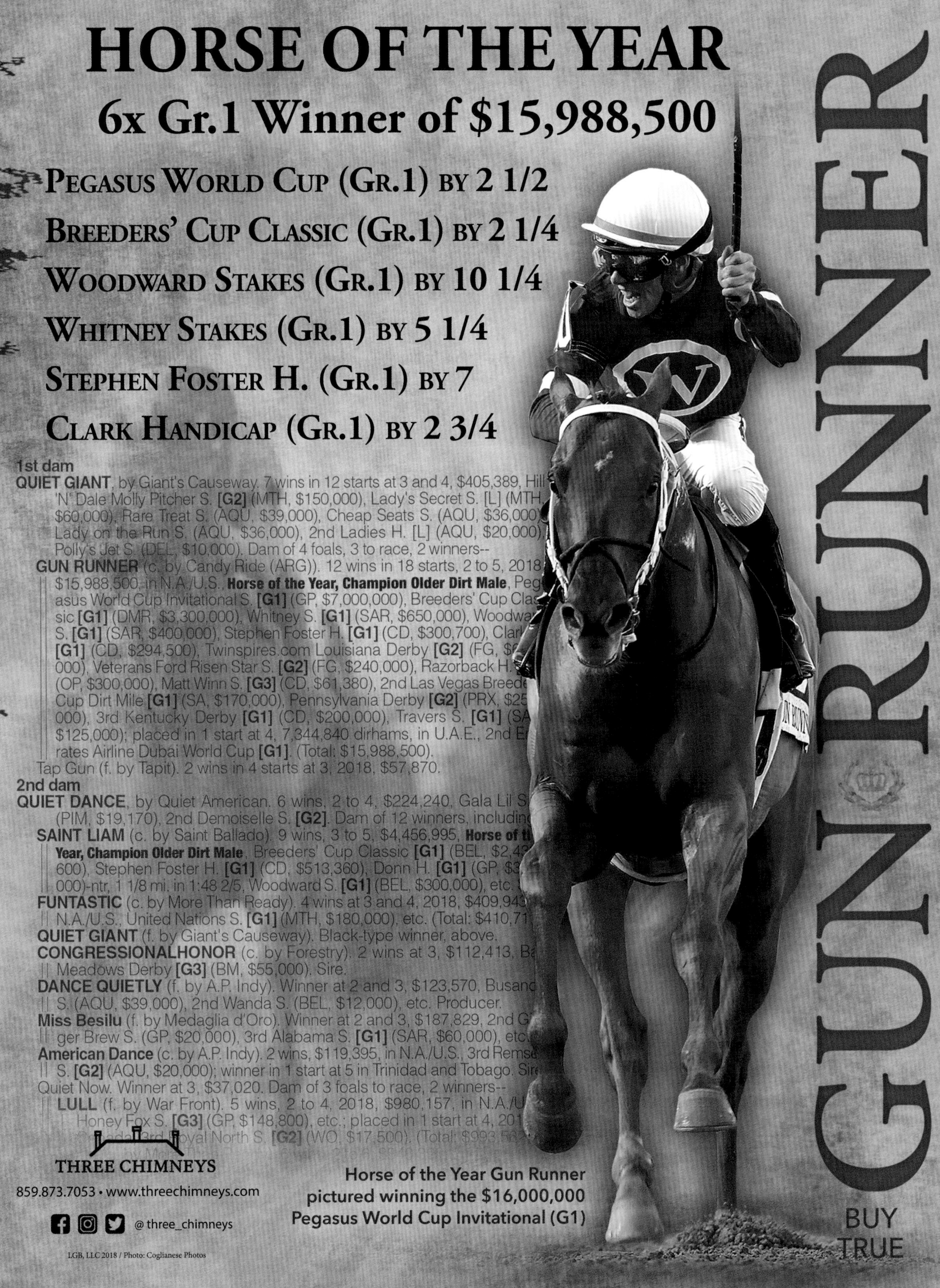

Horse of the Year Gun Runner pictured winning the $16,000,000 Pegasus World Cup Invitational (G1)

aficionado and whip up a storm wherever she goes.

It has been the perfect marriage of ability and attitude that has won her the love of the racing world, but without Dettori to orchestrate the pandemonium there would have been far less outreach to the universe that chooses to exist – for reasons best known to itself – on the indifferent fringes of the Turf.

Sadly, but not tragically, it was when most eyes were on her, when her magnetism and the allure of the Arc combined to capture the attention of Europe and beyond, that her aura of invincibility finally fractured.

The build-up to what threatened to be an unprecedented third success had been feverish. Dettori spoke of the draining nature of the media attention but, as ever, fielded it with a showman's flair. "She's the best in the world," he reassured us, "but make no mistake, this is no penalty kick. She's doing something that's never been done before and she has to bring her A-game, has to get a good draw, get some luck. It's going to be hard."

How right he was. We were worried about the ground: 'tres souple' was how the French described it, but that sounded far too polite to do justice to the mud that splattered the undercard. We hoped she would still be on her mettle at the end of what had been a short, three-race season, and she was, but not quite in the same way as before.

Facing a field of just 11 rivals, she was never far away from the pace and, when she kicked past the leader Ghaiyyath two furlongs from home, leaving Sottsass and Japan chasing shadows, she looked bound for history. From further back, however, came Waldgeist, fourth in the 2018 Arc and now launching what soon became clear was a murderous challenge for this one.

As he powered past Enable, we knew the dream was over. It was Andre Fabre, with his eighth Arc win, who made the history and it was Waldgeist, another five-year-old, who was the best horse on the day, but Enable and her reputation were in no way lessened by the loss. She had been sent into a battle she had no need to fight, in which the odds had moved against her, but that was the way she

▲ Centre of attention: Enable fans out in force at Longchamp; below, the great mare at York

had always been campaigned and it would have been no time for her owner and trainer to start hiding behind the sofa.

An athlete's worth is judged in victory, not diminished by defeat, and her career has been forged with that oft-ignored sporting reality in mind. Running away from a challenge has never been the way of Enable and because of that we have got to know every glorious inch of this wonderful mare and her almost boundless talent.

In a move that evokes astonishment and gratitude in equal measure, Abdullah and Gosden have decided she should race on as a six-year-old – in the bold tradition of the likes of Winx and Black Caviar, Dahlia and Goldikova – and that means we will have a few more chances to savour her magnificence. Perhaps more records will come her way – maybe even that elusive third Arc – but what she has done already is surely enough for any lifetime.

'Come on Enable'

Nine days after Enable's Arc defeat came the good news that she will be around again in 2020 to have another go.

The decision to keep her in training as a six-year-old was reached only after careful deliberation, as Khalid Abdullah's racing manager Teddy Grimthorpe explained.

"We gave her a good MOT and she passed that cleanly," he said. "Her wellbeing is going to be paramount in all of this. She's not going to be asked to do anything she's not asking to do herself.

"She's always been, I think vocal is almost the right word. She tells you when she's happy, tells you when she's had enough of you, she tells you when she wants to eat and wants to work and how she wants to work. Her powers of communication are pretty good."

Grimthorpe said the Enable team had started with the 2020 Arc and worked back from there, asking themselves key questions. "What are the opportunities and targets if we keep her in training? Is it going to be more of the same, something different, is it going to be something new? All those things come into play and obviously the unfinished business of a third Arc de Triomphe was certainly a very important part of this."

Trainer John Gosden said: "It's a typically sporting and positive decision from Prince Khalid. It's wonderful for her to be racing next year."

Frankie Dettori, who had been crestfallen after Enable's Arc defeat, was delighted by the news, saying: "My girl is staying in training for next year. I can't wait. Come on Enable."

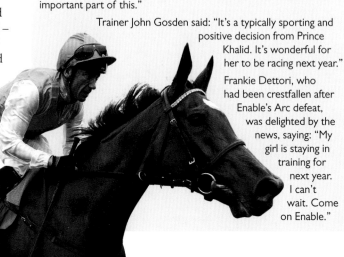

By Lewis Porteous

REPEAT BUSINESS

Stradivarius dominated the Flat staying division again by landing the £1m bonus for the second year running

SO MUCH for once bitten, twice shy. Weatherbys Hamilton, the insurance arm of the historic family firm, once again put its money on the line at the start of the Flat season, offering a £1m stayers' bonus, and once again a remarkable little horse snatched all the booty. In completing what was deemed an impossible quest not once but twice, Stradivarius confirmed himself the best stayer of his generation and invited comparison with the all-time greats.

It is open to argument where the dual Gold Cup and triple Goodwood Cup winner ranks against the stars from the last golden age of stayers in the late 1970s and early 1980s, but what is not in doubt is that Stradivarius dwarfs them all in terms of earnings and perhaps beats them in the popularity stakes too. Stayers on the Flat often win a special place in the affections of racing fans for their longevity and fighting qualities and Stradivarius's following has grown with every mighty deed. As Frankie Dettori put it: "He has got the heart of a lion and the people love him. There's a lot of pressure riding him, but when you're on him he's a joy to ride." And a joy to watch too.

****

STRADIVARIUS defied the odds to land four bonus races – the Yorkshire Cup, Gold Cup, Goodwood Cup and Lonsdale Cup – at the first attempt in 2018 and he started the new season as the dominant force in the staying division, having completed a perfect campaign by also taking the Long Distance Cup on British Champions Day. That might have been enough to put off most bonus sponsors but Weatherbys Hamilton came back swinging, laying another £1 million on the table while potentially increasing the difficulty of landing the bonus by adding more starting points.

Although the final three legs – Gold Cup, Goodwood Cup and Lonsdale Cup – remained

» *Continues page 24*

sky b

compulsory to winning the bonus, the choice of opening race for bounty hunters was doubled from four to eight in 2019, with the Dubai Gold Cup at Meydan, Vintage Crop Stakes at Navan, International Oleander-Rennen at Berlin-Hoppegarten and Prix Vicomtesse Vigier at Longchamp joining the existing list of four British qualifying races.

More qualifying races meant four more potential challengers would be standing in the path of Stradivarius at Royal Ascot in June, assuming he too had won one of the initial races to put himself in the bonus hunt, but any cunning plan proved futile in the end. Stradivarius was just too good for all his rivals for the second year running.

Rated a 50-1 shot for the bonus when it was first tabled the previous year, John Gosden's five-year-old was just 11-2 for the clean sweep this time and 4-5 to come through his qualifying race with a repeat win in the Yorkshire Cup. Six of his seven rivals at York were four-year-olds, including Southern France, who dwarfed the favourite in the preliminaries and gave him a fight on the track, but Stradivarius was comfortably on top at the finish, becoming the first dual Yorkshire Cup winner since Ardross in 1982.

"He was a bit rusty and it turned into a bit of a sprint," Dettori said. "Once he was upsides there was only going to be one winner. He's got me out of trouble so many times and he just sticks his head down and gets the job done. He's a joy to have around. He's a great horse – he's not flash but he's a fighter."

Gosden made clear he had left plenty in the tank for Ascot, where the Gold Cup over two and a half miles awaited in leg two of the bonus series, but the lure of the £1m certainly seemed to have the desired effect and it was not just the connections of Stradivarius whose big-money dreams were still alive at the royal meeting.

Dee Ex Bee, runner-up in the previous year's Derby, was starting to look a big threat to the reigning champ, having collected two qualifying races with wins in the Sagaro Stakes at Ascot and Henry II Stakes at Sandown. Just behind him in the betting was Melbourne Cup

and Dubai Gold Cup hero Cross Counter, a big player if he could see out the extra half-mile at Ascot. Joseph O'Brien had also got a whiff of the money, fielding Vintage Crop winner Master Of Reality, and French challenger Called To The Bar had his shot at the jackpot after winning the Prix Vicomtesse Vigier.

If there was a sense Stradivarius had been a little rusty at York, he was finely tuned at Ascot and was more than up to the task. Briefly the even-money favourite looked like he might be trapped early in the straight but those on his outside simply lacked the gears to keep him hemmed in and the race was over in strides once he slipped the net.

"He's an amazing horse," Dettori gushed after his trademark flying dismount. "He has won two Ascot Gold Cups – his heart is bigger than his body. He doesn't know how to lose. All I have to do is get him among other horses and he does the rest – what a horse. For a stayer, this lad has everything. He loves getting into a fight and he's brilliant to ride."

Continues page 26

How Stradivarius measures up

Stradivarius has been a star of the sport for two seasons – but is he a great champion?

Hype merchants, who think that anything half a per cent above average is "great", see no need even to ask the question. But rational observers think otherwise, and their answer would be negative.

Quantity and quality are the two sharply contrasting ways to assess champions. Stradivarius, with a string of Cup races to his credit, may qualify for the equine pantheon on the score of quantity, but true greatness is about quality, and ratings are by far the best method of measuring it.

In the 1999 book A Century of Champions, Tony Morris and I nominated Alycidon, the 1949 stayers' triple crown winner, as the greatest stayer of the post-war era with a rating of 137.

On the similar Racing Post Ratings scale, Stradivarius is rated only 123 and it is possible to argue that, like Yeats *(below)* and all the other recent prolific Cup winners, he is not even a top-class horse, let alone a great one.

Yeats (RPR 126) is the only horse to win the Gold Cup four times, yet during his monopoly there were times when he was not even the best stayer at Ballydoyle (Septimus was).

No recent stayer can compare with the stars of the last golden age of stayers between 1975 and 1982 – Sagaro, Buckskin, Le Moss and Ardross, who were all in the 132-133 range.

The reason is that, for commercial reasons, most of the best potential stayers no longer run in staying events. The top stayer is consistently the lowest-rated champion in the official world rankings.

Let us celebrate Stradivarius for his many qualities, rather than hype him for what he is not – a great champion.

JOHN RANDALL

Also keen to play on the stayer's fighting qualities, Gosden said: "He'd be a dangerous person to bring with you on a night out. He'd pick a fight with someone who is ten foot taller than him at the bar. He'd probably win too, because he's quick."

★★★★

WITH a sense of history repeating, it was now only Stradivarius who could land the bonus and it was hard to see who was going to stop him at Goodwood or York. That is not to say leg three, the Goodwood Cup, was a substandard renewal. Far from it, with Dee Ex Bee, Cross Counter and Southern France all back for another crack even though their bonus chances had evaporated.

Dettori relied on his partner's speed this time, producing his mount from the shadows of his rivals inside the last two furlongs before outsprinting them to the line. The winning rider even allowed himself time to celebrate in the last 50 yards and that probably had something to do with an official margin of just a neck over Dee Ex Bee, which did no justice to the gulf between them.

"I may have celebrated ten yards too soon but I knew I had it won," Dettori said. "What a beautiful little horse. He felt magnificent. With Stradivarius all you have to do is put him in the fight because he'll come out on top."

An eighth consecutive win left owner-breeder Bjorn Nielsen considering Stradivarius's place among great stayers like Ardross, Le Moss, Buckskin and Sagaro, who all left a lasting impression on him as a youngster.

"He's the best horse around today at that trip and just to be compared to them is a great thing," Nielsen said in the winner's enclosure at Goodwood. "It's unreal and I'm just so lucky. Breeding requires an incredible amount of luck to turn up a horse like him and I've had that luck."

With Stradvarius so dominant and winning in different ways, the opposition had melted away by the time he came to the Lonsdale Cup. He had just three rivals for the final leg and, considering Dee Ex Bee was the shortest-priced of them, there was a sense of inevitability about the result, even if Stradivarius was conceding 3lb to his old rival.

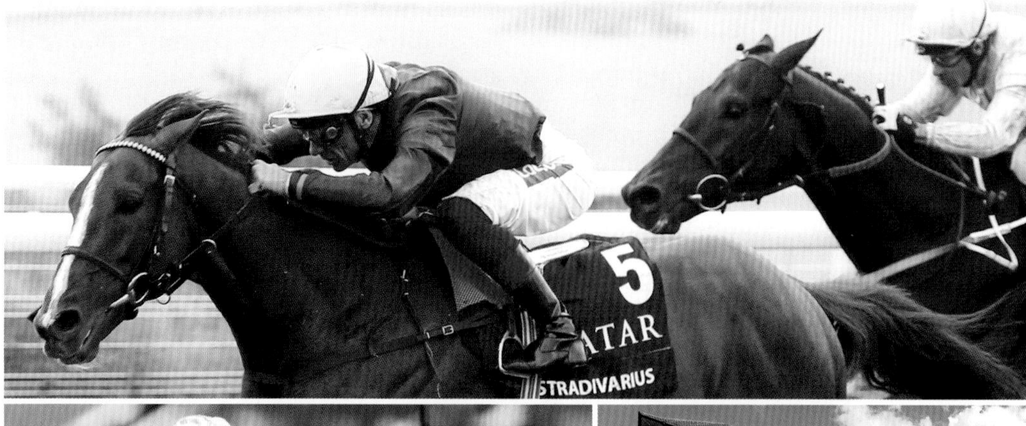

▲ Winning sequence: clockwise from top, Stradivarius and Frankie Dettori score at Goodwood, York and Doncaster following victories (previous page) in the Yorkshire Cup and Gold Cup

▼ The run comes to an end when Kew Gardens beats him by a nose in the British Champions Long Distance Cup at Ascot in October

There was nothing flash on the Knavesmire, yet Stradivarius was utterly dominant as he skipped clear along the inside rail and on to his second bonus, to be split between his owner-breeder, trainer, jockey and the stable staff at Gosden's yard. Victory made it nine wins on the bounce for Stradivarius, leaving connections to pay homage to a magnificent stayer.

"He's a bit like his jockey. He's quite full of himself but at the same time he's a professional. You've got to make him happy and then he'll perform for you," Gosden said.

Including his bonuses, Stradivarius had taken his career prize-money earnings to £4.4 million at York, a phenomenal figure for any racehorse but even more impressive given that he's slogging it out over a staying distance each time.

He didn't stop at York, winning the Doncaster Cup three weeks later to stretch his winning run to ten, but then he was stopped finally when Kew Gardens outstayed him by a nose on testing ground in the Long Distance Cup at Ascot in October.

That denied Stradivarius a second consecutive perfect season but connections shrugged off the defeat. "We were brave to run him but that's not his ground," Gosden said. "He's run an absolute blinder – there's no disgrace in going down by a nose."

Nielsen vowed he would return in 2020 and Kew Gardens – who was being trained for the Gold Cup earlier in the season before being injured – could be back to renew rivalry.

Less likely to return is the £1m bonus, with Hamilton seemingly waving the white flag at York. "To use a prize-fighter analogy, we took on Stradivarius over four rounds last year and were floored. We staggered to our feet, took him on over another four rounds this year and were floored again. Realistically, we have to declare this fight over, and if Stradivarius stays in training it would be difficult to justify carrying on with the bonus."

Gosden's gladiator is more than a bar-room brawler, that's for sure. He is all class, a prizefighter of the highest order.

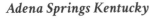

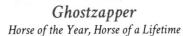

IN THE PICTURE

Piggott's feats immortalised in series of statues

LESTER PIGGOTT'S exploits were recognised across Britain in 2019 with a series of lifesize bronze statues of the legendary jockey.

Perhaps the most fitting monument was unveiled by the Queen on Derby day next to the Epsom winner's enclosure. Piggott holds the Derby record with nine wins and the statue was unveiled almost 65 years to the day after the first of them, Never Say Die in 1954. He was also victorious on Crepello (1957), St Paddy (1960), Sir Ivor (1968), Nijinsky (1970), Roberto (1972), Empery (1976), The Minstrel (1977) and Teenoso (1983).

The Queen was at Epsom for all of Piggott's Derby victories, and in 1957 he rode Carrozza to Oaks success in the royal colours.

Piggott, 83, pictured at the unveiling, said: "I think it has been a great idea – it's marvellous and I'm honoured. I had seen the statue before today and it's very good."

The Epsom statue was the first of nine bronzes by sculptor William Newton to be unveiled in 2019. Other sites included Ascot, in recognition of Piggott's record 116 victories at the royal meeting, and outside the weighing room at York, which was the jockey's favourite track.

Newton said: "I first met with Lester when he was the subject and inspiration for the Derby trophy I made in 2002, so to be asked to create these very special lifesize bronzes is for me just about as important as it gets."

In the same week as the York statue was unveiled, Piggott was honoured in his home town of Wantage, where he was the first boy born in the local hospital, on November 5, 1935. A statue was sited at the town's Vale and Downland Museum to mark the start of a 'Born To Ride' exhibition celebrating Piggott's life and career.

The statues project began with an idea from journalist Neil Morrice, who was joined by Geoffrey Hughes, director of Osborne Studio Gallery in London, and journalist Brough Scott. The statues were commissioned by David and Christopher St George, for whose family Piggott rode many top-class horses including dual Gold Cup winner Ardross.

Scott said: "Everyone forgets, and quite soon everyone may even forget Lester Piggott. This project is to ensure that they don't."

Popularly known as 'The Long Fellow', Piggott had 4,493 career wins – including a record 30 Classics in Britain – and was British champion jockey 11 times.

Picture: EDWARD WHITAKER (RACINGPOST.COM/PHOTOS)

Investec
DERBY
JOCKEY CLUB ROOM
William Newton Esq
Saturday
1st June 2019

Tiger Roll became the first double winner of the Grand National since Red Rum and set up the chance to join the Aintree icon as a hat-trick scorer

GRAND DESIGNS

By Alan Sweetman

THERE will never be another 'Rummy' but in Tiger Roll we have a horse to stand close to Ginger McCain's iconic hero. Having won the Randox Health Grand National for the second time last April, the Gordon Elliott-trained Tiger Roll now has the chance to eclipse Red Rum as a three-in-a-row winner of the great race.

Red Rum, who scaled unparalleled heights in five consecutive Aintree appearances between 1973 and 1977, will never be equalled in terms of his public profile and his impact on the National, a race he helped to save from extinction. Over the years his feat of winning two consecutive Nationals had not been equalled, having proved beyond the likes of Aldaniti, Don't Push It and Many Clouds, and the legend of his hat-trick – finally achieved at the age of 12 after two gallant second places – only grew with the passage of time.

Tiger Roll now has his own place in National history after becoming the first since Rummy to land back-to-back Nationals. The last to do it before that was Reynoldstown in 1935-36 and you have to delve way back into Victorian times to find any others.

Fame plays out in different ways as history moves on. Red Rum became part of the furniture of 1970s Britain, a celebrity who opened supermarkets and made TV appearances. These days, if Tiger Roll continues to work his way into the public consciousness he may become a meme for the Love Island generation.

▸▸ *Continues page 32*

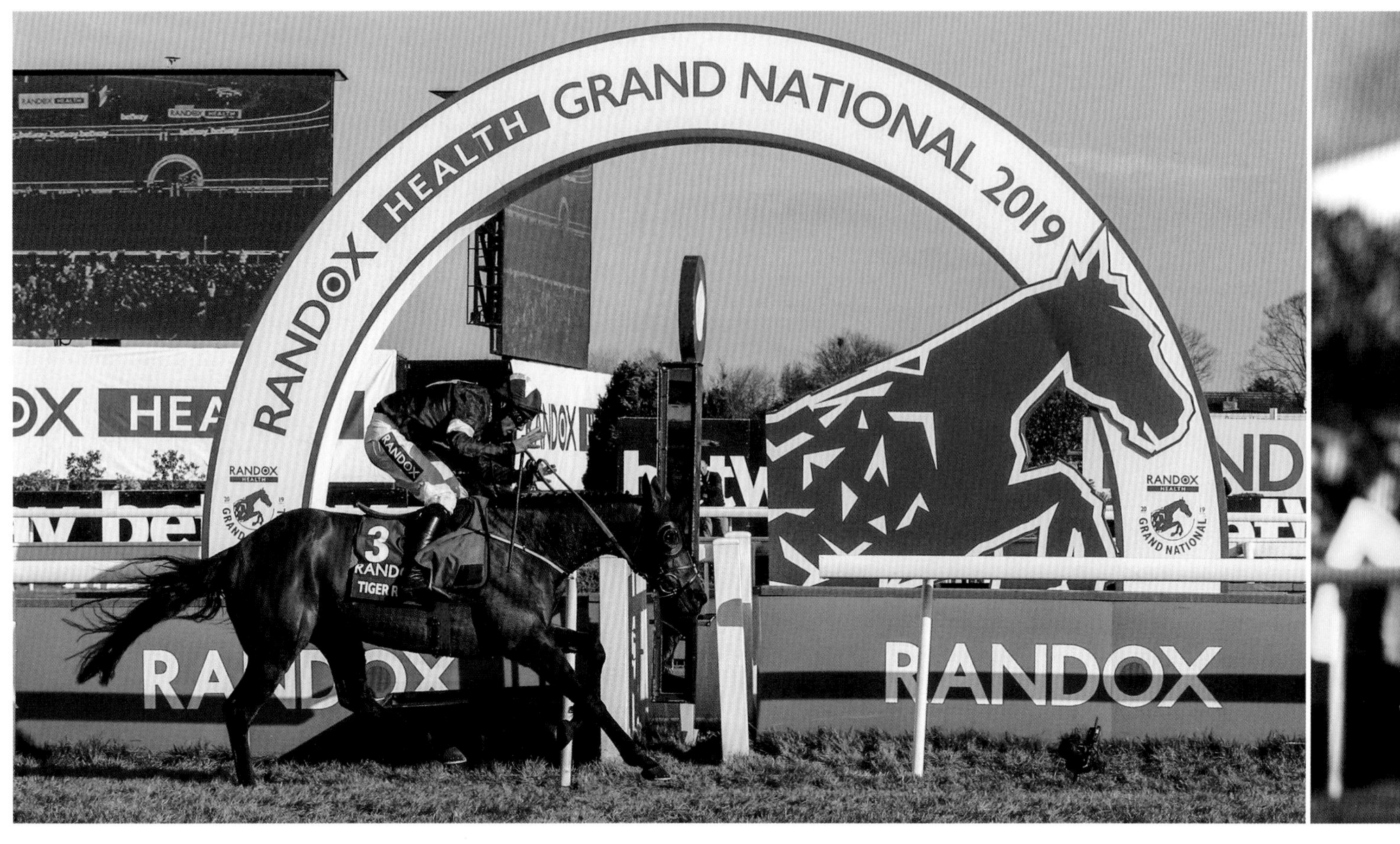

▲ In command: Tiger Roll passes the post for his second National win, more comfortable than the first; right, Davy Russell stands tall as he celebrates their back-to-back successes; below right, owner Michael O'Leary, who later announced a major reduction in his Gigginstown House Stud operation

Things are radically different too in the wider sporting landscape and at Aintree, where the famous fences have long since lost their brutally unforgiving aspect. And yet the National still presents a formidable challenge in terms of stamina, of courage on the part of horse and rider, as well as a more subtle test of a horse's athleticism than in former times.

Every National creates its own distinctive narrative, building layer by layer on the tradition of the race. Thanks to Tiger Roll, the 2019 edition yielded a dual aspect, allowing us to look back in time and appreciate Red Rum's historic feats while projecting forward to the potential for an unprecedented hat-trick in 2020.

In 2018 Tiger Roll achieved his triumph off a mark of 150, carrying 10st 13lb, and was given a flawless ride by Davy Russell, who conserved just enough to get him home by a head from the Willie Mullins-trained Pleasant Company after holding a lead of around six lengths at the Elbow.

Much of the focus was on Russell, eloquent, thoughtful, gracious, who captured the spirit of the occasion. The Cork-born jockey dedicated the victory to Pat Smullen, who had recently received the cancer diagnosis that would bring his career to a premature close, and pointed to the heavens in memory of his recently departed mother Phyllis.

Tiger Roll was surrounded by strong personalities: Russell, who had encountered many bumps on the road to this career-defining moment, the essentially taciturn Elliott, quietly relishing a second Aintree triumph 11 years on from his rookie days with Silver Birch, and the loquacious Michael O'Leary, who had once described the embryonic national treasure as "a rat of a thing".

As for the horse, analysis of his first National win tended to concentrate not on the minutiae of his performance on the day, but rather on the remarkable range of his achievement, played out against the background of a Flat pedigree. He is a thoroughly modern National type whose low-jumping trajectory would assuredly have been a major negative over the old-style fences.

A Triumph Hurdle winner who

Versatility writ large at Cheltenham

Golden Miller stands supreme in the Cheltenham Festival pantheon as the five-in-a-row Gold Cup winner between 1932 and 1936, while Quevega enjoys a unique distinction as a six-time winner of the Mares' Hurdle.

However, the Willie Mullins-trained mare does not come close in stature to more distinguished four-time winners, in chronological order, Sir Ken (three Champion Hurdles and a Cotswold Chase), Arkle (three Gold Cups and a Broadway Novices' Chase), Istabraq (three Champion Hurdles and a Sun Alliance Hurdle), Big Buck's (four consecutive World Hurdles) and Altior (Supreme Novices', Arkle and the Champion Chase twice).

Only two other horses, Willie Wumpkins (a three-time winner of what is now the Pertemps Hurdle) and Tiger Roll, have won four times at the festival since 1945 – Persian War's Triumph Hurdle win which prefaced a Champion Hurdle hat-trick came at the April fixture in 1977.

For sheer versatility, Tiger Roll's feat of adding two Glenfarclas Chase wins to his Triumph Hurdle and National Hunt Chase victories arguably outranks the higher-profile hat-tricks in different races achieved by Flyingbolt (Gloucestershire Hurdle, Cotswold Chase, Champion Chase) and Bobs Worth (Albert Bartlett, RSA Chase and Gold Cup).

A third Glenfarclas win in 2020, on his way to his bid for National history, would add further lustre to the Cheltenham record of the Flat-bred superstar.

returned to Cheltenham three years later to win a four-mile National Chase, he then extended his versatility to the twists, turns and varied obstacles of Cheltenham's cross-country course, warming up for his 2018 National by taking the Glenfarclas Chase under Keith Donoghue, digging deep in the closing stages to resist the French-trained Urgent De Gregaine.

★★★★

BY the time Tiger Roll returned to defend his National title in 2019 he had added to his reputation for versatility when partnered by Donoghue to beat a strong field in the Grade 2 Boyne Hurdle at Navan in February. From there it was back to Cheltenham, where this time he was quite simply in a different league to the usual cross-country exponents, trouncing Enda Bolger's four-time course winner Josies Orders by more than 20 lengths without having to be extended by Donoghue.

Bookmakers immediately went as low as 5-1 for Tiger Roll to repeat his 2018 Aintree win off a 9lb higher mark. When reassessed after Cheltenham, it was apparent he could go off one of the shortest-priced favourites in the history of the National, since he was now officially 8lb well in.

On the day he ended up 4-1 in a market dominated by Irish challengers. Second favourite on 8-1 was the Mullins-trained 2018 National Hunt Chase winner Rathvinden, arriving on the back of a one-race preparation, a comfortable win in the Bobbyjo Chase at Fairyhouse. On board was Ruby Walsh, bidding for a third win in the race following Papillon in 2000 and Hedgehunter in 2005, in front of an audience unsuspecting of his imminent exit from the stage.

Then there was Anibale Fly, 10-1 joint-third favourite, fourth in the race 12 months earlier after finishing third in the Cheltenham Gold Cup. He returned as the Gold Cup runner-up carrying top weight of 11st 10lb. From an 11-strong team, Elliott also provided the other joint-third favourite, Jury Duty, winner of the Grand National Hurdle at Far Hills,

▸▸ *Continues page 34*

Gigginstown scaling-down will have major impact on Irish jump racing

In a year when Brexit supplied the dominant narrative in politics in Britain and Ireland, the biggest story of the racing year in Ireland also involved the theme of departure.

In May, with the new jumps season in its infancy, Michael O'Leary triggered a racing version of Article 50 by announcing a scaling-down of operations under the Gigginstown House Stud banner.

It was a startling decision in many respects, not least for its timing in the month following Tiger Roll's historic Aintree triumph and in the wake of the team's fifth consecutive Irish jumps owners' championship, achieved with earnings of almost €4m and 159 wins, surpassing a previous best of 153 in the 2016-17 season.

The impact, though mitigated by the fact that it will take place over a period of years, will be significant for Gigginstown's trainers and point-to-point handlers, and for breeders, vendors, bloodstock agents and sales companies.

In the short term at least, the decision has potentially radical implications for Gordon Elliott, lengthening the odds that he can depose Willie Mullins from the top spot in the trainers' championship his great rival has occupied for 12 consecutive seasons. Elliott's title ambitions had become feasible when O'Leary took away his horses from the Mullins yard in September 2016 but may now be compromised by a different withdrawal.

At the same time, Elliott will have no trouble filling any empty boxes and he may be able to build up a more balanced team to challenge for Grade 1 races, given that Gigginstown's purchasing strategy was heavily biased towards identifying high-class staying chasers, a policy implemented with conspicuous success by the Ryanair supremo's bloodstock agent brother Eddie.

From modest beginnings with David Wachman in the opening years of the century, O'Leary's interest in jump racing really took off with the victory of War Of Attrition in the 2006 Cheltenham Gold Cup. In the 2009-10 season, with 43 wins and over €900,000 in earnings, Gigginstown ended a 14-season monopoly of the owners' championship by JP McManus.

But this was small beer in terms of what was to come. The 2012-13 season produced the first of seven consecutive three-figure tallies. As Gigginstown and McManus consolidated, other wealthy owners began to exercise major influence as well, and a group of half a dozen or so trainers left their colleagues behind.

When Gigginstown began to monopolise big-value handicaps over fences, and to swamp major conditions races with multiple representation, it created a simmering resentment within the industry. O'Leary also came in for criticism for a perceived lack of loyalty to trainers and for centralising policies in marked contrast to those adopted by McManus with his ever-increasing squad of trainers.

In his role at Ryanair, O'Leary *(left)* has relished criticism and thrived on controversy. It may seem improbable that he was stung by adverse comment about his racing activities, but perhaps the rumbling negativity was a contributory factor to a gradual loss of interest which became more pronounced as his children reached an age where their sporting interests were a more satisfying leisure-time occupation for him.

It may be only the beginning of the end, but the complexion of Irish jump racing will start to change substantially in the season that lies ahead.

ALAN SWEETMAN

New Jersey in the autumn and fresh from a winning return to chasing at Down Royal in March.

Twice placed in the Ultima Handicap Chase at Cheltenham, the Sue Smith-trained Vintage Clouds was the shortest-priced of the home team, aiming to give Trevor Hemmings a fourth win in the race after Hedgehunter, Ballabriggs (2011) and Many Clouds (2015).

Irish trainers were responsible for 18 of the 40 runners, including the sole mare, Magic Of Light for trainer Jessica Harrington. Variations on a Celtic theme were struck by the Scottish-trained 2017 winner One For Arthur and the Welsh-trained 2018 Scottish Grand National winner Joe Farrell.

Vintage Clouds went at the first, where one of the Mullins runners, Up For Review, was brought down and suffered a fatal injury. A mistake at the first seemed to take a toll on Joe Farrell but otherwise there was precious little incident in the race until Jury Duty became one of three casualties at the 18th.

As the contest began to take shape on the second circuit, Irish challengers were to the fore, the free-running Magic Of Light accompanying a Mullins trio of Pleasant Company, Rathvinden and Livelovelaugh. Russell had unobtrusively worked Tiger Roll into a position to track Rathvinden, who blundered at Valentine's but still remained well in the mix.

Tiger Roll landed awkwardly at the fifth-last. Four out, where Pleasant Company unseated, he took another little stumble but lost barely any momentum. From three out he moved ominously well and edged ahead of Magic Of Light between the last two fences. When the mare made a mistake at the last the result was effectively sealed.

Staying on much more powerfully from the Elbow than 12 months earlier, he won by two and three-quarter lengths from Magic Of Light, who kept battling away for Paddy Kennedy, with Rathvinden third, well clear of the Becher Chase winner Walk In The Mill and a staying-on Anibale Fly.

There were 19 finishers, a total that might have been greater but for the fact that several riders accepted the inevitable over the last few fences and sensibly called it a day.

▲ The people's horse: residents in the village of Summerhill turn out to see the local hero from Gordon Elliott's yard

▼ The Racing Post front page the day after Tiger Roll had joined Red Rum as a back-to-back National winner

RACING POST

LEGEND

Remarkable Tiger Roll makes Grand National history with glorious repeat victory

****

WITHIN minutes of the finish, thoughts were turning to 2020. And within hours of his triumphant homecoming to Elliott's local village of Summerhill, Michael and Eddie O'Leary seemed to be laying the groundwork for a "will he run or not?" scenario.

In May, Gigginstown stunned the racing world by setting out their exit strategy. Through the summer it looked as if the build-up to 2020 would involve a long-running poker game between the O'Learys and the BHA handicapper regarding the framing of the weights.

The news the world of jump racing had been waiting for was delivered earlier than expected, in the first days of September. Even before the final British Classic had been run, before Listowel, where the first stirrings of the winter ahead are sometimes detected, Elliott confirmed Tiger Roll would be aimed for the hat-trick, taking in the Boyne Hurdle and a bid for a fifth Cheltenham win on the way.

Tiger Roll now boasts an Irish mark of 171, just 6lb inferior to the Punchestown Gold Cup winner Kemboy and 4lb below the Cheltenham Gold Cup winner Al Boum Photo.

But when Elliott announced the three-in-a-row bid he referenced not to the scale of the task but to his evolving appreciation of Tiger Roll's popularity and status. "He's a people's horse now," he said.

Born in the year after Red Rum's third National win, Elliott continued: "Red Rum was before my time, but you've seen the videos and heard all about him. He was an amazing horse and to be in the same league is unbelievable."

In a modern sporting world where hype often prevails in the most mundane of circumstances, jump racing has the real deal in Tiger Roll, an Aintree legend just one step short of the pedestal occupied by Red Rum.

Multiple winners

Tiger Roll is the eighth horse to win the Grand National more than once and the fifth to score back-to-back victories. He has the chance to become the first to win the race three times in a row.

Peter Simple 1849, 1853
Abd-El-Kader 1850, 1851
The Colonel 1869, 1870
The Lamb 1868, 1871
Manifesto 1897, 1899
Reynoldstown 1935, 1936
Red Rum 1973, 1974, 1977
Tiger Roll 2018, 2019

RANDOX
RANDOX
RANDOX
15

IN THE PICTURE

If The Cap Fits squeezes home in Aintree epic

TIGER ROLL'S second Grand National triumph was spellbinding but for finish of the year it would be hard to better the Ryanair Stayers Hurdle, the main supporting act on Aintree's big day.

Coming to the 13th and last hurdle in the Grade 1 contest, after almost three miles of punishing effort, the odds-on favourite Apple's Jade *(main picture, right)* led narrowly from If The Cap Fits *(centre)* and Roksana, winner of the Mares' Hurdle at the Cheltenham Festival. Apple's Jade clattered the hurdle but If The Cap Fits made a worse error, allowing Roksana to move past into second place. From there it was nip and tuck all the way to the line.

Apple's Jade continued to hold a slight advantage on the far side halfway up the run-in, with Roksana pressing hard on the stands' side and If The Cap Fits recovering his momentum to come back at them. The trio came close together in the final drive to the line and, just as Roksana managed to get in front of Apple's Jade, If The Cap Fits bravely thrust himself between the two mares to get up on the post.

The photo-finish showed the Harry Fry-trained If The Cap Fits had won by a head from Roksana, with Apple's Jade a neck behind in third. "Sorry Dan," said a sheepish Fry to Dan Skelton, Roksana's trainer, as the two former Paul Nicholls assistants shared a handshake after the epic battle. "You'd have been an unlucky loser if you hadn't got up," was Skelton's response.

Harry Skelton, who rode the runner-up, was equally magnanimous, saying: "What a race! Three good horses battling it out on the best day of the year and people should enjoy that – it's what racing is all about and I'm glad to be part of it."

Most elated of all was winning rider Sean Bowen after clinching his first Grade 1 success in the soul-stirring finish. "I thought I'd chucked it away and would have to wait a bit longer for my first Grade 1, but he was brilliant," the 21-year-old said. "There wasn't a whole lot of room and he was sandwiched between two horses but he's gutsy."

Victory at the highest level was important for Bowen, cementing both his position in the top rank and his burgeoning relationship with Fry following the retirement of Noel Fehily. A fruitful career in the big races surely lies ahead but Bowen will never forget his first Grade 1. Nor will those who watched it.

Picture: EDWARD WHITAKER (RACINGPOST.COM/PHOTOS)

Cheltenham Thursday produced the most magical 60 minutes of the racing year with heart-melting success for Frodon and Bryony Frost and then for Paisley Park and Andrew Gemmell

BEWITCHING HOUR

By Lee Mottershead

FIRST there was Frost and first there was Frodon. What followed them in the very next race was similarly magnificent but they were the ones who got us in the mood. The loved-up duo ignited one of the most intensely magical hours in Cheltenham Festival history. They put smiles on our faces almost as wide as the one

▸▸ *Continues page 40*

TOP ODDS
APOLLO

worn by the triumphant rider. Even thinking about it now, many months after the event, the smiles are bound to return.

At the end of his Ryanair Chase racecourse commentary Simon Holt described Bryony Frost and Frodon as "a match made in racing heaven". They were perfect words, as were the ones delivered by Frost in the moments after she became the first woman ever to ride a Grade 1 winner over jumps at the sport's showpiece meeting. There were very many of those words, delivered sincerely and with passion. She also told us what Frodon had said to her, which was an added bonus.

Those at the track were present for something unforgettable, but you did not need to be at the sport's sacred home to be enthralled by what had unfolded and Frost's part in it all. If there has ever been a jockey better able to explain what it feels like to compete on a racehorse, that person's name does not spring easily to mind. For those watching on television or listening on radio, Frost takes the watching and listening experience to a new level. On this day, and across the whole season, she took her career to a new level as well.

The campaign ended with the Ditcheat team member crowned champion conditional jockey. The 50th of her 50 successes came on the final afternoon at Sandown, the equine ally being another confirmed four-legged friend in Black Corton.

▲ Battle hardened: clockwise from top left, Frodon gets off to a winning start last season in the Old Roan Chase; going down fighting in the BetVictor Gold Cup; powering home in the Caspian Caviar Gold Cup; victory in the Cotswold Chase is in sight

No horse, however, has done more for Frost than Frodon, who struck four times during the season, never more memorably than on that Thursday in March.

He had won the Old Roan Chase at Aintree in late October before going within two lengths of defying 11st 12lb in the BetVictor Gold Cup. Next time out he did defy that burden, bounding up the Cheltenham hill with the sort of gusto and relish that has become his trademark to land the Caspian Caviar Gold Cup.

The official comment-in-running says he "pinged two out". Frodon does a lot of pinging and he pinged plenty more when upped in trip for the Cotswold Chase,

▸▸ *Continues page 42*

which brought another Cheltenham victory in January.

That made Paul Nicholls and owner Paul Vogt think hard about the Gold Cup. Eventually they thought against it. Perhaps Frodon would have won the biggest prize of all but he definitely did win the Ryanair Chase. Truth be told, such was the euphoria it seemed as though we had all won, even those of us without a penny on him.

****

LOTS of people did have lots of pennies on him, for Frodon was sent off just 9-2 for a deep renewal. The previous year's Racing Post Arkle Chase hero Footpad was 7-2 favourite to claim a contest in which his stable companion and previous Ryanair winner Un De Sceaux was also in the field. Monalee and Road To Respect, like Frodon, could have run in the Gold Cup but came here instead. Also participating was 33-1 shot Aso, who deserves to be recognised as both the eventual runner-up and the only horse to head Frodon, who looked well, jumped well and, apart from the ground in between the final two fences, made every yard of the running.

At this point, we could begin a prosaic attempt to describe the closing stages but nobody could possibly do that better than Frost herself. The floor, Bryony, is yours.

"Two out," she said, "we landed a bit tight, but at that moment he leant into my hands and shook me up. He said: 'Don't you dare let go of this. I want you with me because I cannot do it by myself. Are you with me or are you not? I need to hear you growl at me.'

"The reins grabbed my fingers, so I grabbed hold of him. I felt the determination within Frodon. His ears were flat back and his head was stretched out as far as it could possibly be. He was attacking that final fence. That's all he wanted. 'Find a stride for me,' he was saying. I had to say back to him: 'I am trying, Frod.'"

You can imagine her saying it. "I am trying, Frod." Your heart melts. But anyway, back to Frost.

"Going into the fence, he was telling me, 'I've got it, I've got it,'" she said. "Through the whole race we were so together and never more so than in that split second. At the back of the fence he gave a mighty push. He was grabbing hold of every inch of the grass up that hill.

"When we passed the line I remember looking down at him, thinking: 'You wonderful, wonderful character. How on earth you pulled that out, I don't know – but I do know because I was there with you.'"

And we were there with them. The third afternoon of the festival's four afternoons is generally the least anticipated and the Ryanair Chase is a championship prize some jumps connoisseurs would rather did not exist. This time, helped by what Paisley Park accomplished 40 minutes later, the Thursday afternoon became the most memorable of the week. Frodon is fabulous but the principal reason for our joy was the jockey. Frost is one of the best things to have happened to racing in an awfully long time.

⏩ *Continues page 44*

RACING POST
ON SUNDAY
£2.90
'Then Lalor won. I felt as though Richard was telling me I could do it and shouldn't give up'
CUP QUEEN BRYONY
Frost and Frodon light up Cheltenham in Caspian Caviar Gold Cup romp
Plus a rousing farewell for The New One – all yesterday's big stories and Alastair Down's verdict, pages 2-5
LIVERPOOL v MAN UTD
Premier League wisdom in Racing Post Sport, with live action also including Southampton v Arsenal, starts back page

RACING POST
ON SUNDAY
£2.90
MULLINS
VIKING FLAGSHIP
GOLD CUP HERE WE COME
Frost and Frodon light up Cheltenham in Cotswold Chase

▾ Special bond: Bryony Frost and Frodon after their Ryanair Chase victory; left, the Racing Post front pages the day after the Caspian Caviar Gold Cup and Cotswold Chase

Title character

Six years after Lucy Alexander topped the conditional jockeys' championship, Bryony Frost became only the second woman to lift the trophy. She did that on the day she won two races. The first had been a race against time.

Four days after capturing the Ryanair Chase on Frodon, Frost suffered a Southwell fall that left her with a broken collarbone. She returned from injury on the season's final afternoon at Sandown, making her comeback aboard trusted friend Black Corton in the Oaksey Chase. His 11-length victory in the Grade 2 contest was Frost's 50th in a campaign during which she was also forced to sit out most of the summer due to a racing crash that left her with an arterial aneurysm.

While recovering from the collarbone fracture, Frost had spoken to the Racing Post at the Oaksey House rehabilitation centre in Lambourn, providing a fascinating insight into her own psyche and reinforcing the impression she is wonderfully straightforward and fascinatingly complex at the same time.

"To me, I'm a separate person," she said. "I have this really strange way of never looking at myself as me. I struggle to say 'I'. It's always 'we' because it's me and my horse. It's not me. I find it impossible to think of it being about me.

"This body isn't actually mine. My body is my career and my horses' careers. It's so weird. It's like I'm stood over there looking at me over here."

"We were so in sync our heartbeats were probably together," she said in the moments after the race, somehow conjuring up a line any writer would have been proud to produce after copious thinking time. "I love you mate," she had earlier told Frodon during an ITV interview. "Is he your best friend?" asked Oli Bell. "I've got lots of best friends, I'm really lucky," she answered.

★★★★

TRUTH be told, we all want to be Bryony's friend, as one member of the press pack made clear after we had listened to her recounting what had happened. "I think I've just fallen in love again," said the journalist. He had been married for less than three months at the time.

Frost does not have a husband but she does have a father, Jimmy, who won the Grand National when he was a jockey and now supplies his daughter with winners as a trainer. They had walked the track on Ryanair morning. On Ryanair evening they returned to the West Country with other family members, stopping for a burger dinner at the Grade 1-class Gloucester Services. When they returned to Frost's sponsored car, which carries her name, they found someone had left a note on the windscreen, saying they had watched the race on television and had wanted to say well done.

The following morning a large picture of Frost's beaming face appeared on the front page of The Times. She was interviewed live on BBC Breakfast and even made an appearance on Radio 4's Woman's Hour. She was box office.

"If I had to paint the perfect racehorse it would be Frodon," was something else she said during one of her numerous media encounters that followed the greatest day of her racing life.

Frost would be the first to admit she is not a perfect jockey but she is an exceptionally talented jockey who brings happiness into people's lives. That was never more true than on the day she and Frodon sent us soaring.

Golden hour: how the story was told to the ITV Racing audience

2.51
They're off in the Ryanair Chase

2.56
Frodon crosses the line first, a length and a quarter in front of Aso

2.58
Oli Bell starts his on-course interview with Bryony Frost, whose first words are all about Frodon: "He's got his day, guys. He is Pegasus, he has got wings"

3.01
Frodon and Frost start their triumphal walk in front of the grandstands. "These are pictures you're going to see plastered all over the papers," says Ed Chamberlin

3.05
Frost is greeted by a fist-pumping Paul Nicholls as she comes into the winner's enclosure

3.12
The Frost family is interviewed en masse by Alice Plunkett. Mum Nikki is first to speak: "I'm just so proud of her, that was an amazing ride"

3.14
Frost goes up to the presentation podium, having become the first woman to ride a Grade 1 winner over jumps at the festival

3.17
The runners are in the parade ring for the Stayers' Hurdle. "Ooh, we're trying to regroup here after the emotion of the Ryanair," says Plunkett as the first horse she focuses on in her paddock tour is Paisley Park. She points out the browband specially made for the day in the colours of West Ham United, the team supported by owner Andrew Gemmell

3.21
The jockeys are getting mounted for the Stayers' and heading out on to the track

3.27
The runners are at the post. "Can the fairytale happen for Andrew Gemmell?" asks Chamberlin

3.31
They're off in the Stayers' Hurdle

3.37
Paisley Park wins by two and three-quarter lengths from Sam Spinner. "On a day full of stories, Paisley Park writes another chapter," says commentator Richard Hoiles

3.40
The camera switches to a beaming Gemmell. "I can't believe it's happened. I hope it's the first of many," he says

3.45
Gemmell meets Paisley Park on the walk to the winner's enclosure and leads him in. "Simply amazing," says Chamberlin

3.47
As three cheers go up for Paisley Park, Brough Scott sums up: "I've got tears in my eyes. This is as emotional a day as I've had at the races. I'm so proud of what racing can do"

Paisley Park kept the feelgood factor going with a wonderful victory for blind owner Andrew Gemmell, trainer Emma Lavelle and jockey Aidan Coleman

DREAM TEAM

By Peter Thomas

ON A fairytale Thursday afternoon, it was going to take a fantastical story, even more fantastical than the week usually demands, to get in on the act. Glass slippers and magic pumpkins were never likely to capture the headlines from Bryony Frost and Frodon, and unfeasibly large beanstalks were a million to one, but the Cheltenham Festival has a knack of turning the most unbelievable raw material into glorious reality and the 2019 Stayers' Hurdle obligingly laid a shiny golden egg.

The fable was a heady mix of equine near-death and human triumph over adversity, punctuated at every twist and turn by the more familiar festival currency of excellence. At its simplest it was a highly likeable trainer and jockey combining to break new ground in their careers with a fast-improving hurdler, but the waters surrounding such a thoroughly passable plot ran very deep indeed.

With the best will in the world, Andrew Gemmell was an unlikely owner of any racehorse, let alone a champion like Paisley Park, and an unlikely participant in the wild and colourful whirl of Cheltenham. In fact, he wouldn't object to being called an unlikely racegoer, full stop. Blind since birth, the 66-year-old had been permanently denied many of the sensory pleasures of the sport that

▸▸ *Continues page 46*

most of us take for granted. As a child he was captivated by radio commentaries of old Derby winners, but he had never seen a horse pass the post in glorious victory. His satisfaction from the game had to come by less conventional, less understandable routes but he was an enthusiast, a thrill seeker and a racing man through and through, and that was what mattered to the Prestbury Park crowd who took him to their hearts.

Paisley Park, likewise, was something of a marvel to those who knew his story. As 11-8 favourite for a festival championship, on the day he looked for all the world like a ready-made superstar; the racecard, however, paints a two-dimensional picture of a living, breathing creature, and there was more to the brilliant seven-year-old than met the eye.

As a gifted but erratic five-year-old, just a couple of days on from a promising second on his debut, he had been laid low by a bout of colic that nearly killed him. Nursed back to the land of the living by the expertise and kindness of those charged with his care, he returned to the yard of his trainer Emma Lavelle, "properly skin and bone" as she described his condition, but at least ready to begin the long haul back to race fitness.

Lavelle, the well-educated daughter of an eminent surgeon, could never be described as underprivileged, but her career had been blighted by the effects of oilseed rape at her old yard in Hampshire, and the fraught rebuilding of her new yard in Wiltshire represented a make-or-break opportunity to revitalise a promising career.

Together with her husband, the former jump jockey Barry Fenton – who had refused to leave the sales without the horse he eventually snapped up for a bargain £60,000 – she poured heart and soul into the making of a champion.

Then there was Aidan Coleman. In a trivia quiz, few would have guessed that the Cork-born jockey's tally of Grade 1 victories in 13 years in the saddle was precisely zero before Paisley Park came along. His raw talent, you might have imagined, would have landed him a hatful, but he was now 30 years old and 2018's Long Walk Hurdle with Paisley Park had been his one and only.

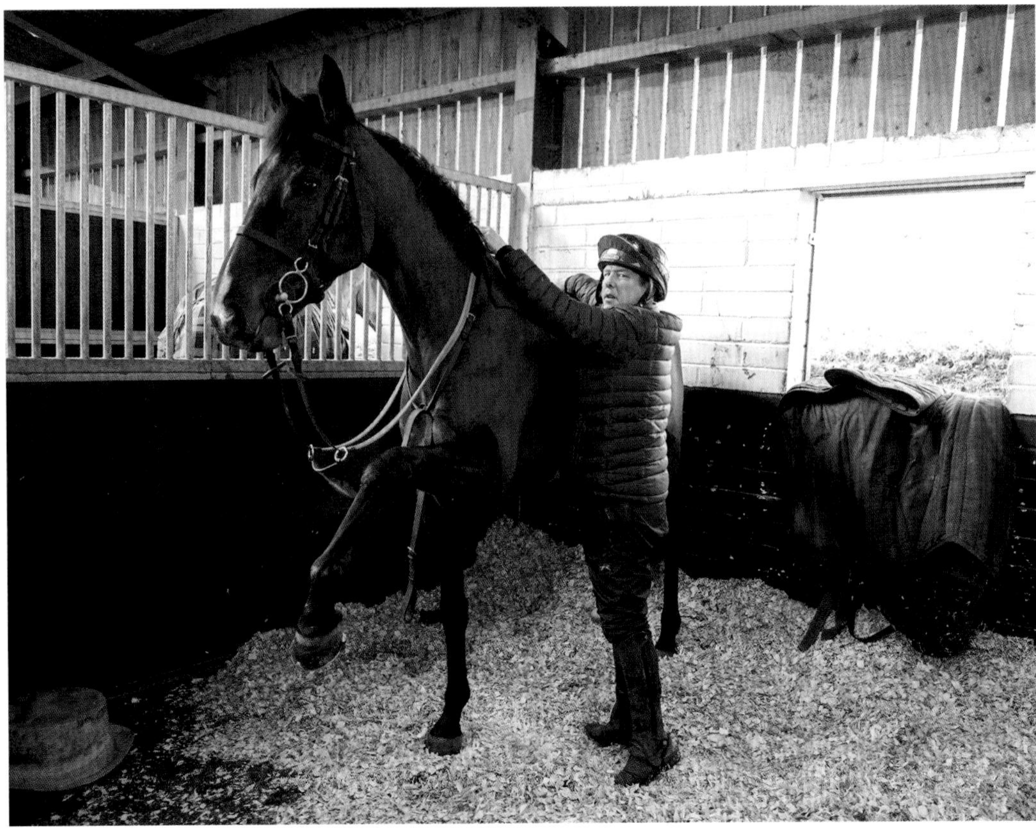

▲ Home team: Barry Fenton with Paisley Park in his box; below, trainer Emma Lavelle. Together they poured heart and soul into the making of a champion

****

PERHAPS there are many such unlikely gatherings of disparate and deserving racing characters whose efforts go unnoticed by the gods of the Turf, but this clan of the sightless, the almost dead and the professionally frustrated were not to be among them. The stage was set for what may not have been the greatest story ever told but is a story that will go down in festival folklore.

"It was unreal," recalls Gemmell, reliving the swirl of emotion and action on that unmissable Thursday afternoon. "I was really tense at the start of the day but luckily I'd had a runner a couple of races earlier [Flemcara, owned in partnership with The Frisky Fillies, tenth in the Pertemps Final] and although it wasn't very good, that didn't matter because it eased the tension slightly. I'd still say I wasn't very good company until the race was over, though.

"I was in the owners' and trainers' enclosure and everybody else was eating but I couldn't be bothered. Then an Irish guy came up to me and said 'you look like you need a double brandy', so I had one, just to ease me down slightly, and I felt a bit better after that."

It wasn't long before this most enthusiastic and likeable of owners – a music fan who named his best horse after the Minnesota recording studio of one of his great heroes, Prince – was eased back up again. Paisley Park was a banker for many – on the back of his wins in an Aintree handicap and three Graded races, most recently a 12-length success over the Stayers' course and distance in the Cleeve Hurdle – and the pressure of favouritism was well and truly on.

It was an occasion that transcended betting, however. The Shropshire lad, a son of two GPs and a syndicate man of many years' standing, revelled in the fact that "after all this time I've finally got a horse of my own that's turning out to be very

▸▸ *Continues page 48*

special", and he was determined to enjoy the moment. Having been lured into gambling at an early age – "I had a good bet on Right Tack and Geoff Lewis in the 1969 Guineas and got more and more interested" – he still had the punter's instinct but was on the trail of something bigger this time.

In his childhood, Gemmell had drifted off to the tones of David Coleman and Richie Benaud telling tales of sporting greatness. Now he was listening to Ian Bartlett on the Cheltenham speaker system, painting a picture of his own personal moment of history in the making, and if there were notes of caution in the commentary, they failed to dent the owner's confidence.

"When he said Paisley Park was hitting his flat spot, I'm past the stage where I worry about that," Gemmell explains. "I know one day he may come unstuck but I really don't worry about it and as far as I was concerned, apart from a ricket at the last, everything in the race was fine. One of my friends was getting despondent but I took no notice and all of a sudden he came from about sixth to lead at the last, which was amazing, but that's him, turbo-charged."

As Paisley Park made his surge to the front, with Coleman conspicuously aware of the superior machine beneath him, Gemmell was caught up in the Cheltenham mayhem, the giant tumble dryer of an experience that hurls emotions this way and that and wrings every last drop of feeling from those who commit themselves to the moment. This was our man's moment and nobody was going to take it away from him.

"It's not so much pleasure while it's happening, more tension as the race is unfolding," he says. "But I hate it when people start telling me I'm going to win, I can't handle all that, so I tell the people I'm with to shut up and let me listen to the commentary. There are one or two serial offenders but I think they know now it's not to happen again."

****

AS A regular at West Ham, at cricket grounds and tennis arenas around the world, Gemmell is well used to the confusion of those who wonder how he can love sport so much when he can't see it. He's sightless, not soulless, though, and at the races he finds himself in his own milieu, among his own people – people who mobbed him when Paisley Park scooted up the hill to see off Sam Spinner and Faugheen, and who continued to share his joy wherever he went for weeks afterwards.

"There are so many levels of enjoyment in racing, the thrills and the disappointments all rolled into one, and I love everything about it, the action and the crowd," he says. I was the only owner who went over when our Ascot Gold Cup winner Trip To Paris was second in the [2015] Caulfield Cup and the Australian media latched on to me, so that had prepared me a little bit, and I did enjoy it at Cheltenham.

"I think people can tell I'm a proper racing fan and wherever I've been since Cheltenham they've been coming up to me – they wanted selfies with me at York! It feels strange, but people mean well, so why not do it? Even on the Flat courses, a small meeting at Nottingham on a Sunday, they still do it, so you've got to embrace it and make the most of it. If they're prepared to talk to you, it's downright rude not to talk to them, and I'm just glad they're pleased."

Cheltenham moved on quickly to the next race, as is the nature of the festival, but for Gemmell the moment lingered as he counted his blessings in being part of such a memorable day, and then, in good time, began looking ahead with the rest of us to another season.

▲ Victory walk: Paisley Park and Aidan Coleman make their way through the cheering crowds to the winner's enclosure where Andrew Gemmell and Emma Lavelle were celebrating

'I think people can tell I'm a proper racing fan and wherever I've been since Cheltenham they've been coming up to me – they wanted selfies with me at York!'

"My worry was that the fairytale was over for the day when Bryony won the Ryanair," he admits, "but it carried on. It was hard to believe there might be a second but that's just what happened and the whole afternoon produced a lot of memories for me.

"It was a massive tribute to Emma and Barry and I'm not convinced we could have done that in her old yard. I never gave up hope with the horse, even in the worst days, and I'd have to say it turned out to be a blessing in disguise that it was such a dry summer in 2018 that we didn't school him over fences and get tempted down that road.

"It's been astonishing how well things have gone since then – I'm sure missing Aintree and Punchestown was the right decision, to leave something in the tank – and the only worry is that you have to ask yourself if it can ever go that well again. There's possibly Benie Des Dieux to contend with in the new season but let's hope we can beat her, and there's no reason at all why he can't have another good go at it. There's no question at all of even considering the possibility of chasing, not for another year at least – why do something that silly?"

It seems the stage is set for another fairytale season and nobody would rule out the possibility of another happy ending for the remarkable team behind Paisley Park.

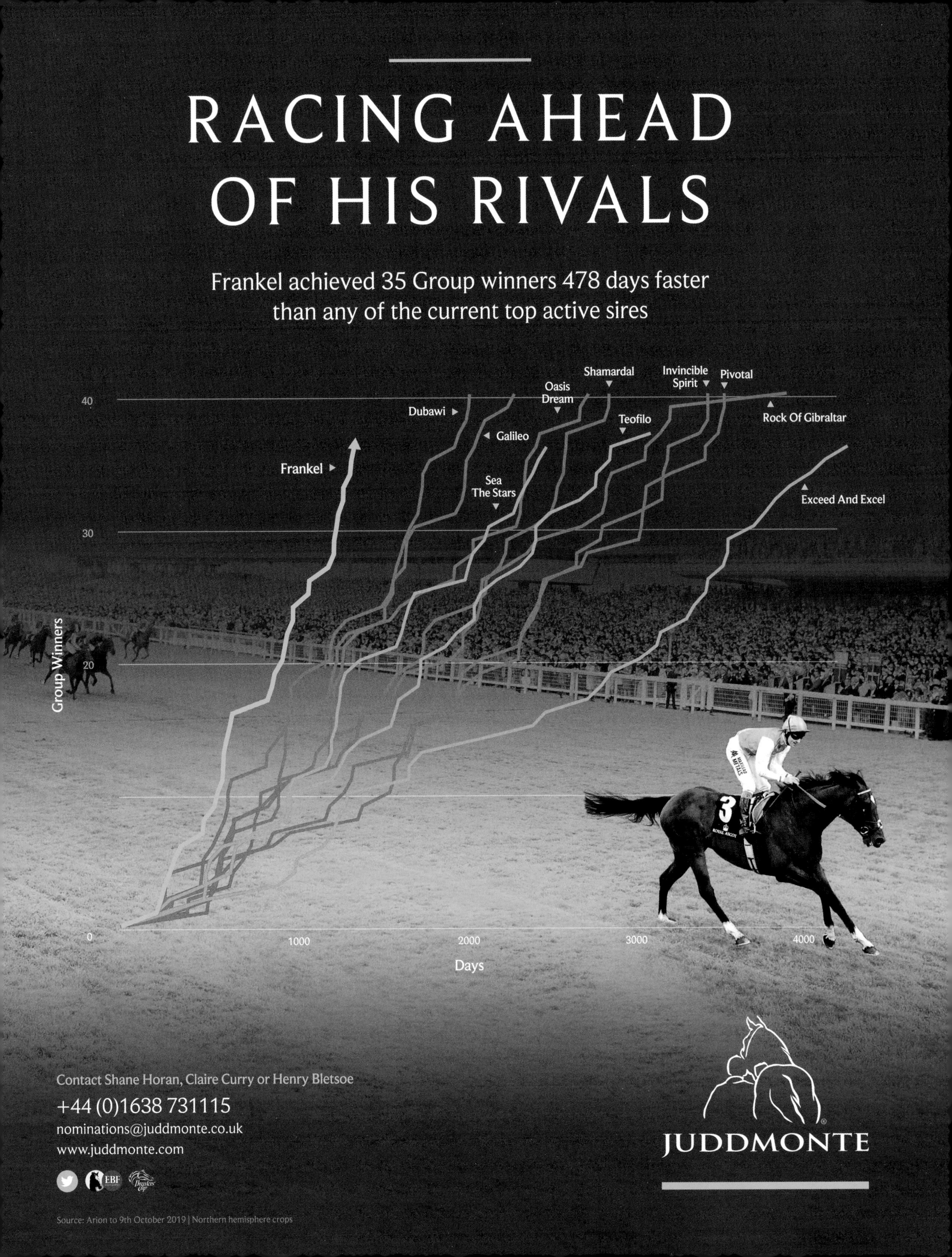
RACING AHEAD
OF HIS RIVALS
Frankel achieved 35 Group winners 478 days faster
than any of the current top active sires
Shamardal
Invincible Spirit
Pivotal
Oasis Dream
Dubawi
Teofilo
Rock Of Gibraltar
Galileo
Frankel
Sea The Stars
Exceed And Excel
40
30
20
0
Group Winners
1000
2000
3000
4000
Days
Contact Shane Horan, Claire Curry or Henry Bletsoe
+44 (0)1638 731115
nominations@juddmonte.co.uk
www.juddmonte.com
JUDDMONTE
Source: Arion to 9th October 2019 | Northern hemisphere crops

Fast forward from Cheltenham Thursday to Goodwood Thursday in August and racing had an uplifting vision of diversity, inclusivity and internationalism, starting with a groundbreaking success for teenager Khadijah Mellah

GLORIOUS

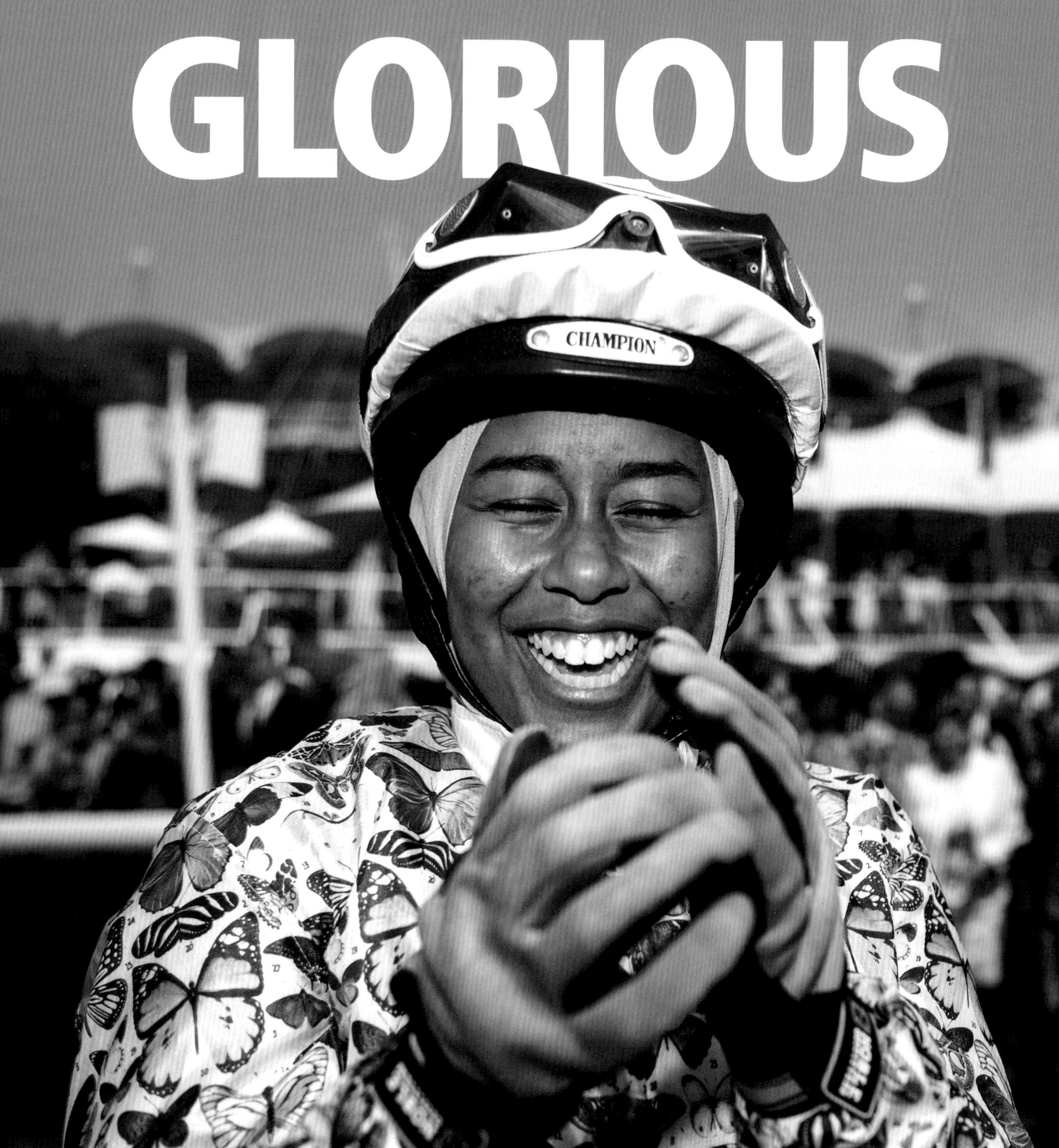

By Robbie Wilders

SOMETHING extraordinary has to happen for racing to make the evening news bulletins, followed by the front page of The Times and the breakfast TV sofa the next morning. At Goodwood on August 1, something extraordinary happened.

Khadijah Mellah was already the focus of attention as she went out to compete in the Magnolia Cup, the charity race that opened the third day of the Qatar Goodwood Festival. In becoming the first person in Britain to ride in a race wearing a hijab, she was making a piece of history. When she raced back down the straight and flashed past the post in front, wearing not just that hijab but a smile as broad as the Sussex Downs, it was clear this was a huge chunk of history.

Mellah's story was remarkable simply for the fact she was an 18-year-old from Peckham but the cultural and sociological significance went much deeper. At this quintessential British summer race meeting, for so long known as Glorious Goodwood, her victory became a symbol of diversity and inclusivity, and for racing it conveyed a message to the wider public that here is a sport which embraces participants from all walks of life, regardless of gender, race or religion.

For Mellah, it was an adventure and a massive test of nerve. She was the youngest of the 12 jockeys in the Magnolia Cup, an invitation race for women guest riders that has raised more than £1.5m for charity since its inception in 2011 and was run this year in support of Wellbeing of Women. Among her rivals from the worlds of business, sport, fashion and media were professional event rider Sophie van der Merwe, Olympic gold medal-winning cyclist Victoria Pendleton, The Apprentice finalist Luisa Zissman

Continues page 52

and Racing Post journalist Kitty Trice. Many of them had been riding horses since their early years, whereas Mellah had not started until her teens with the Ebony Horse Club in Brixton and had sat on a racehorse for the first time only four months before Goodwood.

Before the race, the enormity of the occasion was almost overwhelming for Mellah. "I wasn't used to seeing so many people and there were so many cameras and people looking for information," she said. "At the start it was dead silent and I wanted people [other riders] to start talking. I thought 'Oh my God, will someone smile please?' I didn't really know what I was doing. It was crazy."

The race is run over five and a half furlongs on Goodwood's sharp, downhill course and for an inexperienced rider simply to hold a powerful thoroughbred together and give a competent performance is an achievement. What Mellah did went way beyond that. "I'm quite competitive, so I wanted to win this race, but I never expected to," she said. "When we set off there were three horses in front of me and the kickback was flying in my face and I decided to pull out and see what happened. When I passed the post I couldn't believe it."

Mellah had crept steadily forward near the stands' rail and hit the front close to the line on the Charlie Fellowes-trained four-year-old Haverland, who was a willing and kind partner but had won just once before in 13 starts. Horse and rider had teamed up for only two fast gallops before the race and this was the quickest Mellah had gone on horseback in her life.

This was a charity curtain-raiser to the 'proper' racing, which featured the Group 1 Nassau Stakes, and yet suddenly it was a huge story. "It's a dream result – and it wasn't fixed!" said Goodwood's owner, the Duke of Richmond, as he came down the steps to the winner's enclosure. Tears mixed with smiles as Mellah came back in front of the packed stands and then

▲ Picture perfect: Khadijah Mellah with her mother Selma after winning the Magnolia Cup on Haverland

▼ Mellah on the front page of The Times the morning after her momentous win

THE TIMES

Overpriced and outdated

Stormont's royal portrait farce ends in restoration of Queen

Blood test can detect onset of Alzheimer's

Facial recognition tells bar staff who's next

into the winner's enclosure, where she jumped off Haverland and into the arms of her mother, Selma.

Around the enclosure were more family and friends, including Naomi Howgate, her first instructor at the Ebony Horse Club. "At Ebony it's not a competition, but I told Khadijah I wanted her to forget everything I'd told her before," Howgate said. "I told her to go out there and win. She rode that race like a pro. She was just brilliant."

It was a joyous occasion. "I've known some of these people for five or six years and they've watched me grow up, so for them to be here is wonderful, especially Naomi," Mellah said. "I'm just shocked. There are no words to describe this. I'm still trying to figure out how it all happened and I'm so grateful to everyone who has come along to support."

One of them was her younger sister, Tuka. "I've been waiting for this day for so long and always knew she could do it," Tuka said. "I would see her

▸▸ *Continues page 54*

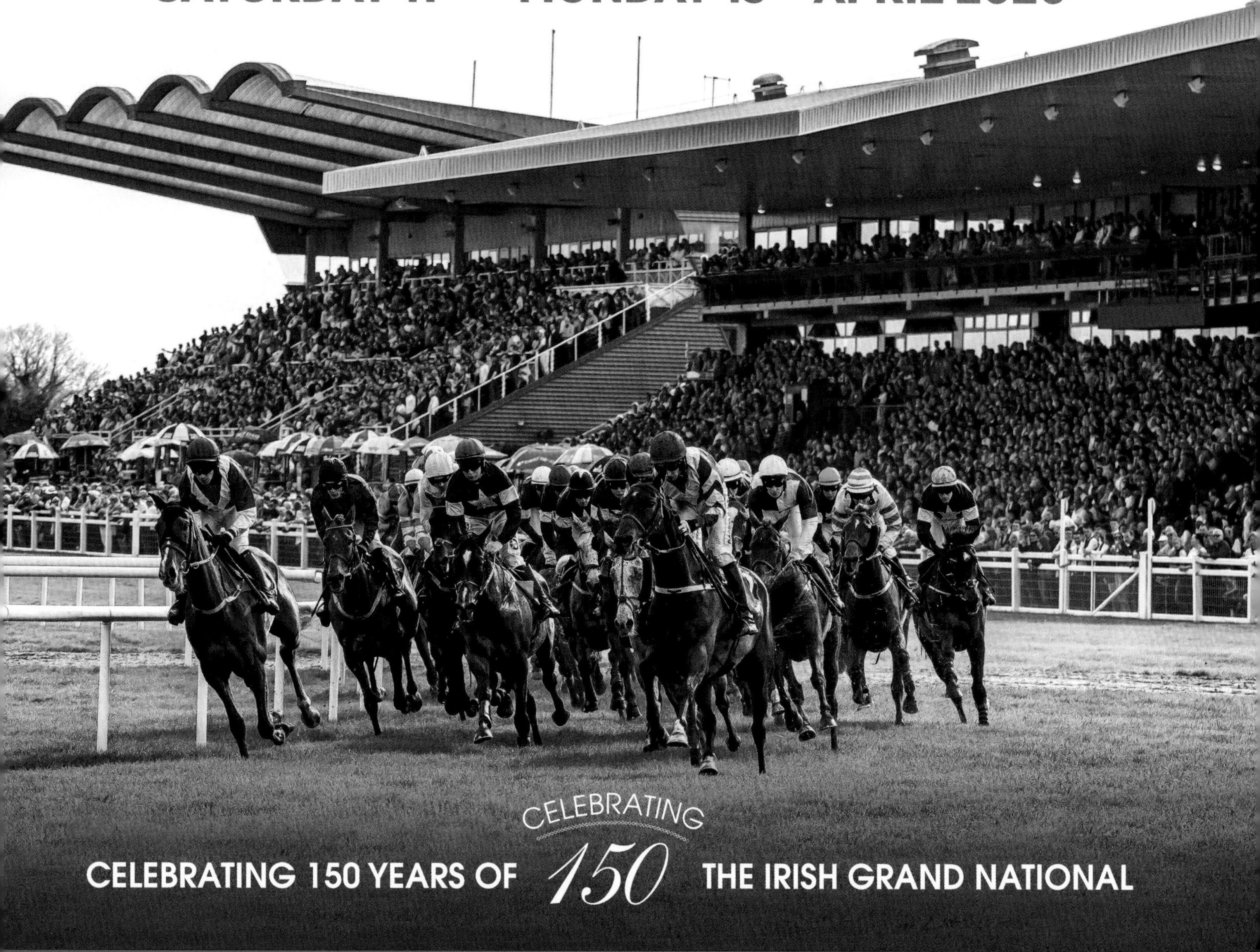
CELEBRATING 150 YEARS OF CELEBRATING 150 THE IRISH GRAND NATIONAL

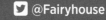

before bed and she would make loads of prayers for it. She has worked so hard for this and she deserves it."

★★★★

OLI BELL, the ITV Racing presenter, was close at hand and he was also in tears. A patron of the Ebony Racing Club, he had come up with the idea of one of the club's riders taking part in the Magnolia Cup and was executive producer of a documentary film about Mellah's journey, called Riding A Dream. "She's become an inspirational woman," Bell said. "For her to win . . . I'm going to cry now."

Fellowes was equally emotional. "I'm speechless, shaking, I can't believe that," the Newmarket trainer said. "Khadijah gave the horse the most unbelievable ride. She was so cool. She followed the right horse through and she did absolutely brilliantly. She's the most incredible young lady you will ever come across. How she has done that is beyond remarkable.

"About six weeks ago Oli rang me and asked if I had a suitable horse, and Haverland is ideal. I knew he would look after her. The two of them have become the most fantastic partnership, but never did I think they could win the race. Every single time we've asked Khadijah to come forward she has done so, emphatically. She's the most wonderful young lady I've ever had anything to do with – she has a smile that lights up our yard."

Mellah paid her own tribute in return. "Initially, riding out at the yard was quite difficult because it was such a new experience, but Charlie and Chris Wall and all the trainers I've ridden out with have been amazing in helping me. I didn't really know how to ride and Charlie has been so amazing. I can't thank him enough," she said.

As for her mount, she added: "I've been riding Haverland a lot at Charlie's and I love him so much. Horses bring me immeasurable amounts of happiness. I've always loved them and always will and I hope to carry on riding."

On the wider significance of her success, she said: "It shows ambitious women can make it and that's all I want to represent. I've had so much support and I can't wait to see other stories of other women getting into the industry and doing amazing things."

Fellowes hoped the positive images would dispel the perception of a lack of diversity in racing. "I think racing is very diverse. I think it has a reputation that it's not and it's a closed shop, but I definitely don't think that's true," he said. "You only need to come to Newmarket to see the multitude of cultures that are part of the industry to understand that. Her success showed that to the wider world and the media attention we've seen has been unrivalled. I don't think there's been a story in racing that has caught so many people."

The trainer's view on diversity found support from Khadijah's brother Abdus, who is part of the multicultural racing scene in Newmarket, where he rides out for Wall. Like his sister, he is keen to become an amateur jockey. "I started riding in Newmarket and it was bloody brilliant," he said. "Racing is much more than what people think. Behind the scenes so many of the work-riders are multicultural. When

▸▸ *Continues page 56*

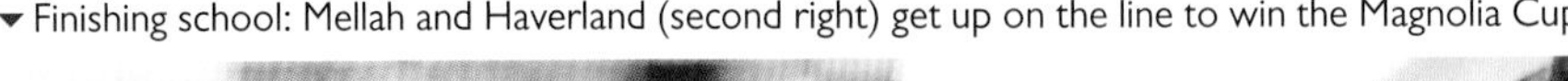

▲ Prep school: Khadijah Mellah at the British Racing School in Newmarket as part of her training for Goodwood
▼ Finishing school: Mellah and Haverland (second right) get up on the line to win the Magnolia Cup

'Thanks to her the sport may benefit'

Lee Mottershead, a member of the BHA's diversity in racing steering group, on Khadijah Mellah's historic victory

When Khadijah Mellah finished the Magnolia Cup in front, an image was painted not just of what racing should be but of what racing can be. It was a beautiful picture on a beautiful day.

It was not simply what happened, it was the reaction to it happening. People at Goodwood recognised the significance of her success and they welcomed it with relish.

When the BHA created the diversity in racing steering group, it was because it could see the sport needed to be more diverse and inclusive. The sport is too white and too male. Khadijah Mellah is not white and she is not male. She is a British Muslim and she raced at one of racing's most iconic venues wearing a hijab.

We saw it and we loved it. More importantly, so will others, thanks to the widespread media coverage Mellah's victory ensured.

This was all about her, but thanks to her the sport may benefit. People who have felt racing was not for them may think again. Let us hope so.

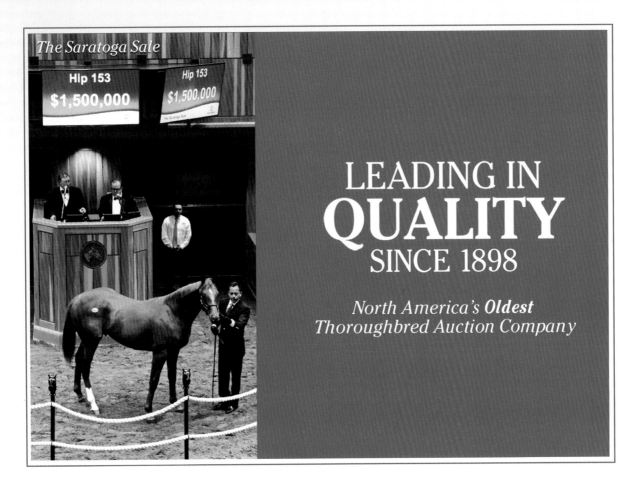

you come to the races you might only see predominantly white jockeys, but as time goes on that might change."

****

THIS was also a story about how charities such as the Ebony Racing Club can connect horses and young people who might not otherwise have the opportunity to enjoy that interaction. Promoting their valuable work was a fundamental reason why Bell wanted to put a rider in the Magnolia Cup.

The club, which was formed in 1996, has 160 members and describes its work as "transforming young lives through horses in south London's most disadvantaged communities". Mellah found out about the club by chance when her mother saw a leaflet at a nearby mosque and she was on a waiting list for two years before she could join.

David Fleming, the club's engagement manager, said: "We have a load of kids here who are very talented. We're very keen on getting more kids into racing and other aspects of horsemanship such as eventing. If they want to take it further that's fantastic, but everyone here has one thing in common: they all love horses. People in the local area are very proud of the work we're doing. We have great kids and volunteers."

Another of the Ebony kids is Andrew Smith, 16, who was keen on an equine studies college course. "I gave it a chance here and realised I was naturally talented. I love the people and it's a really positive place," he said.

Reflecting on the profound impact the club has had on her, Mellah said: "The Ebony Horse Club means the world to me, I love that place. I spent a lot of my childhood growing up there and I've made a lot of friends for life. It's helped me gain a lot of connections and opportunities."

When the opportunity to ride in the Magnolia Cup came up, Mellah grabbed it with both hands. And in the minute or so it took her to race down the Goodwood straight, she made a difference.

Kieran Shoemark put his riding career back on track after suspension and treatment for alcohol addiction

GOODWOOD REVIVAL

By Lewis Porteous

KIERAN SHOEMARK'S focus was clear. Vividly, his mount in the two-year-old fillies' maiden on the Thursday of the Qatar Goodwood Festival, may have been a 16-1 shot but Shoemark was determined to seize the initiative from the widest draw in the 15-runner contest. The idea of taking control had wider significance for a young jockey who had fought a battle just to be at the races and it was about to bring him high-profile reward on one of the summer's biggest stages.

Shoemark jumped Vividly out of the gates, moved smoothly all the way across to the opposite rail inside the first furlong and set out to make all the running. Frankie Dettori, riding one of the joint-favourites, was the only one able to throw down a challenge in the straight but Shoemark, showing tremendous strength and determination, had judged the pace so astutely that he was able to hold on by a short-head.

It was quite some ride to repel Dettori, who was at the top of his game throughout 2019, but Shoemark's performance could be taken as an analogy for the long, hard journey that had brought him to victory at Glorious Goodwood. Single-mindedness, courage, strength, determination – he had needed all of those, and more, to get him there.

While most people were raising a glass on New Year's Eve, Shoemark was in the final period of a 28-day stint in rehab, battling to overcome his addiction to alcohol. Bank House rehabilitation centre in Nottinghamshire was an unorthodox place to see in the new year, but considering he would be standing in the Goodwood winner's enclosure seven months later, looking and feeling like a man with everything to live for, it was time well spent for Shoemark.

Shortly after his Goodwood success, the 23-year-old rider spoke candidly about his addiction and recovery, revealing just how far he had plummeted and the routine that ensures he never returns to the same depths.

"I remind myself every day of the position and place I was in," he said. "It's very important to reflect on that, otherwise I could get ahead of myself and fall back into old habits. It's above everything else in my mind and I think it always will be."

There is no way of playing down the habits that locked Shoemark away in a bleak void for so long. He had attended his first Alcoholics Anonymous meeting three years before entering rehab – "everyone knew I wasn't a so-called normal drinker," he said – but had never really confronted the problem head-on and eventually found that drinking became a trigger for occasional drug use. A racecourse test revealed a positive for cocaine, three days after he had used the banned drug, and he was suspended in November 2018. Only then did he commit to the rehab programme at Bank House, leading eventually to a winning return to race-riding on Heroic – trained, like Vividly, by Charlie Hills – at Lingfield on June 1.

Astonishingly, even at his lowest, Shoemark somehow managed to control racehorses travelling at 40mph during his years of battling addiction. Whether it was as an 18-year-old spending his winter riding in Australia or during his ding-dong battle with David Egan for the apprentice championship in 2017 – a year when he also landed a Royal Ascot winner – his dependence on alcohol was never far away.

"Misery and constant fear" is how he sums up his previous existence. Fear of getting caught and the misery of what was to come each evening. It was an exhausting cycle and one he struggled to break. "I can't stress how bad it was – I was texting other jockeys and valets to see if the testers were at the races and all that crap you don't need. I was here in body but I wasn't here in mind," Shoemark said.

"I suppose I was running; it was complete denial. I didn't know right from wrong – I was completely twisted."

His dependence on alcohol became so great that his riding was getting in the way of his drinking rather than the other way around. His lifestyle was unsustainable, with his cravings increasingly wandering beyond drink.

"I've never taken drugs while I've been sober but it was getting to the stage where I'd have half a pint and it was on my mind. It was probably going to get to a point where drink didn't have to be involved. That's why getting caught was the best thing that ever happened to me.

"I've got nothing to hide now. I was taking drugs every weekend without fail and maybe once in the week as well. Once I started, I couldn't stop, and that's just me with everything."

****

IN JUNE 2018 Shoemark suffered a sickening fall that left him sprawled on the turf at Lingfield with six broken ribs and a punctured lung. While doctors raced to stabilise the stricken jockey, his first thought when he regained consciousness was not what damage the fall had caused but what damage he would soon be inflicting on himself. This was rock bottom and his drinking spiralled totally out of control.

"I remember waking up in hospital and thinking this is bad news now," he recalled. "Two months off and it was just socialising and drinking, and my career never got back from that injury before the ban."

It was on November 14 that year, just as it seemed there was no return, that he was inadvertently directed back to the right path. With cocaine in his system, he was

▸▸ *Continues page 58*

selected for a random test at Kempton. Back at the same track 15 days later he was handed a six-month ban. There was embarrassment when he had to vacate a packed changing room before the meeting had even begun, but there was also huge relief. For the first time in years he could stop running.

"When I got to the car I just breathed a huge sigh of relief. I'd been getting no buzz out of race-riding and hated it in the weighing room. I felt guilty all the time, it was just relentless."

Professional Jockeys Association chief executive Paul Struthers was quick to offer the help and support Shoemark needed. The rider was banned on the Thursday and by the following Tuesday he was off to rehab, paid for by the PJA. Had Struthers not reacted so quickly and proactively, Shoemark thinks he may well have reverted to flight mode, but instead he was booked into Bank House for what turned out to be the best Christmas gift he will ever receive.

"I actually loved it in there and met people who follow my career now. It's group sessions, counselling and AA meetings. You're living with people who are going through the same thing. You might have a bad day but there are 20 others around you having a good day. You can get among other alcoholics who think the same as you and that's how the rehab works."

Living back at home with his parents in Stow-on-the-Wold and with the security of a job just 40 miles away with Hills in Lambourn, Shoemark has been sober since he left rehab in January. Previously exhausting, his life is simple nowadays, with an uncomplicated routine the key to staying on track. He rides out in the morning, goes on to the races and returns home for dinner and bed, allowing him to concentrate solely on what he is paid and loves to do.

While the majority of his wins in 2019 were for his new boss, Shoemark also partnered winners for the likes of Sir Michael Stoute, Henry Candy and Charlie Fellowes and his natural flair in the saddle is shining once more. He certainly made the difference aboard Vividly at Goodwood, a win that was as satisfying as it was important for his rehabilitation. "To get a winner there was pretty special and for my boss Charlie Hills made it that little bit more important. I was very fortunate he gave me a chance when I came back. I love going into the yard.

"I had a lot of help from the horse at Goodwood, but I know what I'm doing now. I was going out to make the running and it paid off. I feel like I'm winning races I shouldn't be and that's what makes a top jockey. I buzz and thrive off winners now."

With his addiction firmly under control, Shoemark is in a healthy place and works hard to stay there, allowing not a week to pass without visiting his local AA meeting. "If you want to beat it, you've got to talk to like-minded people who have been through or are going through the same situation. Get yourself to the AA meeting, get your arse on the seat and do what they suggest. As long as you listen, leave your ego at the door and be honest, you can do it."

Shoemark did it and 2019 was the year he got his personal and professional life back on a winning track.

Zero tolerance but more understanding

The racing authorities continue to have a zero-tolerance policy on drug and alcohol positive tests but there is a growing understanding of the need to offer jockeys more help and education.

BHA figures show drug tests increased from 350 in 2006 to 520 in 2018 and the number of breath tests for alcohol rose from 309 to 1,894 in the same period. The number of positive samples remains small (for cocaine, eight in Britain and 16 in Ireland in the six years from 2013 to 2018) but there has been a worrying rise in the past year.

When William Carson was suspended for six months in September, following a positive test for a metabolite of cocaine in March, he joined Kieran Shoemark, Callum Rodriguez and Kevin Lundie on a list of jockeys who have served BHA-imposed bans recently.

In July the BHA launched an integrity education programme on a range of regulatory issues, including drugs and alcohol.

A BHA spokesman said: "Racing has very clear rules on the use of drugs and alcohol. The safety, health and welfare of all our jockeys is paramount and so we take a strict approach to substances that may impair judgement when riding in races or in training.

"Nevertheless, we're aware that a range of sports, including ourselves, are seeing an increase in positives for cocaine, as is wider society. We are working in collaboration with riders, through the Professional Jockeys Association, to understand why this may be happening and how it may relate to the use of prohibited drugs outside of racing. We're looking at how we might support jockeys with better education and information."

Leading the way: Kieran Shoemark heads the field before winning on Vividly at Goodwood

BIG FOR JAPAN

Deirdre pushed back the boundaries of international racing with a Group 1 triumph for Japan in the Nassau Stakes

By Nick Pulford

THE Thursday of the Qatar Goodwood Festival was glorious in terms of stretching racing's horizons and the Nassau Stakes, the Group 1 highlight of the card, played its part in a momentous day with victory for the Japanese mare Deirdre.

While not as groundbreaking or front-page headline-grabbing as Khadijah Mellah's feat in the Magnolia Cup, Deirdre's success was an important marker on the international racing map. Almost two decades after the breakthrough Group 1 victory of Agnes World in the 2000 July Cup, Deirdre became only the second Japanese-trained winner at the top level in Britain with a late swoop under super-cool Oisin Murphy.

Seiko Hashida Yoshimura, the daughter of trainer Mitsuru Hashida and racing manager to owner Toji Morita, summed up the significance of Deirdre's achievement. "This is very important not only for us but also for the whole of Japan to come over to Britain and have a big-race winner," she said. "It shows it's not just possible to come here and compete but that it's also possible to win. Hopefully we can have a good influence on Japanese racing with this win."

Goodwood, though, was plan B for Deirdre, who had been beaten when going for her primary target at Royal Ascot, just as Agnes World had been all those years ago when second in the King's Stand Stakes before going on to Newmarket glory. In Deirdre's case, she did not get close in the Prince of Wales's Stakes at the royal meeting, finishing just over 13 lengths behind Crystal Ocean as she came home sixth of the eight runners.

Connections felt there was a legitimate excuse with the soft ground at Ascot, however, and were encouraged enough to make her the first Japanese-trained runner at Goodwood, especially after a sparkling workout in the lead-up to the Nassau. By then, the five-year-old mare had been in Britain for almost three months, stabled at Jane Chapple-Hyam's Abington Place yard in Newmarket, and her acclimatisation to the rhythms of British racing was enhanced further with an away day to Goodwood in July.

Everything seemed set for a better showing and it was significant that Deirdre was taking on her own sex this time, as she had when winning her sole Grade 1 in Japan, the 2017 Shuka Sho for three-year-old fillies. She was also taking a drop in class, even if the Nassau is labelled in the same Group 1 bracket as the Prince of Wales's. Five of her seven rivals at Royal Ascot had a Racing Post Rating in the 120s and Crystal Ocean ran to 128 in victory, whereas Hermosa's Irish 1,000 Guineas RPR of 117 was the best on show in the Nassau.

Yutaka Take, the 50-year-old Japanese riding legend, had been in the saddle at Ascot but he did not return for Deirdre's second assignment and the ride passed to Murphy. This was no chance booking, with Murphy having ridden 25 winners in Japan during a two-month winter stint, and the young star once again demonstrated his fast-maturing talent.

This time the ground was good and Murphy played a perfect waiting game on the 20-1 shot as the market principals, dual Guineas winner Hermosa and recent Group 2 scorer Mehdaayih, ensured a quick pace with their early battle for the lead. That was always likely to set up the race for a swooper and, while Mehdaayih

Continues page 62

kept on bravely after Hermosa had faded a long way from home, Murphy read the race perfectly. He saved every inch on Deirdre and kept to the inside rail at the cutaway in the straight before launching a strong run to cut down the gallant Mehdaayih in the final 100 yards, scoring by a length and a quarter.

"That was a special performance from Deirdre," Yoshimura said. "It was a very big challenge to come here. We have been in Britain for three months with Deirdre and we're so pleased that we kept believing in her. A lot of credit has to go to Oisin Murphy. We didn't give him any instructions and just decided to let him ride the horse in the way he felt right. He's a brilliant jockey."

Murphy had hoped his winter stint in the Far East would have the knock-on effect of putting him in line for any Japanese runners in Europe and he was delighted to deliver a landmark win. "I'm so glad the Japanese have brought a horse here and she has performed," he said. "I've been telling people since I came back from Japan of the regard they hold their horses in, and it's fantastic they've won a Group 1 race here. She was already a Group 1 winner but it's great to do it in Britain."

Deirdre came out of the race as the top-rated runner, having earned a career-best RPR of 118, and Murphy was full of praise for her effort in conceding weight to the three-year-olds Mehdaayih and Hermosa. "She's a big, masculine mare, and I'm not surprised she was able to carry the 60kg [9st 7lb], which is far more than she would be used to carrying in Japan. I kept looking at her price but thinking she had a wonderful chance. She had worked brilliantly, but to go and win against a decent field was something else."

John Gosden, Mehdaayih's trainer, was magnanimous in defeat and appreciative of the wider significance of Deirdre's win. "To bring Deirdre over here from Japan and win a Group 1 like this, at a great festival, is fantastic for international racing and for Japanese racing. If we were going to be beaten, I'm delighted to be beaten by the Japanese.

"I saw Deirdre as a threat. I've seen her train across the road in Newmarket and I know her form. She's a tough racemare, a real pro, and her owners are the most charming people. It's a fabulous result for racing. We've had two fabulous results today, the charity race and this. It's wonderful for racing and wonderful for the country."

On such a boundary-pushing day, racing was the biggest winner.

▲ Perfect timing: Oisin Murphy brings Deirdre (far side) past Mehdaayih to score a landmark win in the Nassau Stakes; below, Murphy hugs trainer Mitsuru Hashida

'A life-changing experience for us all'

Instead of heading back home after her Nassau Stakes victory, Deirdre took up extended residency in Newmarket and her connections looked around Europe in search of more glory.

The Deirdre effect was felt next at Leopardstown, where her participation in the Irish Champion Stakes made her the first Japanese-trained runner in Ireland. Originally scheduled for a 6.35pm start time, the big race was brought forward to 4.15pm so that it could be shown live in Japan.

Deirdre did not let down her fans at home and, with better luck, she might have given them another Group 1 triumph to cheer. She was travelling well under Oisin Murphy but ran up behind a wall of horses on the inside rail two furlongs out. Magical, the 11-10 favourite, had flown by the time Murphy pulled around the back of the field to challenge down the outer and, despite a flying finish by Deirdre, fourth place was the best they could manage.

The general feeling was that Deirdre looked at least the second best on the day and might have challenged Magical with a better passage, with Murphy giving a frank appraisal of the race a few days later. "I was gutted," he told Sky Sports Racing. "The best jockeys are judged on their performances on the big days and I ran straight into a hole. It was my fault."

Connections attached no blame to Murphy, who was on board again in the Qipco Champion Stakes at Ascot. Deirdre moved up a place from Leopardstown to finish third this time but again Magical took the honours and her winning margin over the Japanese mare was three lengths, exactly as it had been at Leopardstown.

The soft ground at Ascot was not in her favour but this was not a time to dwell on what might have been in different circumstances. For Deirdre's team there were only positive thoughts of their mare and the whole experience of racing in Britain.

"She is so tough and we are so proud of her," said trainer Mitsuru Hashida's son and assistant Yoshi. "We cannot say thank you enough to this amazing horse. All of our team love Britain and British racing. It is so special. Every race has given us unforgettable memories. It has been a life-changing experience for us all. We are almost crying."

Murphy paid tribute to their sporting enterprise. "They've done a great job with her," the rider said at Leopardstown, "and I think it shows how good Japanese horses are. She's done Japan proud."

He wasn't wrong there.

sky bet
York

IN THE PICTURE

Long-term plan pays dividends as Mustajeer mops up £1m Ebor

MUSTAJEER made history at York in August when he landed the Ebor, the first £1m handicap to be run on the Flat in Britain. The Ger Lyons-trained six-year-old took the £600,000 winner's share of the monster pot with a three-quarters-of-a-length victory over Red Galileo, who earned almost £180,000 for finishing second.

First run in 1843, the Ebor has long been one of the most prestigious staying handicaps but its allure has increased following a massive prize-money injection from sponsors Sky Bet, who agreed a five-year deal with York in 2018. The purse went up by 75 per cent to £500,000 in the first running under their banner and doubled for 2019 to become the richest handicap in Europe.

One trainer who certainly had his eye on the prize was Lyons, who sent Mustajeer across the Irish Sea to finish fourth in the 2018 Ebor and immediately targeted a return trip for the £1m contest, persuading owner David Spratt to hold off on an Australian campaign and go back to York again. "Ger said, 'Wait, this is a proper horse, let me train him properly' and he's got it spot on," said Spratt, who had bought Mustajeer for 50,000gns in 2017 out of a Sheikh Hamdan Al Maktoum sales draft.

Lyons was busy working back in County Meath on Ebor day and was represented at York by his daughter Kerri, but the next day the trainer told Racing TV's Luck On Sunday: "The plan was set in motion when he finished fourth last summer. We thought 'they're making this a £1m race, it would be rude of us not to go over and have a go at it'.

"Very seldom in our game does it work out. If you'd given me fourth place money before the race, I'd have taken your hand off. That's not being pessimistic, it's just realistic. To see him win as he did was phenomenal."

The race was given a flashy build-up under the new sponsorship, with the 22 jockeys introduced to the crowd one by one in the style of big-fight boxers, and the bout came down to an experienced title winner versus a young challenger.

Mustajeer was ridden by Colin Keane, the 2017 Irish champion, and he struck for home with a furlong and a half to run. Cieren Fallon, the 20-year-old son of six-time British champion Kieren Fallon, launched a desperate late bid along the rail on Red Galileo but it was Keane who had landed the knockout blow with his confident early move. A clear case of fortune favouring the brave.

Picture: EDWARD WHITAKER (RACINGPOST.COM/PHOTOS)

BOUM TIME

Al Boum Photo and Paul Townend laid the ghost of infamous defeat with an emphatic victory in the Cheltenham Gold Cup

By David Jennings

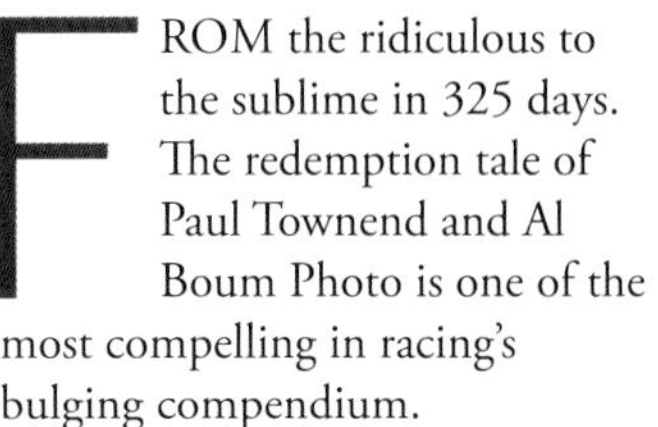

FROM the ridiculous to the sublime in 325 days. The redemption tale of Paul Townend and Al Boum Photo is one of the most compelling in racing's bulging compendium.

We must rewind to April 24, 2018 for the ridiculous. A video of the Growise Champion Novice Chase at Punchestown, posted on YouTube by Attheraces, has had almost 100,000 views. If you have seen the race, you know why.

Townend had the race at his mercy on Al Boum Photo, only for him to swerve violently right in an attempt to bypass the final fence, taking Finian's Oscar with him. The jockey thought he heard a shout; he heard wrong. It earned him a 21-day ban for dangerous riding. It could have cost him his job with Willie Mullins. It could have cost his boss the Irish trainers' title. It could have cost him his career. Instead it was merely the edgy opening chapter of what turned into a fairytale for the 29-year-old.

Fast-forward to March 15, 2019 for the sublime. The unexposed novice chaser from 11 months ago, who had defeat snatched from the jaws of victory in that infamous race at Punchestown, negotiated the last safely in the Magners Cheltenham Gold Cup and stormed up the hill to win the most coveted prize in jump racing. Townend was doing the steering and this time he headed straight for the line.

It was the sincerest apology Townend could have given Mullins and owners Marie and Joe Donnelly. The trainer had sent out four runners in the Gold Cup, searching for his first winner in two long decades of trying, and Al Boum Photo was the only one still standing at the end. Most importantly, he was standing in the no.1 spot.

Townend was still thinking of that pernicious Punchestown moment, even in the ecstasy of winning the Cheltenham Gold Cup. "From the time I was an apprentice I've had Willie behind

▸▸ *Continues page 68*

me, all the way up through my career. To walk into Punchestown the next day with him having my back was a huge thing. It happened, but it's in the past now. Al Boum Photo is a Gold Cup winner. I think I owed it to the horse. I'm so grateful to Willie and the owners for sticking by me. To repay them with a Gold Cup is the best feeling in the world."

Having reflected back on that dark day, Townend was able to enjoy his golden moment. "You dream of winning the Gold Cup as you grow up. I can guarantee it's as good as you dream it's going to be. It's some feeling to cross the line, I swear to God."

****

AL BOUM PHOTO arrived at Cheltenham with plenty to prove. He had run only once since the Punchestown fiasco and that was in a Listed chase at Tramore on New Year's Day when his nearest challengers were stablemates Total Recall and Invitation Only. Now he would be facing more serious contenders from his own yard who had notched Grade 1 victories on the road to Cheltenham – Savills Chase winner Kemboy and Irish Gold Cup scorer Bellshill – as well as favourite Presenting Percy, King George VI Chase winner Clan Des Obeaux and defending title-holder Native River.

If Al Boum Photo's lack of hard yards at the top level was one question mark, another was his fall in the 2018 RSA Chase on his only previous visit to Cheltenham, which left Ruby Walsh with a broken leg. He had fallen at Limerick earlier in his novice campaign too and arrived for the Gold Cup with only four completed chases behind him. He had yet to win beyond the 2m5½f of his Tramore success and now he had to go another five furlongs over the testing Cheltenham undulations.

Mullins admitted afterwards Al Boum Photo was "my third or fourth choice" but said there were good reasons behind the light campaign. "His run at Tramore was not the usual sort of prep run for a Gold Cup but that was it because of the ground. The horse has been good and sound and we didn't get another run because there was no ground to run him on. I knew he would go on the ground [good to soft at Cheltenham] and we always thought he would stay."

It was harder for punters to know what to expect from Al Boum Photo and he was allowed to go off at 12-1. Bellshill, the choice of stable jockey Walsh, and Kemboy were both preferred in the market and Patrick Mullins was on board Invitation Only, a 33-1 shot. Three of the Mullins quartet had departed by the tenth fence, however, and Al Boum Photo was the only one left.

"I wasn't feeling very good with a circuit to race, that's for sure," admitted Mullins after Kemboy unseated David Mullins at the first fence, Walsh pulled up Bellshill after eight fences following a series of errors and Invitation Only suffered a fatal fall.

Townend sure was feeling good. Recounting his race, he said: "I got into a beautiful rhythm everywhere. I wasn't where I wanted to be over the first two, but I got a couple of good jumps and from there everything flowed for me. There were horses struggling around me and it was just happening for me. I knew if I kept upright, I had a good chance."

'There were horses struggling around me and it was just happening for me. I knew if I kept upright, I had a good chance'

Everything might have flowed perfectly for Al Boum Photo but this Gold Cup was a brutal affair. Only nine of the 16 who started managed to complete.

Native River, who had dominated from the front the previous year, could not get to the head of affairs until the 12th fence. Until that point the previous year's runner-up, Might Bite, had blazed the trail. Thistlecrack

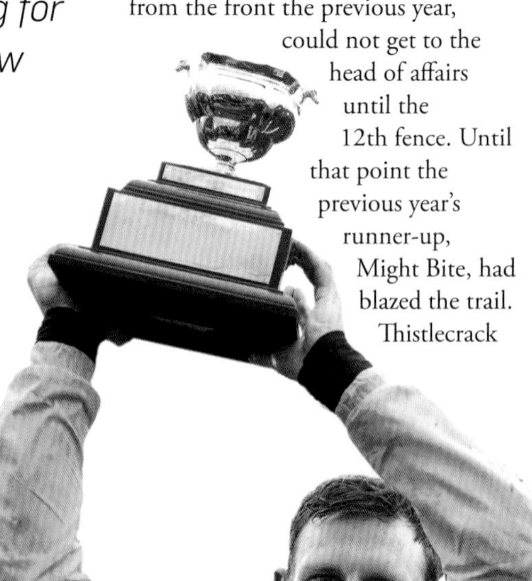

struggled from the start, while Presenting Percy, the impressive RSA winner at the 2018 festival, never looked happy at any stage under Davy Russell.

Clan Des Obeaux sneaked into contention on the home turn but his stamina ran out after the second-last. He was not the first King George winner and certainly won't be the last to succumb to the gruelling uphill climb to the line. It was here that Al Boum Photo came into his own.

Townend threw him into the second-last and the seven-year-old responded in style. They popped the last three lengths clear and Bristol De Mai could not sustain his challenge. It was left to the stamina-laden Anibale Fly to try to land the final blow but he could not get close enough. This was Al Boum Photo's day.

★★★★

MULLINS had laid the Gold Cup hoodoo to rest but his thoughts were with Townend. "It's fantastic to win the Gold Cup but for Paul to ride it is the real result for me," he said. "Paul started off when he was 17 and has always been so natural and so good. He was riding as a claimer for me and won the Galway Hurdle for John Kiely. That really put him on the scene. He has just been unlucky that he's there alongside Ruby and, any time Ruby is free, Paul gets to ride the second horse. He's a fantastic rider."

The trainer felt the owners had also received due reward for loyalty and perseverance. "I'm delighted for Marie and Joe Donnelly. We've had a few upsets, one or two horses weren't as good as we thought they were, but they've put in a huge commitment to the yard," he said.

"There was no question of Paul not riding the horse. Marie and Joe rang me the morning after Punchestown and said to tell Paul that they've had a great life in racing and that was only a small disappointment. There was never a doubt or a word that he wouldn't ride their horses – they said it was just one of those days. They are proper sporting people."

On that golden day in March these proper sporting people – the Donnellys, Mullins, Townend – had their proper sporting reward.

▲ Photo call: Paul Townend shouts with delight as he crosses the line in the Cheltenham Gold Cup ahead of Anibale Fly and Bristol De Mai; below left, Townend lifts the trophy

▼ The following day's Racing Post front page

RACING POST

Search 'Racing Post App' for must-have news, insight and fast results £3.20

ONE FOR THE AL BOUM

Townend's finest hour – on horse who gave him worst moment in the saddle

Mullins ends Gold Cup hoodoo – reports and Alastair Down, pages 2-17

TIPPING GOLD

Paul Kealy tipped 12-1 crackers Al Boum Photo and Ch'Tibello

Tom Segal tipped Ch'Tibello, 5-1 Early Doors and Gold Cup runner-up Anibale Fly ante-post at 50-1

DON'T MISS TODAY'S BEST BETS

Pricewise, pages 24-25

Saturday Sizzlers, page 27

New number one

Springtime was a whirlwind for Paul Townend. Not only did he win the Magners Cheltenham Gold Cup on Al Boum Photo, he was crowned Ireland's champion jump jockey for a second time and promoted to number one at Willie Mullins' all-conquering Closutton stable following the retirement of Ruby Walsh on the first day of May.

"Strange is probably the right word for it," said Townend when asked what life without Walsh is like at Closutton. Looking ahead to the possibilities his new job would bring, he added: "I'm looking forward to riding in the big races more often in England. Before Ruby retired I used to love it when there was a big race in England as it meant Ruby was riding there and I was going to pick up a few nice rides at home.

"Any professional sportsperson wants to be on the big stage and operating at the highest level, so hopefully I'll be able to do that."

The truth is that Townend has been operating at the highest level for quite some time, even when Walsh was still around. Benie Des Dieux's victory in the Grande Course de Haies d'Auteuil in the middle of May brought up his half-century of Grade 1 wins. She was his 49th top-tier winner too, having landed the Irish Stallion Farms EBF Annie Power Mares Champion Hurdle at Punchestown.

The understudy stepped up to the lead role while Walsh was sidelined with a succession of injuries in 2018 and Mullins has every confidence Townend will continue to prosper.

"He worked very hard while Ruby was off and it paid off – he definitely deserved the title last season," the champion trainer said. "He has played second fiddle to Ruby so often and, when he was still in front halfway through the season, I said I would let him have a good crack at it.

"I'd be hoping Paul can build on that now and win a few more. He's got all the talents a jockey needs to be a multiple champion."

Willie Mullins reflects on a memorable year that brought success in the Cheltenham Gold Cup and Irish Grand National at long last

GLORY DAYS

By Tony O'Hehir

WILLIE MULLINS' chances were dwindling fast in the Cheltenham Gold Cup. He started with four runners but three had gone before a circuit had been completed. Kemboy, the most fancied of the quartet, unseated Mullins' nephew David after the first fence, Bellshill was pulled up after a catalogue of errors and Invitation Only departed at the tenth with a fatal injury. Al Boum Photo, the mount of Paul Townend, was the only hope.

It was a familiar story of Gold Cup misfortune. From Florida Pearl's first attempt at the prize 20 years before, Mullins' quest had repeatedly come up short. Six times he had saddled the runner-up – Florida Pearl, Hedgehunter, Sir Des Champs, On His Own and Djakadam (twice) – and the fates always seemed to conspire against him.

"I was thinking the Gold Cup just wasn't our race," he says, recalling that disastrous first circuit of the 2019 edition. "We always wanted to win it and, while it would be wrong to say we were obsessive about winning it, my gut feeling at the halfway stage was that we were going to have to wait at least another year."

Mullins, the most successful trainer in Cheltenham Festival history, revealed later that he had started to doubt himself. "We've been very lucky with our Champion Hurdle horses as we've had some fantastic winners of that event and maybe I started to think my method of training is more suited towards two-mile horses. We've had some nice staying chasers such as Hedgehunter, who won the Grand National, but I did just start to wonder whether we were training our horses to be too fast for the Gold Cup."

With only one horse to occupy his mind on the final circuit, it began to dawn on Mullins that all was not lost this time. "I could see Al Boum Photo was travelling sweetly and jumping well. Also Paul's body language, and knowing the way he rides, encouraged me. Horse and rider were in a perfect rhythm."

As he watched through his binoculars,

Mullins saw Townend put Al Boum Photo into contention. In fifth place passing the stands with a circuit to run, Townend was fourth over the open ditch in the back straight and moved up to dispute third with Clan Des Obeaux after jumping the next ditch. As they turned to run down the hill, he was close behind leading duo Native River and Might Bite and soon angled out to throw down his challenge.

"I worried whether the horse would pick up when Paul asked him but he certainly did that and went away to win well," Mullins says. Al Boum Photo led soon after turning for home and stayed on too strongly for the dogged Anibale Fly as the fancied contenders faded away.

"It was a fantastic feeling when he won and a great result for all involved. I was especially delighted for Paul because of what happened at Punchestown the previous season when he got his wires crossed. Al Boum Photo's owners Joe and Marie Donnelly stood by him, we all did. They took that blow on the chin and for them winning the Gold Cup was reward for their loyalty."

Another name to the forefront of Mullins' mind after the Gold Cup was that of Mick O'Toole, himself a Gold Cup-winning trainer, who died in 2018. "Al Boum Photo's Gold Cup win would never have happened without Micko. He introduced me to Joe Donnelly and the brief he gave me was to buy a Gold Cup horse for Joe and Marie."

In finding that horse for the Donnellys, Mullins had unearthed his own Gold Cup winner after years of searching. Al Boum Photo was his 65th festival winner, putting him one ahead of Nicky Henderson in the all-time standings and making him leading trainer at Cheltenham for the sixth time in nine years.

"We celebrated that night and the reaction when we got home was amazing," he says. "It clearly meant a lot to the folk in our locality to have a Gold Cup winner and the amount of calls, texts and messages of congratulation we received was staggering and much appreciated."

★★★★

A MONTH later on Easter Monday at Fairyhouse, another gap in Mullins' CV was filled when Burrows Saint gave him a first win in the BoyleSports Irish Grand National, leading home a one-two-three for the yard ahead of stablemates Isleofhopendreams and Acapella Bourgeois.

Mullins explains it was a win with special historical significance for his family. "My father [Paddy] won the Irish National four times and when Vulpine gave him his first win in the race in 1967 it was the first big race he won during his long and successful career. So it meant a lot to us to win the race after many years of trying."

This time Walsh was on board the winner, the latest big-race triumph for the most successful trainer-jockey combination in Irish jump racing history. A few weeks later there was another when Kemboy, who had bounced back from his Cheltenham exit with a convincing victory over Clan Des Obeaux in the Betway Bowl at Aintree, relegated Al Boum Photo to second place in the Punchestown Gold Cup. The significance of that victory was revealed to Mullins in the winner's enclosure when Walsh announced he was retiring from the saddle.

Recalling the emotional occasion, Mullins says: "I wasn't expecting Ruby to bow out and the first I knew about the decision was when he jumped off Kemboy. He caught me on the hop.

"We had tremendous success together over the years and it was the end of an era. I knew the day would come but not as suddenly as it did. But I suppose announcing his retirement after winning the big race of the week at his home track, with all his family there, was a fitting way to bring his remarkable career to an end.

"I was delighted to see him going out on his own terms. He first came to us when he was 16 and it's great that he's still involved in the yard, where his knowledge and input remain a huge asset."

A 13th Irish trainers' title was already in the bag before Mullins sent out 13 winners at the Punchestown festival, the annual climax to the season in Ireland. Novice hurdler Klassical Dream completed a hat-trick of Grade 1 wins, Un De Sceaux won the BoyleSports Champion Chase for the second consecutive year and a new star was born in Chacun Pour Soi, who landed the Grade 1 Ryanair Novice Chase from Defi Du Seuil and the Mullins-trained Duc Des Genievres, both of whom had landed big prizes at the Cheltenham Festival.

"Chacun Pour Soi is a really exciting horse and to see him, on only his third start over fences, beat the JLT winner and the Arkle winner in the style he did was an awesome performance," Mullins says. "For many reasons it was a memorable and successful season for the yard."

That was emphasised when Klassical Dream and Chacun Pour Soi topped their respective two-mile novice categories in the 2018-19 Anglo-Irish Jumps Classifications and Kemboy was the overall champion with a rating of 177, 2lb ahead of Al Boum Photo.

With his usual breadth of quality and quantity, Mullins can look forward to another exciting season at the big festivals. But the highs of the 2018-19 campaign will be hard to beat.

Magic numbers

How the key figures stood for Willie Mullins in 2019

13 Irish jumps trainers' titles

65 Cheltenham Festival winners

6 Cheltenham Festival top trainer awards

1 Cheltenham Gold Cup winner

1 Irish Grand National winner

3 Divisional champions in the 2018-19 Anglo-Irish Jumps Classifications

◀ Boum town: Willie Mullins parades Cheltenham Gold Cup winner Al Boum Photo in Leighlinbridge near his Closutton yard

FINAL FLOURISH

Ruby Walsh had long wanted to go out on a high and the ultimate big-race jockey got his wish at the Punchestown festival

By Richard Forristal

IN THE end you could say that nothing became Ruby Walsh's career quite like the leaving of it. It was close to perfect, as meticulously orchestrated and exquisitely executed as it could possibly have been. At Punchestown, on Kemboy, for Willie Mullins and in a Gold Cup, with most of his family there to share the seminal moment. And in glorious victory, of course. Walsh knew what he wanted to do and implemented his plan with all the conviction you would expect of him.

It was a fitting finale for jump racing's big-race rider extraordinaire, a totemic figure who checked out with 59 Cheltenham Festival triumphs, 213 Grade 1s and 2,756 winners. He won Cheltenham's big four races at least twice apiece, two Grand Nationals and a record five King George VI Chases, among so

many other big-race triumphs, and was inextricably linked with modern greats such as Kauto Star, Big Buck's, Hurricane Fly and Master Minded.

Walsh had long been renowned for being surgically detached from his emotions while he went about his work but keen-eyed spectators had been speculating since the turn of the year that he was getting unusually animated in his celebrations. The first reported sighting of Walsh expressing a notable degree of rapture was as he crossed the line victorious on Invitation Only in the Goffs Thyestes Handicap Chase at Gowran Park in January. If the fist pump he thrust across his body had connected with anyone, it would have been lights out. It was Kloppesque.

We witnessed similarly enthusiastic celebrations aboard Klassical Dream at Cheltenham and Kemboy at Aintree, and in hindsight his third Irish Grand National success could be presented by the prosecution as the single most damning piece of evidence of his altered perspective. As Burrows Saint stepped over the line to deliver Mullins a landmark first win in the Fairyhouse showpiece, his old ally stood bolt upright in the irons, punched the air and gesticulated to the crowd again when he regained his seat.

There were high fives and generously reciprocated pats on the back with colleagues and then he planted a kiss on his sister Katie's cheek as he leaned over to hug her. Poor girl was only trying to conduct her mounted post-race interview for RTE television.

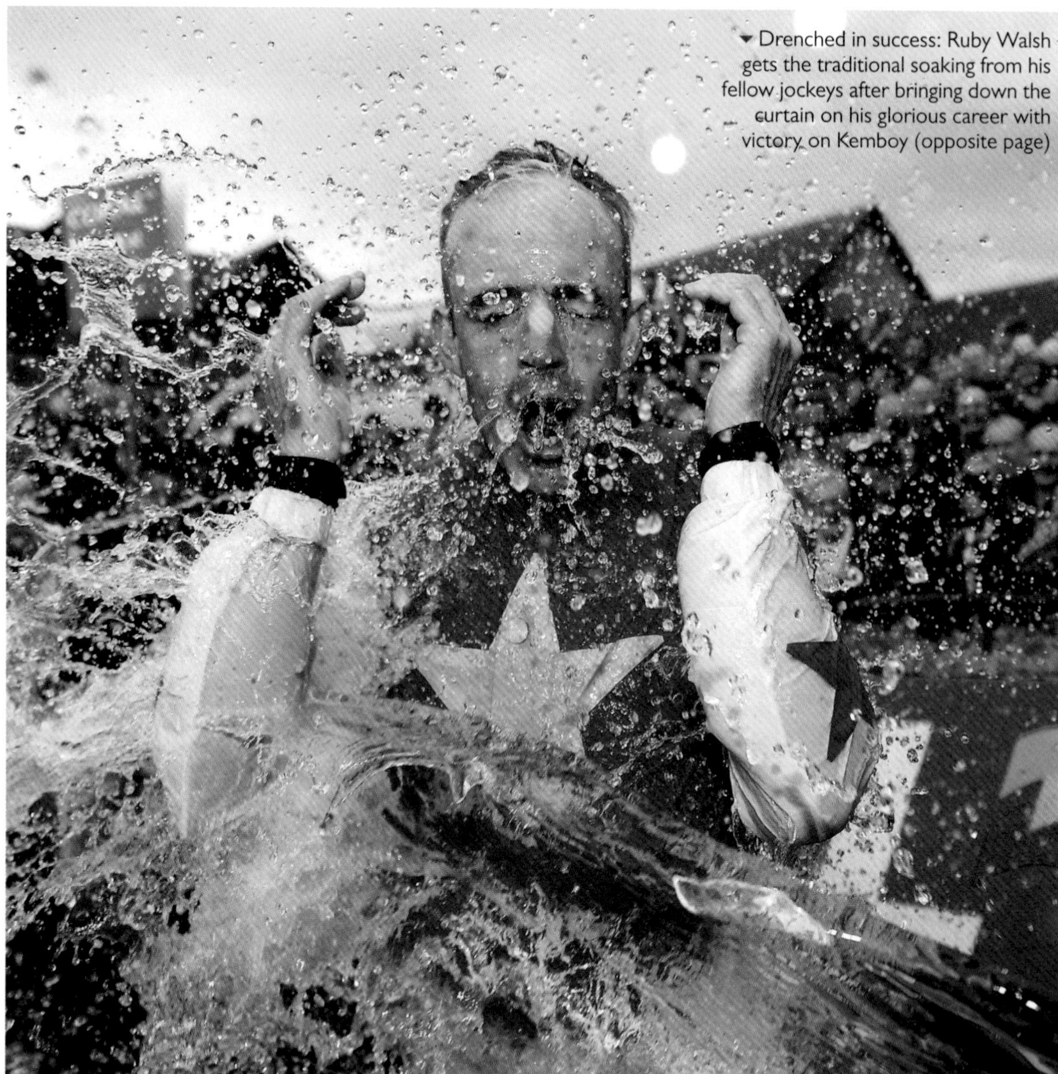

▾ Drenched in success: Ruby Walsh gets the traditional soaking from his fellow jockeys after bringing down the curtain on his glorious career with victory on Kemboy (opposite page)

★★★★

THIS wasn't the cool, dispassionate assassin racing fans had come to know and worship over the previous 25 years. To that guy, high-profile success was a matter of routine. That guy used to fold up his rifle and casually saunter back to his station while the pandemonium he had created unfolded all around him. It was just business.

However, there had been whispers for months that Walsh, in his 40th year, was relishing each marquee win in the knowledge that it might be his last. When Aintree rolled around, the whispers grew louder, but third was the best Rathvinden could manage behind Tiger Roll in the big race. The Grand National proved historic for different reasons, so Walsh had to wait for his moment.

Given the subsequent fervour of his Irish Grand National success, it's a small wonder he didn't decommission his weapons right there. But Walsh had long ago put on record how he would like to make his departure and he subsequently confirmed that it was always going to be Aintree or Punchestown. Plundering the most valuable jumps race in Ireland wasn't going to prompt him to deviate from how he had envisioned his exit unfolding.

"I'd love to get off one in Punchestown, pull the saddle off and tell Willie that I won't be out for the next one. That's how I'd do it if I had my choice," he had said in the past. That concept of getting as far as Punchestown one day and calling time was something he had spoken about hypothetically for years. A fairytale Grand National swansong in Liverpool would have been a worthy alternative, but the Irish equivalent wasn't an adequate catalyst.

While Burrows Saint's win was special, Walsh has never been the type to get carried away by a moment, and a long goodbye in the mould of AP McCoy's wouldn't have been his thing either. He never craved that sort of attention.

When the subject was broached at his Kilcullen home in the months beforehand, his wife Gillian provided the sort of reassuring counsel he desired. "We looked at what way to go about it and she just said 'stick to what you always said you would do – just get off one and walk away'," Walsh later reflected. "It's all about big races and you want to go out on a big one. Punchestown is home and I've been coming here since I was a kid."

Fate can be a cruel mistress, but she had his back this time. Walsh's desire to be true to his word was threatened every time he threw his leg over a horse and getting the opportunity was something that had privately preoccupied him ever since Al Boum Photo crashed out at the second-last in the 2018 RSA Chase and left him with a freshly broken leg, having just recovered from the fracture he suffered when Let's Dance fell at Punchestown the previous November.

"That's how I'd do it if I had my choice but you don't often get to do things your own way or have a choice in these things," he once said when speaking about plan A, the exact version of which was in the making for over a year. "When a decision is made in your head it's

▸▸ *Continues page 76*

easy enough to say it and I made it a good while ago. When I broke my leg in Cheltenham last year I felt I couldn't do that again," he revealed at Punchestown.

****

PUBLICLY he had moved to dispel the rumours in the spring. Twice the 12-time Irish champion proactively stated he wasn't going anywhere, that he fully intended to be riding at the 2020 Cheltenham Festival and that he was like a bad smell – he'd linger a bit yet.

That wasn't something he had to say so explicitly, but perhaps he didn't want Mullins getting wind of the notion that retirement was near. The champion trainer duly insisted in the winner's enclosure at Punchestown that he didn't know what was coming. "It was a surprise to me," Mullins said. "We don't discuss the 'R' word in our house for either man or beast and it caught me on the hop completely.

"He got off the horse. I said, 'Well done' and he said, 'You'd better find a rider for Livelovelaugh later'. And I was wondering was he dehydrated or something and couldn't race for the rest of the day. And then he said, 'I'm finished'. Then it dawned on me that he'd just announced his retirement."

If Walsh really did catch Mullins completely unawares after unsaddling, his boss was slightly later to the party than many observers. The wave started it all. It wasn't a fist pump, it was a wave, and a pretty unambiguous one. We all saw it as he flashed by the line on Kemboy and every journalist with a rapidly diminishing deadline immediately began to curse Punchestown's penchant for twilight fixtures.

"He's doing it, isn't he?" was the vibe within a panicked press room. But then Walsh was interviewed by RTE as he circled out on the track and he threw everyone off the scent. The interviewer dangled a loaded question in front of him, but he didn't bite.

Was he not going to do it after

▸▸ *Continues page 78*

Life at the top: Ruby Walsh's career highlights

Full name Rupert Edward Walsh

Born May 14, 1979

Father Ted Walsh (trainer of Papillon)

Apprenticeship Amateur rider with Ted Walsh, Willie Mullins, Enda Bolger

First mount Wild Irish, 5th in bumper, Leopardstown, May 17, 1995

First winner Siren Song (trainer Ted Walsh), bumper, Gowran Park, July 15, 1995

First winner over obstacles Katiymann over hurdles, Leopardstown, May 22, 1996

First big-race winner Garaiyba (1996 GPT Galway Handicap)

First winner in Britain Major Jamie (1997 William Hill Hurdle, Sandown)

First Grade I winner/First Cheltenham Festival winner Alexander Banquet (1998 Champion Bumper)

Grand National winners Papillon (2000), Hedgehunter (2005)

Cheltenham Gold Cup winner Kauto Star (2007, 2009)

Champion Hurdle winners Hurricane Fly (2011, 2013), Faugheen (2015), Annie Power (2016)

Queen Mother Champion Chase winners Azertyuiop (2004), Master Minded (2008, 2009)

World/Stayers' Hurdle winners Big Buck's (2009, 2010, 2011, 2012), Nichols Canyon (2017)

Ryanair Chase winners Thisthatandtother (2005), Taranis (2007), Vautour (2016), Un De Sceaux (2017)

Six-time Cheltenham Festival winner Quevega (2009-14 Mares' Hurdle, Grade 2)

Other notable Cheltenham Festival winners Azertyuiop (2003 Arkle Chase), Denman (2007 Royal & SunAlliance Chase), Celestial Halo (2008 Triumph Hurdle), Vautour (2014 Supreme Novices' Hurdle, 2015 JLT Novices' Chase), Faugheen (2014 Neptune Investment Novices' Hurdle), Douvan (2015 Supreme Novices' Hurdle, 2016 Arkle Chase), Un De Sceaux (2015 Arkle Chase), Yorkhill (2016 Neptune Investment Novices' Hurdle, 2017 JLT Novices' Chase)

King George VI Chase winner Kauto Star (2006, 2007, 2008, 2009, 2011)

Irish Gold Cup winners (Leopardstown) Neptune Collonges (2009), Quel Esprit (2012), Bellshill (2019)

Punchestown Gold Cup winners Imperial Call (1999), Commanche Court (2000), Neptune Collonges (2007, 2008), Boston Bob (2014), Kemboy (2019)

Irish Grand National winners Commanche Court (2000), Numbersixvalverde (2005), Burrows Saint (2019)

Irish Champion Hurdle winners (Leopardstown) Brave Inca (2009), Hurricane Fly (2012, 2013, 2014, 2015), Faugheen (2016)

Grande Course de Haies d'Auteuil winner Thousand Stars (2011, 2012)

Nakayama Grand Jump winner Blackstairmountain (2013 – his richest prize, £465,162)

Grand National Hurdle winner (Far Hills, USA) Rawnaq (2016)

Australian Grand National winner Bashboy (2015)

Highest-rated mounts (Racing Post Ratings) 191 Kauto Star (2009 King George VI Chase by 36 lengths), 186 Master Minded, 183 Denman

Most consecutive wins on one horse 16 (Big Buck's 2009-12)

Most Grade I wins on one horse 16 (Hurricane Fly 2009-15)

Leading jockey at Cheltenham Festival 11 times (record)

Total wins at Cheltenham Festival 59 (record)

Champion amateur rider in Ireland 1996-97, 1997-98

Champion jump jockey in Ireland 12 times (record): 1998-99, 2000-01, 2004-05, 2005-06, 2006-07, 2007-08, 2008-09, 2009-10, 2013-14, 2014-15, 2015-16, 2016-17

Leading jump jockey in Britain (prize-money) 2006-07, 2007-08, 2008-09

Most wins in an Irish season 131 (2007-08, 2016-17)

Most wins in a British season 81 (2004-05)

Most wins in a season (Ireland & Britain combined) 200 (2006-07, 2007-08)

Total wins over jumps in Ireland & Britain 2,756 (Ireland 1,980, Britain 776)

Compiled by John Randall

▲ Racing icons: Walsh on the big stage with (from top) Kauto Star, Big Buck's, Hurricane Fly and Master Minded

all? It didn't make sense. Was the press pack, so eager to pay worthy tribute to a colossus who had bestrode the game for a quarter of a century, to stand down? It was like waiting for smoke from the Vatican.

As Walsh rode back to the winner's enclosure, the sense that something was stirring grew stronger. A giddy, expectant swarm of people had descended in and around the parade ring, far more so than would normally be the case for a Walsh-Mullins Grade 1 win, not least when you consider the stable's recently crowned Cheltenham Gold Cup hero Al Boum Photo had been vanquished in the process.

On dismounting, after a short debrief you could see Walsh steal a word in Mullins' ear. Then they smiled knowingly at each other and Walsh made a beeline for the weighing scales. Once he had done that, the parade-ring announcer Brendan McArdle collared him on the podium. This time Walsh pounced on the bait. The reason he had to play the poker face earlier was because he didn't want to announce anything publicly until he had informed Mullins of his decision.

That job done, now all he needed was a platform. McArdle threw a routine question about the victory his way, Walsh answered hastily and then answered a question he wasn't asked. "That's it – I'm not going out on the next one. I'm finished. I wanted to go out on a winner like I said I'd always do at Punchestown," he told McArdle.

"You say go out on a winner, but you've plenty more Gold Cups in you?" McArdle posed, slightly taken aback and unsure how he should respond to such a momentous statement. "No, you'll never again see me on a horse," Walsh volleyed, cracking into a smile as he realised the magnitude of what he was doing. "I'm finished. That's it – it's all over."

And so it was. An elegant punctuation mark on an epoch-defining legacy – exactly how its author intended.

Ruby on . . .

Horses
People often think jockeys get attached to their horses but we don't. The trainer has a much bigger emotional attachment to the horse than the jockey because they spend so much time together. The jockey just gets on and off

Journalists
I hate lazy journalism. I pick reporters up, and broadcasters up, on simple things like form. I hate sloppiness. I hate bullshit – that's probably the best way of putting it

Proudest moment
Winning the Grand National when I was 20. My dad had trained the horse, Papillon, and that gave me the most pride

Big races
I grew up watching the big races on Grandstand on Saturdays and that's what I wanted to do – to ride the big winners on the big days. And that's what I chased – the good horses

Injury
The physical pain goes – it's gone in two hours, three hours – but that's nothing compared to the mental pain you then face. You're watching somebody riding a horse you should be riding and you're cooped up – it's the mental torture of what you're missing

Losing his spleen
When your spleen is gone it's gone. It would have been worse if it was a kidney or my bladder. Take an antibiotic and a few injections and away you go. As long as it's not your brain or your neck, the rest will heal

Others on Ruby . . .

It's the end of an era. What a riding career. What a career he's had with me, what a career he had with Paul Nicholls **Willie Mullins**

We had some amazing times – Ruby's a brilliant jockey and a great friend. I'm just glad to see him go out in one piece as he's had some horrific accidents and he's done amazingly well to come back **Paul Nicholls**

The fact he's gone out on his own terms is brilliant. That was always the main thing. I'm just thrilled he's come out in one piece **Ted Walsh, who famously teamed up with his son for Grand National success with Papillon**

He was like Lionel Messi on a horse. What he had is uncoachable, unteachable – better than everyone else **Sir Anthony McCoy**

I've been my brother's agent since he was 16. We've had some horrible times but mainly amazing times. I'm very lucky I can call Ruby my brother **Jennifer Walsh**

◂ Ruby Walsh celebrates his 2019 Irish Grand National victory on Burrows Saint

Neal & Palmer
OF JERMYN STREET
Made to measure,
Ready to wear
Accessories and Hire
service available
11 Piccadilly Arcade
London, SW1Y 6NH
Call +44 (0)20 7495 4094
www.nealandpalmer.com

WINNING STREAK

Altior retained his Champion Chase crown and overtook Big Buck's as the world record holder for the longest winning sequence over jumps

By Graham Dench

WE learned long ago that where Altior is concerned it's never over until it's over and it was the same old story in his two big races of the springtime. He kept on winning, of course, but made us sweat as he equalled Big Buck's on a world record of 18 straight wins over jumps with a fourth successive Cheltenham Festival victory in the Betway Queen Mother Champion Chase. Then, when landing odds of 1-6 in the bet365 Celebration Chase for the outright record ought to have been a formality, anyone unfamiliar with Altior's running style would probably have bet against him when he received a reminder on landing over the third-last fence.

That's Altior for you. He's no Sprinter Sacre – the former stablemate with whom he is inevitably compared, and a two-mile chaser who did it all so effortlessly in his pomp – but the 7lb gap between them on Racing Post Ratings is not the whole story. When he is asked to dig deep, Altior's famous turbo has kicked in time after time. His last couple of furlongs are almost invariably his strongest and he always finds a way.

Racing Post Ratings credited Sprinter Sacre with a peak figure of 190 and his best official mark was just 2lb lower. Altior's best RPR, achieved when beating Min by seven lengths in the 2018 Queen Mother, is 'only' 183, and officially he lags much further behind, having seemingly plateaued on 175, the mark he was awarded after that race.

Underlining their relative standing, when the Racing Post ran its 50 Great Two-Mile Chasers series early in 2019 it was Sprinter Sacre who topped the list, ahead of Arkle's brilliant stablemate Flyingbolt and Desert Orchid.

Altior came in at number eight, behind recent champions Master Minded and Moscow Flyer as well Dunkirk and Badsworth Boy from earlier vintages, but ahead of Kauto Star and Viking Flagship. Had the series been run after Altior had scooped the record he might have been a place or two higher, but he would not have threatened Sprinter Sacre's supremacy.

▸▸ *Continues page 82*

Joint-third overall

Altior completed a fourth consecutive unbeaten campaign in 2018-19 and was the champion two-miler again in the Anglo-Irish Jumps Classifications but he was not the best chaser around.

Top five chasers in Britain and Ireland in 2018-19

177 Kemboy
176 Cyrname
175 Al Boum Photo
175 Altior
172 Tiger Roll

Official ratings

Yet Nico de Boinville, who is uniquely placed as the only man to have ridden both horses in competition over obstacles, believes there is not much in it and that Altior might yet scale the Sprinter Sacre heights in ratings terms as well as achievement.

Back in January he said: "I'd say we're nearly there. The sequence of wins Altior has conjured up is some record and he's still relatively young. Altior has the chance to go higher. And the way he races, being slightly behind the bridle, will stand him in good stead in terms of longevity. Sprinter did everything at 100mph hard on the bridle. That's where his problems came from."

★★★★

ALTIOR'S latest season started in December with the Tingle Creek Chase, the race he had missed in controversial circumstances 12 months earlier when Nicky Henderson took him out on the Wednesday and gave him a wind operation two days later, despite having reported him firmly on course at the start of the week.

Unusually the biggest scare in the Sandown contest came very early on, when Altior stood a long way off the second fence and brushed his hind legs through it as he landed steeply, but his jumping was good all the way down the back straight. Nevertheless, having jumped the third-last virtually upsides the 2016 winner Un De Sceaux – a regular sparring partner of Sprinter Sacre – it was only on the run-in that he finally asserted himself by powering up the hill for a four-length success.

There was nothing to test him in the Unibet Desert Orchid Chase and he won as he pleased at odds of 1-8, and it was a similar story at even shorter odds in the three-runner Matchbook Clarence House Stakes at Ascot, where his performance was marred only by a tendency to jump repeatedly out to the left.

Cyrname, who had put up a breathtaking front-running display in the earlier bet365 Handicap Chase at Ascot, would probably have proved a tougher opponent on the latter course than Fox Norton, who was returning from a long break, but having come

home seven lengths clear without having at all a hard race Altior now needed only one more win to equal Big Buck's and two for the outright record.

Expectation ahead of the Queen Mother Champion Chase would have been keen enough even without the prospect of equalling the record Big Buck's set at Newbury in 2012, but there's no doubt the shot at history added another layer to the anticipation.

At 4-11 against eight opponents headed by 2018 runner-up Min, who had also been second when Altior broke his festival duck in the 2016 Supreme Novices' Hurdle, he was the banker of the meeting for many. Though almost unbackable in singles, Altior will have featured in thousands of multiples, yet there was a heart-in-mouth moment at the water jump

▲ Record player: from left, Nico de Boinville salutes a second Queen Mother Champion Chase victory on Altior; celebrations in the Cheltenham winner's enclosure; Altior in his box at Nicky Henderson's Seven Barrows yard

▼ How the Racing Post reported Altior's 19th consecutive win

RACING POST

HOW TO BOOST RACING'S FINANCES

PREMIER LEAGUE WISDOM

Mighty Altior makes history

Henderson superstar seals record 19 wins in a row

All the reports and analysis from a memorable end to the jumps season at Sandown, pages 2-5

when he made a pretty serious error as he chased the front-running Saint Calvados and, although he looked to be going comfortably enough heading down the hill towards three out almost upsides the leader, the pack was still tightly grouped.

When De Boinville made his move turning for home Altior went perhaps a length and a half clear, but Politologue was going just as well and Sceau Royal was seemingly running all over both of them. The winning streak looked like it might be over and record hopes gone when Sceau Royal, yet to come off the bridle, jumped past on the inside at the last, with Politologue still not out of it, but Altior had other ideas, and when it came to a fight there was only going to be one winner.

Altior initially rolled in towards Sceau Royal after a smack, and De Boinville had to pull him off and switch his whip to his left hand, but Sceau Royal had flattered again and as the trio got down to it, with Altior sandwiched between his two opponents, the famous turbo kicked in yet again and he started to assert.

The final margin over Politologue was a decisive enough length and three-quarters and win number 18 was in the bag, but Nicky Henderson described watching the race as "hell" and added: "It's seriously like hitting

Longest winning streaks in Britain

Wins	Horse	Biggest wins
21	Meteor (1786-88)	16 races at Newmarket
19	Skiff (1825-26)	King's Plate at Perth
19	Sweetmeat (1845)	Doncaster Cup
19	The Hero (1846-47)	Ascot Gold Cup
19	ALTIOR (2015-)*	2 Queen Mother Champion Chases
18	Eclipse (1769-70)	11 King's Plates; sire of Meteor
18	Big Buck's (2009-12)	4 World Hurdles

** Up to end of 2018-19 season*

your head against a brick wall. The only nice bit is when it stops."

★★★★

SECURING the outright record over jumps on the last day of the season in Sandown's Celebration Chase against four rivals – one officially rated 24lb inferior and the other three already beaten at least once by Altior in the current campaign – ought to have been something of a lap of honour, but the hot favourite didn't make it look easy.

Making the running this time, but jumping repeatedly out to the left again down the far side, Altior had Sceau Royal travelling ominously well again on his inner as he touched down at the Pond Fence, three from home. With Sceau Royal's rider Daryl Jacob sitting motionless, De Boinville felt obliged to give Altior a wake-up call and after landing over the second-last, where Sceau Royal was far from fluent, he was a good two lengths up.

But Sceau Royal proved a more determined rival this time and was back with a chance starting up the run-in, only for Altior to summon hidden reserves yet again and come away in the last 100 yards to score by two and a half lengths. With God's Own and Vosne Romanee within seven and a half lengths at the line this was by no means vintage Altior, on ratings at least, but it was the record that mattered.

After Altior had returned to a rousing three cheers, De Boinville summed it up when he said: "He's a class act. No other horse has ever achieved what he has done. He is very special."

He certainly is.

'He's very good at telling you things'

New challenges lay ahead for Altior as the curtain came down on the 2018-19 season, among them a record that has stood for well over 200 years. Altior's winning streak at the end of the season left him needing just two more victories to equal the British all-time record winning sequence set on the Flat by Meteor, who after finishing second in the 1786 Derby won his next 21 races. Three more wins and he would hold that record outright.

While there is such a shortage of credible opposition over the minimum trip that the easy thing seemed to be sticking to two miles, Nicky Henderson threw a major unknown into the equation by confirming his intention to step Altior up in distance, reasoning that those closest to the dual Queen Mother Champion Chase winner were in agreement that he was winning at two miles despite the trip, and not because of it.

Altior himself was sending out a clear signal, evidently, for at Sandown on the final day of the season Henderson said: "He's very good at telling you things and he told us one thing today and that was 'go further'."

One attraction of a step up in trip was that it offered Altior an opportunity to raise his game and attain even bigger figures. It's a truism that a racehorse can only beat what is put before him but Altior's style of running – racing behind the bridle and usually doing little more than is necessary, as Big Buck's did too – means his ratings have been held down over two miles by the lack of viable opponents.

In short, it was clear by the end of last season that he needed stronger opposition in order to achieve the truly stellar figures achieved by Sprinter Sacre or Kauto Star. If one could create an ideal rival to take Altior's figures to that sort of level he might well be a free-going chaser who leaves nothing behind and is already of broadly similar merit.

A Kemboy or a Cyrname perhaps.

IN THE PICTURE

Lambourn legend Corky Browne ends star-studded career

ALBERT 'CORKY' BROWNE, Nicky Henderson's legendary head lad, announced his retirement in June at the age of 77 after a career associated with many of the great names of British jump racing.

Widely regarded as a genius with horses' tendons and limbs, Browne played an integral role in the five-time champion trainer's Lambourn operation. They joined forces when Henderson started training in 1978 and the stable's roll of honour featured two Cheltenham Gold Cups, a record seven Champion Hurdles, six Queen Mother Champion Chases and three King George VI Chases.

Among the stable's stars were Altior, Sprinter Sacre, Long Run and See You Then, the three-time Champion Hurdle winner of the 1980s whose fragile legs were famously held together by Browne's skill and patience.

"It's been a massive part of my life; 41 years I've been with Nicky and I've enjoyed every year, month and day," Browne said. "The whole lot was special and things got bigger and bigger until it became the empire it is now. You'd never dream it would become this big, but it did – more than 3,000 winners."

Henderson paid tribute to his right-hand man's part in the success story. "It's been an amazing journey," he said. "Things grew, but I think the big horse for us and one who would have struggled to do what he did without Corky was See You Then. That was his masterpiece. Unfortunately, horses get injured and the most important thing is to mend them and that has been one of his greatest assets. He was someone I could rely on solidly and I knew I could call on him any hour of the day."

Browne, originally from County Cork, moved to Lambourn in 1962 and soon started work at Fred Winter's all-conquering stable. He enjoyed early big-race success when he took 50-1 shot Anglo to Aintree for the 1966 Grand National – he had promised Diane he would marry her in the event of victory and was true to his word – and remained with Winter through the golden age of Bula, Crisp, Lanzarote and Pendil in the 1970s.

"I've had a great run, far better than most in the game. I've worked for two great trainers in Fred and Nicky, and if I get another ten years I'll be more than happy," said Browne, who was planning to spend more time playing golf and snooker, and with his family.

"Diane will have to get used to having me around the house. She'll probably end up shooting me, but if it hadn't been for her I probably wouldn't have got through it all. She has put up with a lot, because I'd take my worries home sometimes."

Picture: EDWARD WHITAKER (RACINGPOST.COM/PHOTOS)

Cyrname, Clan Des Obeaux and Frodon were major contributors to a title-winning resurgence for Paul Nicholls

NEW WAVE

By Nick Pulford

THE 2018-19 season was a tale of the unexpected for Paul Nicholls. Some surprising names emerged as contenders for top honours, not least himself in the trainers' championship, and that changed the mood at Ditcheat entirely. As he looked ahead to this winter's campaign and the spring festivals of 2020, he was more buoyant than he had been in years.

"This is without a shadow of a doubt the strongest team we've had here since the days of Kauto Star," he said at his annual owners' day in the autumn. "It was always going to be near impossible to replace the likes of Kauto, Denman, Big Buck's and those other good horses. But the ones we have for this season look the strongest batch we've seen at Ditcheat since that golden era."

What a difference a year makes. In the autumn of 2018 Nicholls did not think he had a stable full of potential stars and could not see how he would beat Nicky Henderson to the trainers' title. He was sure to be as competitive as ever on the big Saturdays but his stocks of ammunition for the Grade 1 and festival races seemed to be running low. With Harry Cobden still finding his feet as the new stable jockey, it looked likely to be a season of transition rather than transformation. Then along came Frodon, Clan Des Obeaux, Cyrname and Topofthegame to lead the revolution.

"Even I was gobsmacked by the improvement some of the horses showed. I could never have predicted the likes of Frodon and Clan Des Obeaux would win those big Grade 1s," Nicholls said. "If I'd said in the autumn Frodon would win at the festival and Clan would win the King George you'd have laughed at me."

Clan Des Obeaux jumped into the spotlight when he gave Nicholls his tenth King George VI Chase triumph. He was the stable's second-string behind Politologue according to the betting but Cobden chose to ride him and was convinced he was right. "I think he's got the most fantastic chance," the young jockey told a journalist who came across him walking the course before racing.

Cobden remained confident, both in his mount and himself, as a dramatic race unfolded. Two major rivals departed early when Bristol De Mai fell at the final fence on the first circuit and wiped out Waiting Patiently, with Clan Des Obeaux only narrowly avoiding the havoc. There were still two Cheltenham Gold Cup heroes and a pair of King George winners to beat but it was clear from a long way out they were all Cobden's for the taking. The nerveless rider, only recently turned 20, did not take the last of them, Thistlecrack, until the final fence and then

▸▸ *Continues page 88*

betfair
DODSON & HORRELL

wrapped up the Christmas showpiece by a length and a half.

"To win races like this one means more than anything, I promise you," said Nicholls, who had won little of this magnitude since his ninth King George with Silviniaco Conti four years earlier. Twelve months after that, shortly before King George day in 2015, Clan Des Obeaux had opened his account for Nicholls in a juvenile hurdle at Newbury. "We'll mind him," the trainer said that day. The minding had worked rather well.

Nicholls had achieved notable successes before Clan Des Obeaux landed the King George. Dynamite Dollars won the Grade 1 Henry VIII Novices' Chase at Sandown and stable favourite Frodon performed admirably under top weight in Cheltenham's pre-Christmas double-header, finishing second in the BetVictor Gold Cup before taking the Caspian Caviar Gold Cup. The day after the King George there was another Grade 1 win with Quel Destin in the Finale Juvenile Hurdle at Chepstow.

The season was catching fire for Nicholls but he was still inclined to play down his chances of wresting the trainers' title away from Nicky Henderson, the champion in the previous two seasons. "Nicky has some super, super horses. We're just getting there slowly. I think it'll be hard but, you know me, I'm competitive. I never give up."

The embodiment of that never-say-die spirit was Frodon and his rider Bryony Frost, who continued to climb the ladder together with another Cheltenham victory in the Grade 2 Cotswold Chase, a Gold Cup trial at the late January meeting. They were headed towards the Cheltenham Festival after that, ultimately for the Ryanair Chase rather than the Gold Cup, and many hoped Cyrname would go there too after his sensational burst on to the scene.

Having been beaten on his first two starts of the season, Cyrname produced a stunning performance at Ascot in mid-January when he ran away with a 2m5f handicap chase by 21 lengths, earning a Racing Post Rating of 178, and then he did likewise in the Grade 1 Ascot Chase over the same course and distance a month later. He left Waiting Patiently, the 2018 winner, 17 lengths adrift in second place to record an even higher RPR of 181.

With his pronounced preference for racing right-handed, Cyrname was not sent to Cheltenham by Nicholls and owner Johnny de la Hey, nor did they send him anywhere else for the rest of the season. Big plans were already in mind for the new season and he had done more than enough for now.

****

THE winners had not been flowing at the Cheltenham Festival for Nicholls in recent years but the tide was about to turn there as well. Topofthegame was first to strike in a high-quality

▸▸ *Continues page 90*

Cobden shines in top job

Harry Cobden was only 19 when he was appointed stable jockey by Paul Nicholls in May 2018 but he thrived on the pressure in his first full season, which brought King George VI Chase success on Clan Des Obeaux and a maiden century of winners.

Having started riding out for Nicholls at the age of 13, Cobden felt prepared when the opportunity came. "There were a lot of jockeys in front of me when I went to Paul's but at that age that's a good thing because you learn so much," he said in a Racing Post interview. "It was always very competitive and still is. I was very keen and ambitious, and from the day you start you half want them to move over and let you through, but Rome wasn't built in a day and it was a great way to progress. I was fortunate to be riding a lot of good horses from a young age and that helped massively."

On his boss, Cobden added: "Paul is a genius, he sees everything and will always tell you when you've done wrong." The boss, meanwhile, claimed – possibly tongue in cheek – that his young stable jockey is "a cocky little ***t whose a*** I still have to kick from time to time".

The confidence of youth shone through in the King George both in Cobden's choice of ride – he went for 12-1 shot Clan Des Obeaux over 5-1 fourth favourite Politologue – and his execution of the race. "People said I wasn't on the stable first string and the betting suggested I wasn't, but I thought I was, that's for sure," he said. "I wouldn't very often be on the one I didn't want to be on. Nine times out of ten it would be my choice and that was certainly the way it was in the King George."

That was one of four Grade 1 victories in 2018-19 for Cobden, who ended the season with a career-best 109 winners, and he put down another important marker with a first Cheltenham Festival success for Nicholls on Topofthegame in the RSA Novices' Chase. Just as he had in the King George, Cobden played a cool waiting game before unleashing his winning effort.

"I didn't say too much to Harry about how to ride him," the trainer said after the RSA. "I left it to him and just told him to take his time whatever he did – and he gave the horse an absolutely brilliant ride."

Endorsements do not ring more loudly than that.

▾ Easy does it: Cyrname and Harry Cobden run away with the Grade 1 Ascot Chase in February

renewal of the RSA Novices' Chase, holding off Henderson's Santini by half a length with the Gordon Elliott-trained favourite Delta Work a close third in a thrilling contest.

That victory was a festival first for the Nicholls-Cobden partnership and was also notable for ending a four-year Grade 1 drought at the festival for the trainer since Dodging Bullets won the 2015 Queen Mother Champion Chase.

The wait for the next one would last only 24 hours and this one was extra special as Frodon and Frost scrapped their way to an incredible victory in the Ryanair Chase on a magical festival Thursday. Nicholls, such a staunch supporter of Frost, revelled in the occasion along with everyone else.

"That was awesome – I lost my voice a bit!" he said amid the tumult after the little chaser's battling win. "Bryony deserves it, everyone in the team deserves it and, most of all, the horse deserves it. He's the most amazing horse you'd ever want to train. He's not very big and it's a very special day."

Other memorable days followed as the Nicholls team kept the momentum going through the rest of the season. One came on a quieter day at Cheltenham in April when Kupatana won a mares' novice handicap chase to bring up 3,000 jumps winners in Britain for the trainer, who had turned 57 the day before. Nicholls, who started training in 1991, became only the third trainer to reach the milestone, joining Martin Pipe and Henderson.

That achievement was still on his mind when the season closed at Sandown just over a week later with Nicholls lifting the championship trophy for the 11th time. "My main aim at the start of the season was to get to 3,000 winners, that's what we wanted," he said. "It probably does mean more to win the title now and I think it's one of our greatest achievements, having had a couple of years rebuilding."

Nicholls, who as usual deflected much of the credit to his right-hand man Clifford Baker and the rest of the team, was not the only champion at Ditcheat. Frost won the conditionals' title and Cyrname and Topofthegame were divisional winners in the Anglo-Irish Jumps Classifications.

Unfortunately in early autumn Topofthegame was ruled out for the season with a minor tendon injury but there are still big-race contenders in every corner of Ditcheat. The buzz is back and nobody will be surprised if this season is a vintage one for Nicholls.

▲ Title winners: Paul Nicholls and Bryony Frost with their championship trophies

▼ Megan Nicholls, whose growing success on the Flat included a third win in the Silk Series for female riders

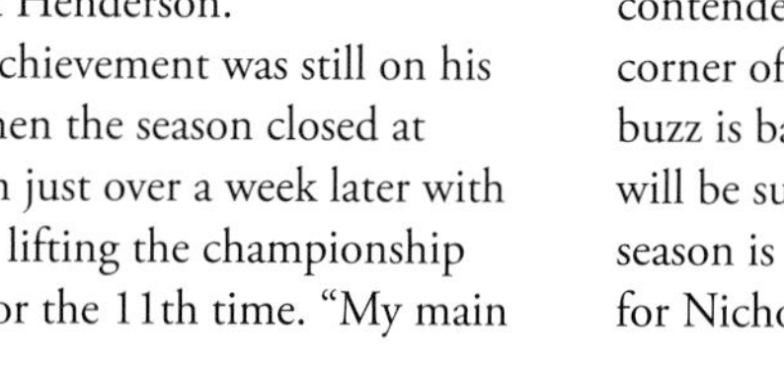

Megan riding high

Paul Nicholls had conditionals' title winner Bryony Frost in his yard in 2019 and the next champion apprentice on the Flat might come from even closer to home.

His daughter Megan, 22, is making rapid progress as a rider, having increased her tally each year since her first winner in 2014. The biggest leap forward came in the latest campaign when she was something of a go-to 3lb claimer and more than doubled her previous best of 13 winners.

"I'm well up on last year's tally and the backend of the season has been awesome. I'm going in the right direction now and long may that continue," said Nicholls, who has ridden winners for Simon Crisford, Richard Fahey and Kevin Ryan among a wide list of trainers.

"I'd love to compete for the apprentice title next season. I ride for some really good trainers and I'm attached to my dad, who will have more Flat runners come the spring, which is also exciting."

'A true inspiration'

Paul Nicholls lost a mentor with the death of Richard Barber in June at the age of 77.

A brother of the 11-time champion trainer's Ditcheat landlord Paul Barber, he was a leading racing figure in the West Country and a huge influence on Nicholls' career.

Barber won the Foxhunter Chase at the Cheltenham Festival four times with Rushing Wild (1992) – a subsequent Cheltenham Gold Cup runner-up for Martin Pipe – Fantus (1995 and 1997) and Earthmover (1998).

Earthmover was later trained by Nicholls to win the Foxhunter again in 2004 and their yards remained closely linked. Barber was responsible for sourcing many future Nicholls stars, including Cheltenham Gold Cup and two-time King George VI Chase hero See More Business and Champion Hurdle winner Rock On Ruby.

Nicholls said: "He trained some great horses and some great people down the years and I wouldn't be where I am today without his help, guidance and friendship, so I have so much to thank him for.

"He was a true inspiration and a massive influence on my career as he bought See More Business and passed him on to me. He was a great man in so many ways and will be sadly missed by everybody in the sport of jump racing."

The large congregation at Barber's funeral included Martin and David Pipe, Philip Hobbs, Dan Skelton and Harry Fry, who was helped by him to become Nicholls' assistant and later to set up on his own.

BRISTOL & BATH:
luxurychauffeurhirebristol.co.uk

BERKSHIRE:
luxurychauffeurhirereading.co.uk

BIRMINGHAM:
luxurychauffeurhirebirmingham.co.uk

BUCKINGHAMSHIRE:
luxurychauffeurhiremarlow.co.uk

CARDIFF:
SOUTH WALES
luxurychauffeurhirecardiff.co.uk

HEREFORDSHIRE:
luxurychauffeurhirehereford.co.uk

GLOUCESTERSHIRE:
jonnyrockschauffeurs.co.uk

OXFORDSHIRE:
luxurychauffeurhireoxford.co.uk

WILTSHIRE:
chauffeurhireswindon.co.uk

WORCESTERSHIRE:
luxurychauffeurhireworcester.co.uk

WARWICKSHIRE:
luxurychauffeurhirewarwick.co.uk

THE BIGGER PICTURE

The Queen feeds some carrots to Ryanair Chase winner Frodon during a visit to the Ditcheat yard of champion jumps trainer Paul Nicholls in March as part of a royal tour of Somerset

TRACY ROBERTS

Older filly Magical was a key performer for Aidan O'Brien as Ballydoyle's Classic winners failed to maintain their form

LEADING LADY

By Alan Sweetman and Nick Pulford

NORMAL metrics do not apply to a summary of Aidan O'Brien's record in any given season. We take for granted the latest Irish trainers' championship – 21 in a row now – and the inevitable roll call of Group 1 wins at home and abroad. Beyond that we judge O'Brien's training feats by unique criteria, trying to decide if a haul of five British and Irish Classic victories constitutes a good, bad or indifferent season for the Ballydoyle operation.

Whatever the overall picture, Ballydoyle's 2019 record in domestic Group 1 races was odd for a stable whose main rationale is to provide a platform for future stallions, with five of its six top-level Irish wins provided by fillies.

Even if the stable's top performers on Racing Post Ratings were colts – Japan and Ten Sovereigns shared that distinction – and Anthony Van Dyck secured the always-coveted Derby win, in

many ways it was the fillies' leader, Magical, who left the biggest imprint on the season.

The four-year-old certainly had a special place in O'Brien's affections following her brave win on soft ground in the Qipco Champion Stakes at Ascot in October, which came six months after the start of a testing nine-race campaign through many of Europe's best middle-distance races.

Before she got to British Champions Day, Magical had run Crystal Ocean close in the Prince of Wales's Stakes in appalling conditions at Royal Ascot, twice finished second to old rival Enable, won the Irish Champion Stakes and finished fifth in the Prix de l'Arc de Triomphe, which came just 13 days before her return trip to Ascot.

Many of O'Brien's horses are noted for their tough constitutions and consistency at the top level, but even the trainer was impressed by Magical's ability to perform well in the highest class, recover and go again.

"When you ask Magical a question she always says yes," O'Brien said at Ascot. "She says yes to everything. Mentally she has never carried a grudge. She is unique. She gives her all and really is the most unbelievable filly.

"The Arc was a strongly run race and she has come out of that and won here. She handles ease in the ground and goes on fast ground. What can you say? She's the ultimate racehorse – that's what she is."

★★★★

AN honourable second to Enable in the 2018 Breeders' Cup Turf, Magical started the new campaign with three consecutive defeats of her stablemate Flag Of Honour, the final one at 2-7 in the Group 1 Tattersalls Gold Cup, and then she headed up to the big league.

In June she made the first trip of her career to Royal Ascot, where she was made 13-8 favourite for a high-quality Prince of Wales's. Her chief rivals, in betting order, were Crystal Ocean, subsequent Arc winner Waldgeist and Sea Of Class, making her first appearance since running Enable so close in the 2018 Arc.

William Haggas had contemplated withdrawing Sea Of Class on account of the soft ground and wished he had after the showpiece event was run in driving rain. "I'm so angry with myself for subjecting her to that awful weather," he said after Sea Of Class finished a bedraggled fifth. "As soon as I decided to run her it bucketed down with rain for an hour."

Magical, proven on soft ground at Ascot after winning the British Champions Fillies & Mares Stakes the previous autumn, coped admirably with the conditions but not as well as Crystal Ocean, who got the better of her by a length and a quarter, with Waldgeist third. "She ran very well and I'm very happy with her," said O'Brien, who by this stage had Derby winner Anthony Van Dyck to lead his middle-distance colts, along with Epsom third Japan.

Soon the Derby order would be turned upside down by Sovereign's shock victory over Anthony Van Dyck in the Irish Derby and Magical was the Ballydoyle number one when it came to the Eclipse at Sandown in early July. Again she had to settle for being number two in the race, this time to Enable, and it was the same story when she met her old rival in the Yorkshire Oaks the following month.

By now Magical was established as a consistent Group 1 performer but her level was in the low 120s on Racing Post Ratings, whereas Enable and Crystal Ocean were in the rarefied air of the high 120s. Once she was taken out of that company for an easier opportunity in the Irish Champion Stakes, she became a Group 1 winner for a third time with a clear-cut success, giving O'Brien his first victory in the race since So You Think in 2011.

The trainer was pleased but was still expecting her to do more. "She had a midsummer break and had her first run back in York," he said. "She was just ready to go to York but she still ran very well. Obviously Enable is a great filly but when we saw Magical run that well, we were looking forward to this and to the autumn after that.

▸▸ *Continues page 96*

It's important when the best horses are around that they run against each other whenever they can, and there is no sidestepping anyone."

****

JUST three weeks later Magical was sent into battle once more against the best when she lined up in the Arc under Donnacha O'Brien, with Ryan Moore on the stable's better-fancied Japan. The market was right about them but they were only fourth and fifth, with Magical possibly paying the price for following the early pace.

Still she was not going to rest, however, and O'Brien jnr was on board again two weekends later at Ascot. She was back to being the highest-rated runner in the £1,358,750 feature and again she took the prize, the most valuable of her career. She sat in second until being asked to assert halfway up the home straight, responding in style to beat Addeybb by three-quarters of a length.

Her jockey, who enjoyed a red-letter day having earlier beaten Stradivarius on Kew Gardens in the Group 2 Long Distance Cup, said: "She's a trainer's dream and a jockey's dream." It's a dream he lives all the time as Magical's regular work-rider.

****

O'BRIEN JNR had started the season on a high with 2,000 Guineas victory on Magna Grecia, a record tenth winner in the race for his father. That was followed 24 hours later by Hermosa's 1,000 Guineas success and everything seemed set for Ballydoyle's Classic generation to shine all season.

It didn't quite turn out that way. Hermosa won the Irish 1,000 Guineas but then her form tailed off, while Magna Grecia disappeared for five months after his Irish 2,000 Guineas defeat, although Circus Maximus did make an impact in the mile division by winning the St James's Palace Stakes and Prix du Moulin.

It was a similar mixed bag with other three-year-olds. Derby triumphs were secured at Epsom and the Curragh but Anthony Van Dyck failed to kick on through the summer and Sovereign did not run again after his surprise success. Japan, third at Epsom, was the one who blossomed in midsummer, reaching full bloom with his narrow defeat of Crystal Ocean in the Juddmonte International at York.

In the sprint division Ten Sovereigns scored an impressive July Cup win but found the drop to five furlongs a step too far when he finished sixth behind Battaash in the Nunthorpe.

Through it all there was always Magical, the iron lady who was not for turning down any challenge. O'Brien even raised the possibility that she could stay in training at five. "It would be unbelievable if she did," he said, "and she would be delighted." She would not be the only one.

Key figures for Aidan O'Brien

5 Classic wins in 2019

7 Derby wins (record) after Anthony Van Dyck in 2019

13 Irish Derby wins (record) after Sovereign in 2019

10 2,000 Guineas wins (record) after Magna Grecia in 2019

8 Irish 1,000 Guineas wins (record) after Hermosa in 2019

50 Landmark birthday on October 16

22 Irish trainer titles, the last 21 in a row

RACING POST

JOSEPH O'BRIEN STABLE TOUR

MAN CITY v LEICESTER

Unstoppable!

O'Brien bandwagon rolls on as Hermosa gives master of Ballydoyle yet another Classic winner

▼ Girls on top: Magical in the winner's enclosure at Leopardstown with Aidan O'Brien and Ryan Moore following the Irish Champion Stakes; bottom, Hermosa (far left) heads to victory in the 1,000 Guineas at Newmarket; previous page, Magical at Ascot after her Champion Stakes success

Aidan O'Brien opened up on a range of subjects in this revealing Racing Post interview in July

Faith, Derby winners and the meaning of racing

By Richard Forristal

IF YOU are expecting the scoop about Padraig Beggy getting a dressing-down for not reading the Irish Derby script properly or John Magnier unleashing the hairdryer treatment after Sovereign's shock triumph at the Curragh, turn away now.

Over the course of an hour-long chinwag in Ballydoyle, Aidan O'Brien is generous with his views and deeply engaging. He often gets characterised in bland terms for sticking rigidly to the Coolmore party line, but that's also a consequence of over-familiarity that does a disservice to his intellect. Peel back a layer beyond the verbal ticks or the hesitant delivery to camera and the astute mind that conducts the single most successful thoroughbred training orchestra on the planet is something in which to luxuriate. We don't hear enough of it.

On this occasion, by his own coiled-spring standards, O'Brien is in relaxed form. Contemplative and ebullient, even. He has plenty to say, but one view he won't validate is the theory that a 33-1 rank outsider foiling an Epsom hero's quest for a Derby double was something that warranted a serious post-mortem.

"In an ideal world, obviously we would have loved for Anthony Van Dyck to win at the Curragh and he'd be a dual Derby winner, but it didn't happen," he says of an event that still left him with a 13th Irish Derby. "All the horses were individually trained and it's far from an ideal world.

"The prices are what the bookies put them in at, but even though we might have horses making the running, everything is spoken about as if it can win. Sovereign was very impressive when he won his maiden at Galway and his form was strong all the way. The market probably overreacted to his Epsom run, but that's how some punters make a lot of money. Picking a horse who is overpriced is all part of it."

Ryan Moore might be forgiven for thinking that eschewing four Classic winners in the space of a month is an accolade he could do without. The intimacies of such a potent and pressurised trainer-jockey relationship will always be off limits, but O'Brien insists Moore copes well with such reversals.

"It's never an issue, and it happens all the time," he responds when asked if the rider gets frustrated.

Does the fact that it can happen so often put a strain on things? "I don't think so," he says with a straight bat. "The way it works is Ryan always rides what we think is the number one horse. I would tell him what I thought and he's always happy to go with that. And if he ever wants to ride another one, there isn't a problem.

"We have always had, and have, a great relationship – very open. It's the same with the lads here, Seamus [Heffernan], [son] Donnacha, Wayne [Lordan], Padraig and Michael [Hussey]. Everyone knows exactly why we do what we do among ourselves. It's an open book. We've had five Classic winners this year with five different riders and we're delighted for all of them."

Moore's time as O'Brien's first-choice rider has made for a pretty stable tenure. His deputy Donnacha O'Brien will squeeze what he can out of his towering frame for as long as he can, but he is now overseeing 25 backend juveniles at David Wachman's old yard near Cashel having already completed his trainer's course. His brother Joseph's training venture began with a similar phased launch, so the blueprint is there for the reigning champion jockey to follow.

"He's a big man and it's hard to believe he's riding at all, but he loves what he's doing," O'Brien muses of his younger son. "He rides two lots here in Ballydoyle and then goes over to the yard. He's doing two days' work every day now but he loves doing it."

▸▸ *Continues page 100*

For all of the privileges enjoyed by the four O'Brien children, they know how to graft. That's an example set by their father, whose relentless, meticulous quest for success shows no sign of abating.

As an archetypal racing clan, the O'Briens are all dependent almost exclusively on the sector for their living. The industry has become an increasingly soft target for vocal and extreme welfare activists and O'Brien opens up candidly when that topic is broached, focusing on the societal benefits of the end product.

"There is always a small percentage of people in all walks of life who will stray and need to be controlled, but there are a lot of professional people who want to ensure everyone is doing the right thing. Racing is well regulated," he begins.

"What the critics have to recognise is racing is all about life. People want to be able to watch sport because it makes them feel good, or they want to be able to compete. This is all part of the circle of life. You can't eliminate risk in anything. There is only one thing certain for us all, that we will only get so far and our bodies will fade and we will move off this earth. Nothing else is certain, so every single day we're here we must appreciate it and enjoy it, and be respectful to ourselves and the animals around us and the people around us.

"The reality of it is that racing is a sport and horses are athletes. Whether it's football or golf or rugby or racing, athletes get injured. We're flesh and blood and there is nothing perfect about anything in life. If a horse doesn't want to race, they will let you know very quickly, and people who care for horses and are looking at them every day, they know when a horse is happy or sad."

O'Brien is in full flow now, the horseman in him vehemently vouching for what he believes in. To illustrate his point, he reaches for his phone and locates a still frame that shows two photos merged side by side. At first glance, it appears to be different horses' eyes, one noticeably listless and dull, the other bright and alert. "That's the same horse," he

▸▸ *Continues page 102*

explains. "He had been sick, and you can see the sadness in his eyes, and the other picture is six months later. It's the people who are dealing with the horses who see these things.

"For the public, it is never any harm to ask questions or give an opinion, because it makes everyone refocus and question themselves, which is never a bad thing. But racing is part of living, and it adds to everyone's lives. We hear about people with mental health issues or depression, racing is something that can lift people out of that dark place and into a place where they can dream."

★★★★

SPORT'S capacity to enrich lives and engender hope is a theme he returns to when the conversation switches to Wexford hurling's resurgence after 15 years in the doldrums.

"The enjoyment people get out of watching it, the feelgood factor," he enthuses. "Sport has that ability to help people feel a bit better about life. It gives human beings something to think about. You go into a different world, and everyone has an opinion on it.

"I don't know enough about it [hurling] to have an opinion, but I love listening to the debates and to the people who do have an opinion. Racing is the same for a lot of people."

You put it to him that victory for the underdog is something that is celebrated with similar gusto when his peers prevail against him. It's a reality to which he is well accustomed.

"With us, we do our very best to win every race," he says. "But we're always delighted for everybody who wins when we don't. Everybody has to live. Like, we don't control fate; fate is controlled, but it's not by us."

And you do have strong faith? "Everyone has faith, but some people will say they have and some people will have it but they don't know they have it. It's a faith. God is what we call God. There's a far greater power than any of us know, and there's no doubt about that.

"Any day any of us get up, we should be thankful that we do get up and that we're healthy. So we control as much as we can but, at the end of the day, we're not the ones doing the controlling. I don't think any human thinks they are."

For someone who has built his legacy by controlling the controllables with a forensic attention to detail, that is a noble perspective. And O'Brien's gratitude is as sincere as his energy is abundant.

'Our bodies only last so long, so the main thing is that your mind stays the same, if you're lucky. Every day you just have to appreciate it and be thankful for it, and do your best for things to happen'

As ludicrous as it sounds, it's not beyond the realms of possibility that his illustrious training career is at the halfway point. Now there's a notion to put the fear of God in even the most fervent atheists among his fellow trainers.

"I feel great," he volleys. "I would look at the people coming along behind us, and see how those you met as kids are all adults now. So even though you might think you aren't changing, something is changing all the time in the environment you're in, and I don't take one thing for granted, ever.

"Our bodies only last so long, so the main thing is that your mind stays the same, if you're lucky. Every day you just have to appreciate it and be thankful for it, and do your best for things to happen."

Awareness, humility and ambition. It sounds like a simple formula, but there's a lot more to it as well. A deep well of substance and an impermeable character are two other attributes that spring to mind.

This is an edited version of an article that appeared in the Racing Post on July 7

▾ Attention to detail: Aidan O'Brien coordinates morning work on the gallops at Ballydoyle

Healthy Gut,
Healthy Horse

HORSLYX
PRO DIGEST BALANCER
SUPPORTS A HEALTHY DIGESTIVE SYSTEM
HORSLYX
PRO DIGEST BALANCER
SUPPORTS A HEALTHY DIGESTIVE SYSTEM
15kg
Mini
HORSLYX
PRO DIGEST

SEVEN UP

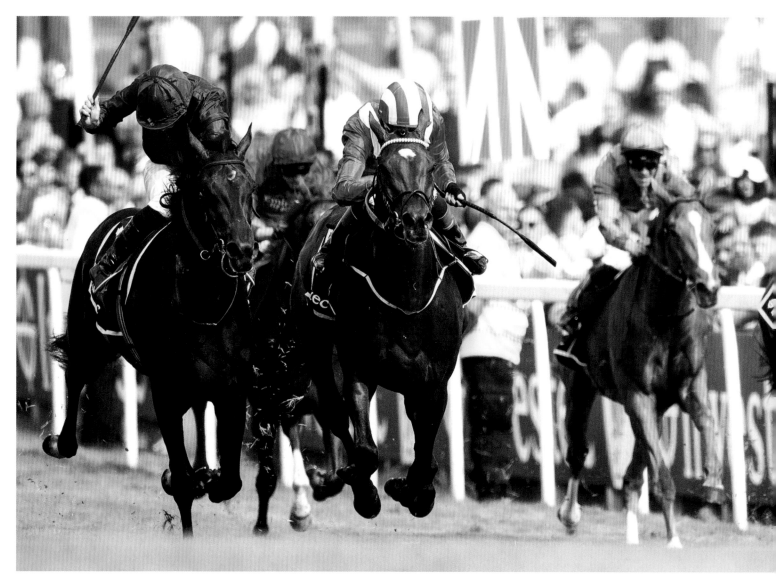

Aidan O'Brien carved another slice of history when Anthony Van Dyck gave him a record-equalling seventh Derby success

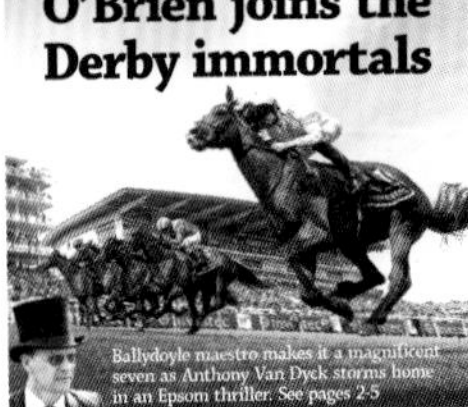

RACING POST

Search 'Racing Post App' for must-have news, insight and fast results £3.20

O'Brien joins the Derby immortals

Ballydoyle maestro makes it a magnificent seven as Anthony Van Dyck storms home in an Epsom thriller. See pages 2-5

By Brian Sheerin

ANTHONY VAN DYCK did not distinguish himself as one of Aidan O'Brien's better Derby winners, either on the day or for months afterwards, but he was an important addition to the canon nonetheless. His victory in a blanket finish, with no more than a length covering the first five, took O'Brien to a record-equalling seventh victory in the great race and, on a day of numbers, became the tenth Derby winner associated with Coolmore supremo John Magnier.

Poignantly, their latest Derby triumph came exactly ten years to the day since the death of Vincent O'Brien, the man who played a pivotal role in the development of Coolmore and Ballydoyle into an all-conquering force and sent out six Derby winners from the County Tipperary stronghold. The man who now rules the celebrated thoroughbred training establishment moved past his predecessor's tally to stand alongside the English trio John Porter, Fred Darling and Robert Robson on a magnificent seven, but typically he did not make a great deal of the moment on a personal level.

"It's incredible to be in the position to be a record holder. We have to pinch ourselves every day," O'Brien said. "We're working with the best people, with the most incredible horses with unbelievable pedigrees and physiques, in an incredible facility. We're so privileged to be a small part of this, all of these people that put so much in on a daily, weekly and yearly basis."

The first of O'Brien's seven

Derby heroes was Galileo, who took the race in 2001 before becoming the supersire he is now, with his latest Classic-winning son Anthony Van Dyck emerging as the 21st Irish-trained winner in the 240th renewal of the great race.

Galileo has now sired a joint-record four Derby winners – his others being New Approach, Ruler Of The World and Australia – but that doesn't tell the whole story of his influence on the Epsom showpiece because he has had four runners-up and four more third-placed finishers and in 2019 all bar one of the 13 runners were by Galileo or one of his sons.

What is even more remarkable is the imprint Magnier has left on the race. While unofficial, the Coolmore supremo's ten wins as owner is the most in the Derby in any category, beating Lester Piggott's nine as jockey. Explaining the laser focus on the race from Coolmore and Ballydoyle, O'Brien said: "The boss [Magnier] always says the Derby is the holy grail and it's the backbone of the thoroughbred. That's why we run so many horses. They are bred, reared and we try to keep them sound to compete in this race. It's the ultimate test in every way, it tests their speed, their stamina and their mentality as well."

★★★★

ANTHONY VAN DYCK ultimately passed the test but the 13-2 shot could hardly have been called a likely winner at the top of the hill. Stablemates Sir Dragonet and Japan, along with the Kevin Prendergast-trained Madhmoon, appeared to be travelling far sweeter but the run-in at Epsom is long and Seamie Heffernan knows this better than most, having been painfully denied Derby glory in the dying strides twice. A Ballydoyle stalwart since 1996, the 46-year-old jockey was having his 12th Derby ride and his crowning moment awaited at last.

In Anthony Van Dyck, he had a willing partner. Having been caught on the heels of the leaders for much of the run-in, Heffernan found a gap opening up on the rails about a furlong from the finish and his mount quickly shot through before stealing home half a length too good for Madhmoon in a thrillingly close finish.

It had been billed as an open Derby beforehand and so it proved. A further nose and two short-heads behind were fellow Ballydoyle-trained colts Japan, Broome and Sir Dragonet, the race favourite and mount of Ryan Moore. On how the Derby was run, Heffernan summarised: "I knew he would do it when I needed him. I decided to go down

▸▸*Continues page 106*

Promise fulfilled

Anthony Van Dyck was just one of the top-ranked juveniles of 2018 to take Group 1 honours as a three-year-old. Having been placed twice at the top level in his first season, he fulfilled that promise with his Derby triumph. Too Darn Hot, the best juvenile of 2018, scored Group 1 wins in the Prix Jean Prat and Sussex Stakes, Ten Sovereigns took the July Cup and Advertise landed the Commonwealth Cup and Prix Maurice de Gheest. Quorto and Jash, the other two in the 2018 top six, were both held back by serious injury as three-year-olds.

Top six two-year-olds in 2018

Horse	*OR*	*RPR*
Too Darn Hot	126	125
Quorto	121	122
Ten Sovereigns	120	120
Advertise	119	117
Anthony Van Dyck	118	119
Jash	118	119

the inside and I needed a bit of luck, but I was always happy." As for his long wait for glory, he quipped: "It was only a matter of time."

The truth is that Heffernan had begun to lose hope he would one day win the Derby. The reliable deputy has seen some of the greats come and go at Ballydoyle. Christy Roche, Mick Kinane, Jamie Spencer, Kieren Fallon, Johnny Murtagh, Joseph O'Brien and more recently Ryan Moore and Donnacha O'Brien have all held sway over Heffernan.

"I've been very fortunate to ride so many big-race winners but the Derby is the race every jockey wants to win, and to do so after years of trying means an awful lot," he reflected. "I had twice finished second in the race, on Fame And Glory and At First Sight, and also third on Idaho. I suppose I was running out of time as far as winning the Derby was concerned, so it's very special to have done it. I'm very grateful for the opportunities I've been given by Aidan and the owners over the years."

Competition on the substitutes' bench has been fierce for Heffernan throughout the 23 years he has been working for O'Brien but success has been plentiful. A key cog in the Ballydoyle machine, Heffernan has amassed eight Classics in his native Ireland – among them Irish Derby winners Soldier Of Fortune (2007), Frozen Fire (2008) and Capri (2017) – and an Epsom Oaks success aboard Was in 2012. There has been Breeders' Cup glory too, when Heffernan gave a masterclass from the front aboard 'iron horse' Highland Reel to win the Turf in 2016.

In his own record-equalling hour, O'Brien heaped praise on Heffernan. "As a horseman and jockey Seamus is second to none. I can't tell you how delighted we are for him," he said. "We've known each other a long time and we worked with each other before Ballydoyle. He puts it all in, day in, day out, and he is incredibly experienced as a horseman."

★★★★

ANTHONY VAN DYCK still had more to prove after Epsom. The Derby form looked solid enough but the tight finish kept his Racing Post Rating to 120, the lowest winning figure since Sir Percy in 2006 and the worst recorded by one of O'Brien's seven Derby winners. He was a long way behind High Chaparral's 130 and Galileo's 127, and it was a sobering thought that Sir Percy had never won again in four attempts.

In 2001 Galileo had gone on from his Derby success to establish himself as a top-class performer in the rest of the season with victories in the Irish Derby and King George VI and Queen Elizabeth Stakes, taking him to a high of 132 on RPRs, as well as a head second in the Irish Champion Stakes following an epic battle with Fantastic Light, in a reversal of the King George placings.

Anthony Van Dyck, the latest son to follow the father, contested the same three races but came up short each time. With Moore taking over from Heffernan in the saddle, he was sent off 5-4 favourite for the Irish Derby but never looked like landing a blow as Epsom also-ran Sovereign (another son of Galileo, of course) left him six lengths back in second in one of the shocks of the season.

Moore stayed on board for the King George, in which Anthony Van Dyck was fitted with cheekpieces for the first time, but the Derby winner went backwards on the good to soft ground, which was in stark contrast to the fast surface at Epsom. He was being ridden more than half a mile out and was tailed off in tenth place, with only stablemate Magic Wand finishing behind him. Way ahead in the distance, Enable and Crystal Ocean were on another level as they fought out one of the races of the year.

That dismal effort proved to be a one-off for Anthony Van Dyck. Following a seven-week break, he returned on better ground in the Irish Champion and ran a fine race to fill the frame behind Magical and Magic Wand in a 1-2-3 for O'Brien. It was much better but still nothing out of the ordinary.

For Ballydoyle and Coolmore, however, Anthony Van Dyck had already achieved the ultimate on that singularly important day at Epsom in June.

Hall of fame

How Aidan O'Brien's seven Derby winners compare on Racing Post Ratings in the race and over their careers

Winner	Year	Derby	Career
Galileo	2001	127	132
High Chaparral	2002	130	130
Australia	2014	125	129
Camelot	2012	126	126
Ruler Of The World	2013	121	125
Wings Of Eagles	2017	121	121
Anthony Van Dyck	2019	120	*120

* Up to end of European Group 1 season

▾ In the pink: Anthony Van Dyck crosses the line to land a seventh Derby for trainer Aidan O'Brien and the first for jockey Seamie Heffernan; previous page, Galileo's fourth Derby-winning son heads to victory in a blanket finish

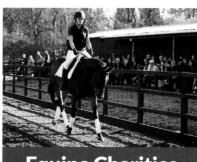

UPWARDLY MOBILE

Japan reached a notable peak with his York victory over Crystal Ocean and could climb even higher in 2020

By Brian Sheerin

COLOURING in the broad outline of the Flat season often requires a purple marker and, having achieved so much despite a far from smooth three-year-old campaign, Japan looks set to keep Derrick Smith's iconic Coolmore silks firmly in the picture in 2020.

A purple and white cavalry has roared through multiple Group 1s in recent seasons with the likes of Highland Reel, Minding, St Nicholas Abbey, Leading Light and Camelot leading the way, and in the latest season Japan – along with Magical – kept the colours well to the fore. With Japan, though, there is the feeling the best is yet to come.

What he achieved in 2019 was impressive enough. Victory at Royal Ascot was followed by back-to-back Group 1 wins before he signed off his three-year-old campaign with a fine effort to finish fourth in the Prix de l'Arc de Triomphe. It was not a bad season by any stretch of the imagination, but one which trainer Aidan O'Brien was always keen to stress was a long way off being ideal.

After landing the Beresford Stakes as a two-year-old, a race in which O'Brien tends to run the best of his middle-distance Classic prospects, Japan spent the entire winter at the head of the betting for the 2019 Derby. However, the Galileo colt faced a race against time after suffering a setback in the spring and eventually made it by the skin of his teeth, having finished fourth in the Dante Stakes at York on his belated reappearance towards the end of the trials. Once he got to Epsom, he ran a stormer in thundering home for third behind stablemate Anthony Van Dyck.

****

GIVEN so much was achieved with Japan despite a lot going wrong, O'Brien has reason to puff out his chest with a view towards next season. With Japan likely to stay in training as a four-year-old, and looking back on the season that was, the trainer said in the autumn: "He's a horse to really look forward to next year. What he did, after everything, was incredible.

"We didn't think he'd make the Derby at the beginning of the season. He was just about ready to go for a piece of work when we ran him in the Dante and then he just improved enough to run in the Derby, where he ran a great race for third."

O'Brien added: "He improved after the Derby and kept on improving throughout the season. He's incredible, what he's done in such a short space of time. It looks as though the lads are going to keep him in training next season and we're all really looking forward to that. He's an exciting horse. He's consistent, he's genuine and he's very comfortable at anything from a mile and a quarter to a mile and a half."

Reflecting on Japan's final start at three, when he ran a respectable race under Ryan Moore to finish fourth behind Waldgeist in the Arc, O'Brien said: "Ryan was following the winner and when it looked like he was going to run into a pocket, he pulled out to go around them. It was some run and Japan got to the last half-furlong before getting tired, but he was entitled to get tired. Like I said, we're really looking forward to next year with him."

For all that the Arc cemented Japan's reputation as a high-class middle-distance operator, it was his victory in the Juddmonte International Stakes at York, where he outmuscled Crystal Ocean by a head, that signified his arrival at the highest level.

Japan had been impressive when landing the Group 2 King Edward VII Stakes at Royal Ascot and in securing his breakthrough Group 1 success in the Grand Prix de Paris at Longchamp, but he took his form to a whole new level by chinning Crystal Ocean, officially rated the best horse in the world at the time.

The York victory moved Japan up to top spot among Ballydoyle's middle-distance horses with a Racing Post Rating of 125 and brought high praise from Moore, a notoriously hard man to please.

"He's beaten a very good older horse there. I know how good Crystal Ocean is and he's a very hard horse to get by," Moore said. "We had a lovely trip. Japan is a very straightforward horse and all he's done is improve since the Dante. He's a beautiful horse with a beautiful mind. Hopefully he'll keep on progressing."

There are genuine reasons to believe Moore's hopes will be fulfilled. The future is bright for the rapidly progressive colt. The future is purple and white.

◂ On the up: Japan in full flow in the Juddmonte International at York; below, after his King Edward VII Stakes victory at Royal Ascot

IN THE PICTURE

Sovereign shines for Beggy in another Derby surprise

THE supersub with the best Derby strike-rate in the weighing room did it again. Remarkably, two years after springing a surprise at Epsom on Wings Of Eagles, the Padraig Beggy lightning bolt struck again at the Curragh with a shock victory in the Dubai Duty Free Irish Derby on 33-1 shot Sovereign.

When he won the 2017 Derby for Aidan O'Brien on 40-1 shot Wings Of Eagles, Beggy was having his first ride in the famous Classic. The following year he finished last on Zabriskie at 66-1 and for his third attempt in 2019 he was tenth behind Anthony Van Dyck aboard Sovereign, a 50-1 shot. The magic seemed to have worn off.

Four weeks later, however, Beggy performed his latest trick. O'Brien had five of the eight runners in the Irish Derby, headed by 5-4 favourite Anthony Van Dyck, and Beggy took his usual position on one of the Ballydoyle outsiders, keeping the ride on Sovereign. The omens did not look good: Sovereign's only victory had been in a heavy-ground Galway maiden the previous autumn and Beggy, the loyal work-rider and sometime race-rider, had not ridden a single winner all season.

Sovereign had been bustled up by Beggy to make the running at Epsom before being swamped early in the straight. The Curragh race started in similar fashion but in the straight there was no catching Sovereign. Beggy turned for home with only stablemate Norway for company and the rest ten lengths or more behind, and he never saw another horse once Norway had been burned off.

Anthony Van Dyck came home six lengths behind Sovereign with Norway holding on for third in a 1-2-3 for O'Brien but in far from the order anyone had predicted. It was a 13th Irish Derby winner for the Ballydoyle trainer, who said: "It wasn't the result we were expecting, but full marks to Padraig, I'm delighted for him. Sovereign wasn't for catching today."

Inevitably, questions were asked of the riders who gave Beggy so much rope but the winning jockey deserved credit for his enterprising and well-judged front running. "I'd say any time you make the running you have to get the fractions right and he did," O'Brien said.

For Beggy there was pure delight in "the race you grew up wanting to win". The 33-year-old rider said: "It's a very good feeling to win the Irish Derby. The Curragh is where I served my apprenticeship with Kevin Prendergast and this means even more to me than winning the Epsom Derby."

The Derby specialist had done it again.

Picture: PATRICK McCANN (RACINGPOST.COM/PHOTOS)

FALLEN HERO

Espoir D'Allen scored a record-breaking win in the Champion Hurdle but joy turned to grief in the summer

By Brian Sheerin

FROM domination to utter desolation. Espoir D'Allen was crowned the new king at Cheltenham in March with a record-breaking 15-length triumph in the Champion Hurdle and hopes were high for a long and glorious reign. In the cruellest twist of fate, however, JP McManus's exciting five-year-old was taken from us just five months later after being injured in a freak accident at trainer Gavin Cromwell's yard.

A big-race victory like Espoir D'Allen's is often described as devastating, and it was, but what happened to him in August was truly so. After a summer break at McManus's Martinstown Stud, he returned to Cromwell's County Meath stable in early August as the 3-1 favourite for the 2020 Champion Hurdle but shortly afterwards suffered a shoulder injury after getting spooked and rearing over following a routine canter.

The extent of the injury was not known initially and Espoir D'Allen was sent to Fethard Equine Hospital for treatment, before a decision was made to put him down a fortnight later. "It is with great sadness that we have to announce Espoir D'Allen had to be put down," Cromwell said in a statement. "John Halley and his veterinary team deemed that it was inhumane to persist with treatment and, on their advice, we made the tough decision."

Just how tough was put into bleaker perspective by Mark Walsh, who rode Espoir D'Allen to his runaway Champion Hurdle victory. "It's a sickening day for everyone concerned," the jockey said. "He could have been anything. It's very sad for JP and Gavin and everyone in the yard. Words can't describe the way everyone is feeling."

It was such a sad end for a young hurdler who shone briefly but so brilliantly. Espoir D'Allen had only ten races but he won nine of them and, in what would turn out to be the last one, he left dual champion Buveur D'Air on the floor and

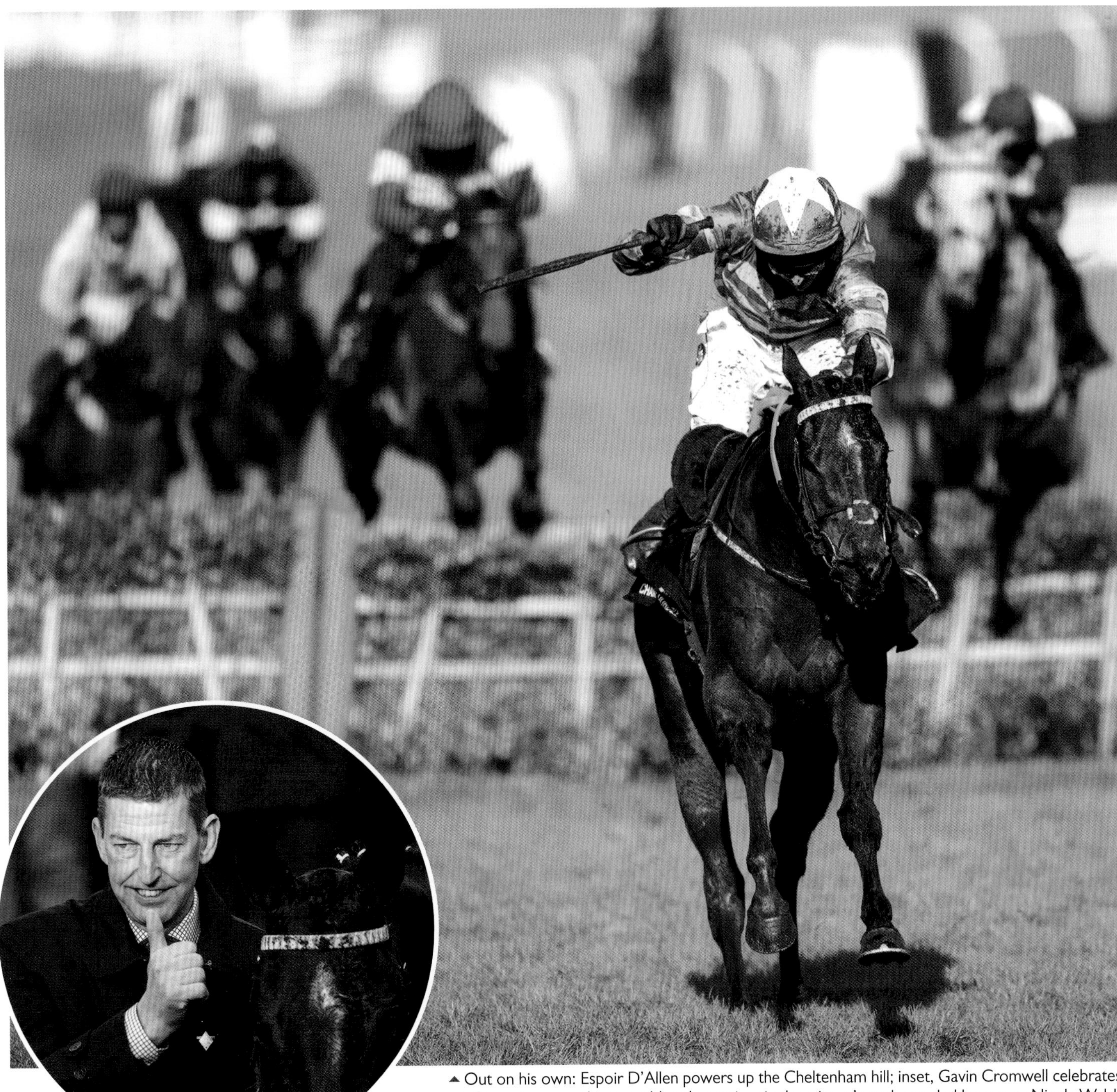

▲ Out on his own: Espoir D'Allen powers up the Cheltenham hill; inset, Gavin Cromwell celebrates
◀ Opposite page, the record-breaker arrives in the winner's enclosure led by groom Nicola Walsh

star Irish mares Apple's Jade and Laurina trailing in his wake. Five-year-olds aren't meant to win Champion Hurdles, especially not in such comprehensive fashion, but there was something special about this one.

★★★★

ESPOIR D'ALLEN went to Cheltenham having completed a Grade 3 hat-trick at Naas, Limerick and Naas again but he had a lot to prove in Grade 1 company and Cromwell made the trip more in hope than expectation. In his mind, a place was the best he could wish for given the strength of the opposition. Something to build on for next year perhaps.

The five-year-old proved he was ready now, however, as a frenetic gallop served up a dramatic race. Buveur D'Air, McManus's leading hope, bidding to join the list of triple Champion Hurdle winners, took a chance at the third hurdle and crashed out. Soon afterwards, Apple's Jade, so used to grinding her rivals into submission and having won the Irish Champion Hurdle by 16 lengths the previous month, was beginning to drop off the early pace.

As one by one his rivals fell by the wayside, Walsh crept into contention on Espoir D'Allen. They moved on to the heels of long-time leader Melon coming down the hill before blowing the race to smithereens off the home turn, drawing almost effortlessly clear to record a stunning success. Espoir D'Allen beat the previous record winning margin of 12 lengths, set by Insurance in 1932 and Istabraq in 1998, and became the first five-year-old to land the prize since Katchit in 2008 – the one before that was See You Then in 1985 for the first of his three Champion Hurdle wins.

"Me and Gavin spoke before the race and the plan was to ride him for a place. We got a place, it was first place!" Walsh joked, adding: "He travelled very strongly and gave me a dream ride. When Buveur D'Air fell, I luckily avoided the fall and got a lovely run

▸▸ *Continues page 114*

through the whole way. For a five-year-old to do that against what we thought was one of the best Champion Hurdle fields for the past few years is unbelievable. He's a right little horse."

For Walsh, McManus's second jockey behind Barry Geraghty, it was a second festival winner. For Cromwell, who has gradually left his farriery business behind as his stable has grown to 50 horses, it was a first. "What can you say? It's unbelievable," said the 44-year-old trainer, wearing a smile that bordered on the bemused. "I know five-year-olds don't have a good record in this race, but we thought he might learn something and potentially come back next year. It was a brilliant performance. I had no idea he was going to do that.

"I was watching them all come under pressure one by one and he was still travelling. I couldn't believe it. I knew he'd stay very well, so I had no fear of him stopping."

****

CROMWELL was not unused to the big occasion. The previous year he had won the Welsh Grand National with Raz De Maree and demonstrated his versatility by landing the Group 2 Prix de Royallieu with Princess Yaiza on Arc weekend at Longchamp. His link with McManus stemmed from a Grade 1 double with Jer's Girl in the 2015-16 jumps season when the owner purchased the mare two days before the first of those wins. The following year, Espoir D'Allen arrived in the yard.

"Charlie Swan [who won three Champion Hurdles on Istabraq for McManus] found the horse in France and he came to me after winning a juvenile bumper over there," Cromwell said. "I had a call from JP's team to say I had a horse coming to me in a couple of weeks, and it was this one. JP has been very good to me and it's great to be able to repay him."

Cromwell, whose father and grandfather were renowned point-to-point men, has had to work hard for his success. So hard, in fact, that as well as tending to his own Champion Hurdle contender, he was shoeing major rival Apple's Jade the week before Cheltenham. "We'll still do a little bit of farriery because it's the only way to make it pay. You need 145 horses otherwise," he said.

His relationship with Gordon Elliott, Apple's Jade's trainer, runs deep. The pair once shared a house and it was Elliott who talked Cromwell round at a time when winners weren't as plentiful and training horses seemed only a distraction from the farriery work, leading Cromwell to contemplate giving up the training.

He doesn't have those thoughts any more. The 2018-19 season was his best yet, with 33 winners in Ireland, and he had gone past that total by early autumn in the new campaign. The simple fact is that Cromwell will continue to train plenty of winners, and he will come across talented horses again, although ones with the raw ability of Espoir D'Allen don't come around very often.

The poignancy of loss is sharply felt when looking back on Cromwell's words as he welcomed his stable star back to the yard in August and looked forward to a "very exciting" season in the top races. "Everyone wanted a Snapchat with him in the yard," he said. "He's become a bit of a celebrity around here. You wouldn't believe the buzz around when he returned – it gave the whole place a new lease of life."

Those feelings would soon turn to despair. A sad end for the shooting star who burned so bright.

▲ Festival joy: Mark Walsh gives a thumbs-up after his runaway Champion Hurdle victory with Espoir D'Allen

FALL AND RISE

Buveur D'Air crashed out of his Champion Hurdle hat-trick bid but recovered his poise at Punchestown

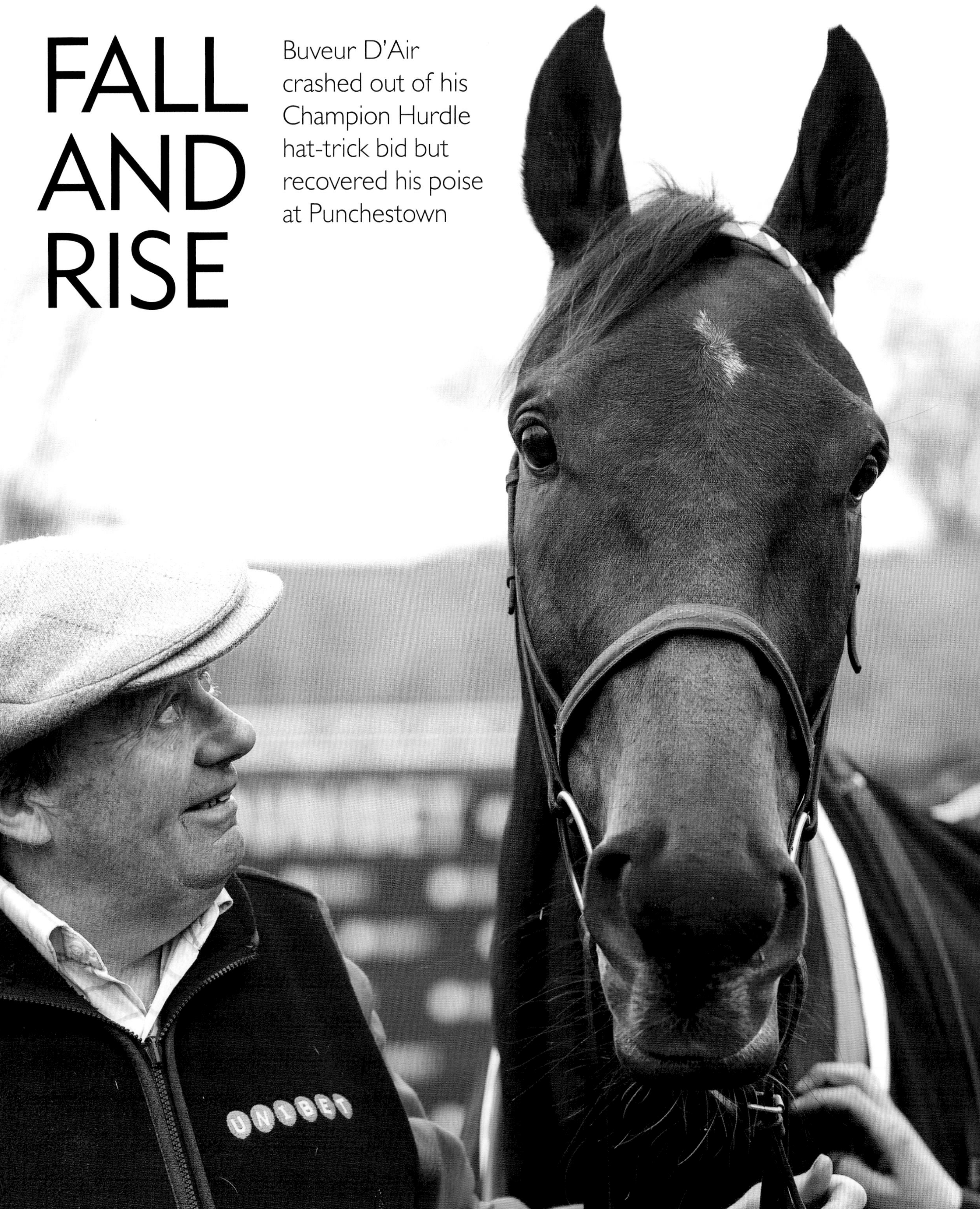

By Richard Birch

BUVEUR D'AIR started the 2018-19 season as a winning machine who seemed on track for a Champion Hurdle hat-trick but it was only after the engine had spluttered a few times that he finally hit top gear again.

Having suffered three defeats in Grade 1 contests and lost his Cheltenham crown, the now former champion was sent to the last big festival of the season on a retrieval mission. Not only did Nicky Henderson's eight-year-old rescue a troubled campaign with victory in the Punchestown Champion Hurdle, he seemed to earn new-found respect. Bizarrely for a horse who had launched his campaign on the back of ten straight wins, he ended the season more admired than when everything had been going right.

Why many racing fans have seen him as functional more than a thing of beauty remains a mystery as the dual Champion Hurdle winner has it all: a Rolls-Royce cruising speed, the ability to clear his hurdles with wonderful precision and a decisive turn of foot. Maybe what counted against him is the fact that he ruled at a time when the number of truly top-class two-mile hurdlers could be counted on the fingers of one hand, but that's hardly Buveur D'Air's fault.

He still looked the one to beat going into the 2018-19 campaign and even more so after a rampant eight-length dismissal of the much-hyped Samcro in Newcastle's Fighting Fifth Hurdle, the winning machine's 11th consecutive success.

Then things started to go wrong. A shock defeat at odds of 1-4 by stablemate Verdana Blue in Kempton's Christmas Hurdle was followed by an unimpressive two-length success over Vision Des Flos and three other markedly inferior rivals at Sandown. Potential Champion Hurdle rivals were emboldened by his lacklustre form and big-race favouritism passed to the Irish mare Apple's Jade, who had cruised to a 16-length win in the Irish Champion Hurdle 25 minutes before Buveur D'Air's Sandown run.

Buveur D'Air was still in the mix, of course, and lined up as 11-4 second favourite at Cheltenham for his bid to join Hatton's Grace, Sir Ken, Persian War, See You Then and Istabraq as a three-time winner of hurdling's greatest prize, but it didn't take long for Henderson's hopes to be dashed. Buveur D'Air, normally the slickest of hurdlers, fell at the third, his crown slipping into the Cheltenham mud as Espoir D'Allen, in the same JP McManus colours, went on to a stunning success.

It was Buveur D'Air's first fall in 15 starts over hurdles but a philosophical Henderson pointed out the quick and accurate jumping that made him so good also carried an element of risk. "With his hurdling, there's such a fine margin, an inch every time, and you only have to get it wrong by half an inch. We all have to take these things on the chin," he said.

The fallen champion stepped up to two and a half miles in the Aintree Hurdle, which he had won after his first Champion Hurdle in 2017, but there was another setback as he suffered an odds-on defeat by Supasundae. Although by no means disgraced on gruelling ground, he again lacked spark under regular partner Barry Geraghty and finished only half a length in front of Ch'tibello, rated 16lb below him on official ratings.

****

THAT was Buveur D'Air's third loss in a row at Grade 1 level but he was about to deliver a jolt to those who believed his best days were behind him. Given a shot at redemption in the Punchestown Champion Hurdle, he came back to form with a vengeance to turn the tables on Supasundae.

Sent off 2-1 joint-favourite with Apple's Jade, with Supasundae at 9-2, Buveur D'Air was partnered for the first time by Davy Russell, who received a late call-up after intended rider Mark Walsh joined Geraghty on the sidelines.

There was an indication that the real Buveur D'Air was back early in the race when the way he arched his back and soared over the second hurdle suggested he was physically and mentally in a good place.

Russell bided his time and sat fourth as Petit Mouchoir cut out the early fractions, tracked by Melon and Apple's Jade. Supasundae hit a flat spot at halfway and was pushed along, but Henderson's resurgent star cantered through the race as if he was merely enjoying an exercise gallop.

After clearing the penultimate hurdle, Buveur D'Air was still tanking along, hard on the bridle, but the big question was would he find? As soon as Russell shook him up approaching the last, we all knew the answer: the fire was back in Buveur D'Air's belly. He produced the burst of speed that had been missing since the Fighting Fifth and stormed clear on the run-in to beat Supasundae by two and a half lengths.

"It's great to see him finish the season back to his absolute best," Henderson said. "He started the season in the Fighting Fifth in a way that made everyone think he was going to be unbeatable. So did I. This was a proper race today. That's what suits him and his hurdling was right back to its usual slickness. We now go into the summer looking forward to next season. He's the one to beat again."

That might not be indisputably true but Buveur D'Air still has the chance to prove himself a legend by joining that illustrious band of three-time Champion Hurdle winners next March. Another victory at Cheltenham would be the best comeback of all.

▸ Air raid: Davy Russell is all smiles after riding Buveur D'Air to victory at the Punchestown festival

◂ Nicky Henderson with his star hurdler

THE BIGGER PICTURE

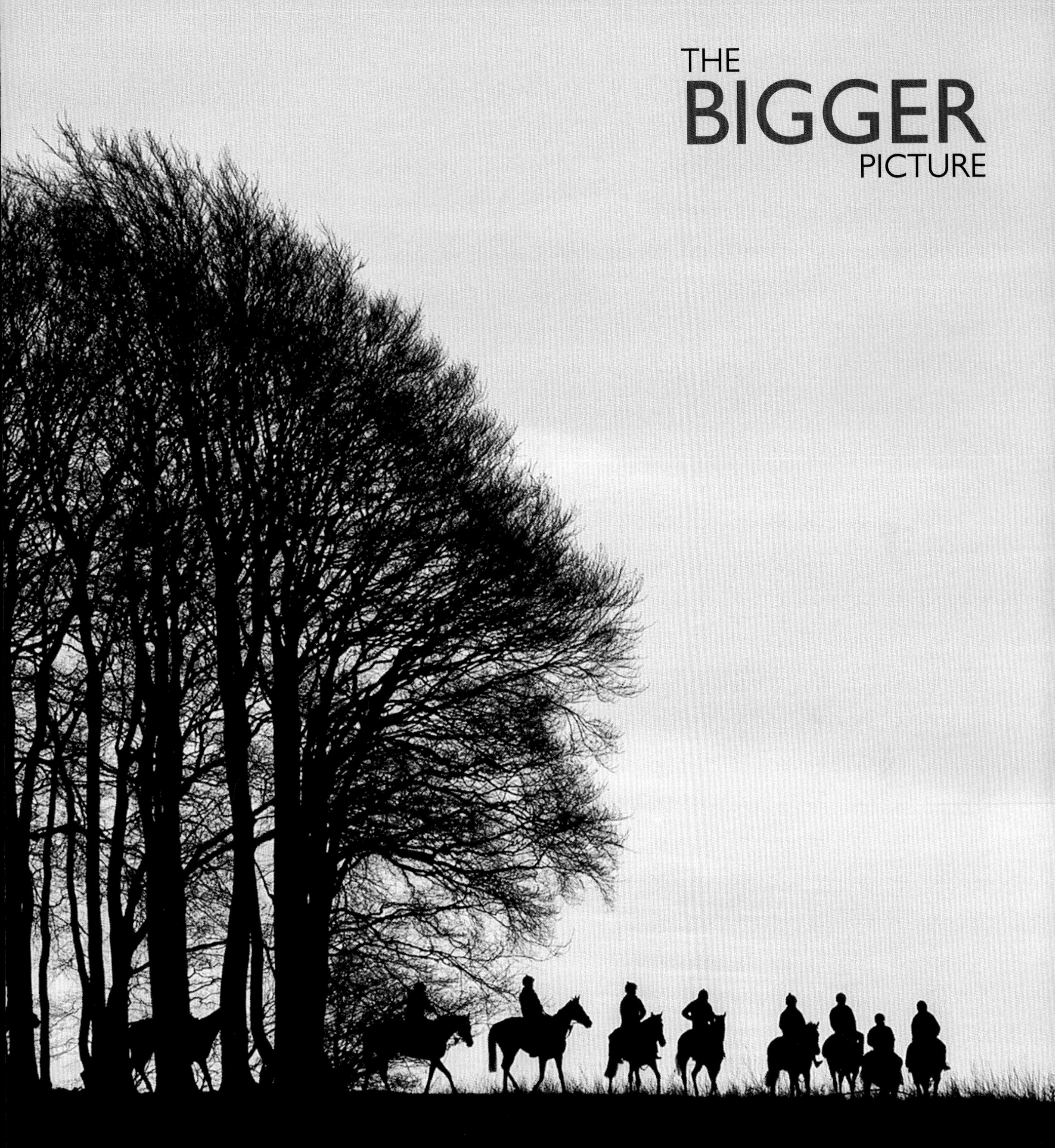

Nicky Henderson's string gathers at the top of the all-weather gallop after working on a bitterly cold January morning in Lambourn

EDWARD WHITAKER (RACINGPOST.COM/PHOTOS)

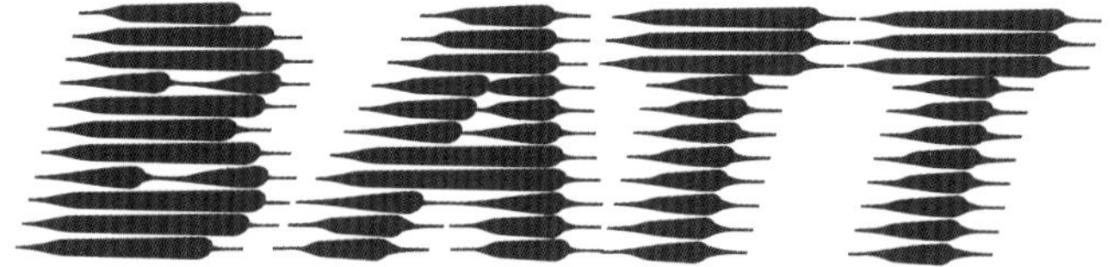

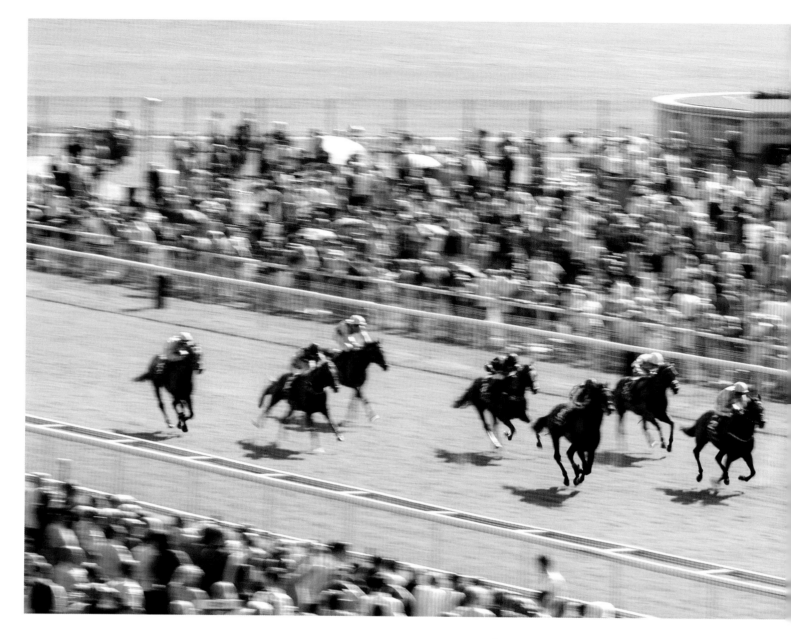

Battaash put his York purgatory behind him with a record-breaking performance in the Nunthorpe

By Nick Pulford

"Insanity is doing the same thing over and over and expecting different results."

IF Charlie Hills had followed the famous dictum often attributed to Albert Einstein, he would not have taken Battaash back to York after a disastrous blowout in the 2017 Nunthorpe Stakes and certainly not after another failed attempt 12 months later. Thank goodness Hills was more inclined to put his faith in Robert The Bruce's adage to try, try and try again because at the third time of asking Battaash finally came good down the York straight with a sprinting spectacular for the ages.

In blitzing the 2019 Nunthorpe field, Battaash lowered the five-furlong course record that had stood for almost three decades since the mighty Dayjur ran away with the Group 1 contest in 1990. In just 55.90 seconds, 0.26sec quicker than Dayjur, Battaash banished all the doubts about whether he could bring his A-game to the Knavesmire. With both sprinters carrying the blue and white of owner Sheikh Hamdan Al Maktoum, there was more than a hint of symmetry to their performances and Battaash's achievement in eclipsing Dayjur's mark now stands as one of the greatest sprinting feats.

It might never have happened. Hills considered swerving the Nunthorpe and heading instead for the Flying Five at the Curragh on Irish Champions Weekend but was persuaded otherwise by the owner. "I'll be honest, part of me wanted to skip this and go to Ireland with him, but Sheikh Hamdan said, 'No, I'll be in York, I won't be in Ireland'," the trainer related after the Nunthorpe.

With the destination decided, the question was whether Hills could get the real Battaash to York. His stable star was coming off the back of an impressive win in the Group 2 King George Stakes at Goodwood but the same had been true the year before and Battaash had disappointed in the Nunthorpe, finishing fourth to Alpha Delphini with a display that Racing Post Ratings made a stone

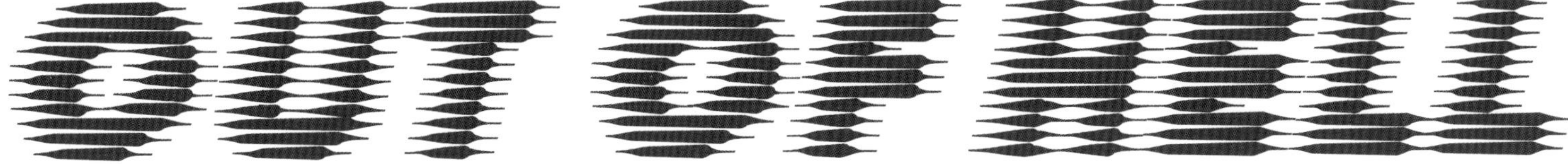

and a half worse than his Goodwood effort just three weeks earlier.

On his first attempt at the Nunthorpe in 2017, Battaash had performed even worse in fourth place behind Marsha. That day the Hills team could barely get the saddle on the three-year-old, who had been gelded as a juvenile but still had serious behavioural issues. When he was good, he was brilliant; when he was bad, he was awful. That August day was his lowest point.

Why he should save his worst moods for York was a matter of some debate but the chief excuse on that calamitous first visit was that he boiled over on the long walk from the stables, while a throat problem compromised his chance in 2018. With surgery having dealt with that issue during the off-season, Hills took steps to keep Battaash calm for his third attempt by boxing him up to York from Lambourn on the morning of the race, rather than the night before, while keeping the lid on him during the King George also proved important. "At Goodwood we were conscious we didn't want him to have too hard a race – in the two years before we'd maybe given him too hard a time," Hills said. "We didn't really want to give him a smack this year. He still recorded a fast time, but we didn't want to ask him for a massive effort."

Another piece in the complicated jigsaw was Battaash's draw in stall one in the Nunthorpe, having been among the high numbers in previous years. That berth on the far side put him close to the pace, set by the outsider Ornate and then Soldier's Call from stalls three and four, and he was able to get into a fast rhythm immediately under Jim Crowley. As Hills said afterwards: "It's a case of getting the sectionals right and using his speed at the right moment. It's hard to ask a sprinter to sprint. It's the worst thing you can do. It's all about balance and getting the horse on an even keel."

July Cup winner Ten Sovereigns, who had edged Battaash for favouritism, also started well

▸▸ *Continues page 122*

enough from stall 11 but by halfway it was clear Crowley had everything under control. Battaash got up to top speed with seemingly effortless ease, hitting a peak of 47.28 miles per hour, and powered clear of his toiling rivals in devastating fashion. Soldier's Call kept on well for second but came home three and three-quarter lengths behind brilliant Battaash.

No wonder Crowley was animated after the race. "I've never before had a buzz off a horse like that," he said. "When I woke up this morning I was excited about it and I was still excited driving to the track. When I asked him to go he finished off the race immediately. He was going so quickly I knew it would need a horse from another planet to come by him in the last furlong. It was unbelievable, my best winner ever."

The same is probably true for Hills, even though his other top horses include 2015 champion sprinter Muhaarar, also for Sheikh Hamdan, and the 2019 Irish 2,000 Guineas winner Phoenix Of Spain. It was certainly an emotional victory after all the trials and tribulations at York in the past. Once the hoodoo had been broken, however, the wonder was not that Battaash had finally won the Nunthorpe but rather why it had taken him so long.

"He loves York now, doesn't he?" joked Hills. "When you look at York you think it should be ideal for him, but sometimes these sand-based tracks don't suit some horses. Not all horses handle York, but he's experienced now and he's doing everything right. He's always shown a great level of ability but now he's putting it all together."

▼ Calm before the storm: Charlie Hills with Battaash at Faringdon Place in Lambourn shortly before the record-breaking Nunthorpe triumph

★★★★

BEFORE York, Battaash had won the Temple Stakes at Haydock before losing to Blue Point in the King's Stand and then bouncing back in the King George – exactly mirroring his start to 2018. What changed, backing up Hills's view about putting it all together, was that York was a triumph, not a disaster.

The Prix de l'Abbaye was the next stop after York for the third year in a row and this time Battaash did not put it all together. Having won the Abbaye in 2017 and finished fourth in 2018, he was a dismal 14th of 16 this time. This was where it all fell apart again. The softest ground Battaash had ever encountered was a legitimate excuse and that one failure should not detract from the most consistent season of his life.

▸▸ *Continues page 124*

The Nunthorpe demolition meant Battaash had reached the high 120s on Racing Post Ratings for the third year in a row – a remarkable sequence of high-level performance, even if he has not always hit that peak as regularly as Hills might like. The York victory earned an RPR of 129, matching his career-best from the 2018 King George at Goodwood, while his previous peak of 128 came in the 2017 Prix de l'Abbaye. To put those figures into perspective, the only other European-trained sprinters since 2000 to reach such heights are Mozart (2001), Oasis Dream (2003) and Dream Ahead (2011).

****

DAYJUR was on a different level again in his remarkable campaign as a three-year-old in 1990, which stretched for more than six months and featured nine races. Trained by Dick Hern and ridden by Willie Carson, he reached 131 on RPR with victory in the King's Stand, then a Group 2, and a phenomenal 136 on three occasions, starting with his four-length Nunthorpe triumph, before winding up his career with 133 in his famously unlucky Breeders' Cup Sprint defeat when he jumped a shadow with victory in sight.

Purely on the clock, however, Battaash had earned the right to be mentioned in the same breath as one of the greatest sprinters of all time. "To lower Dayjur's record is pretty amazing," Hills said. "I thought there would never be a faster horse than him but there obviously is now. Willie Carson said he thought this could be the next Dayjur and he was right. He's a superstar."

Sheikh Hamdan is perhaps best placed to compare his two sprinters and his view in the York winner's enclosure was interesting. "Dayjur was more genuine and straightforward than this horse," said the owner, who pointed to his head when adding: "Battaash is sometimes a little bit . . ."

Yes, but at his best Battaash is sometimes more than a little bit brilliant.

New generation quick to shine

Three-year-olds performed with great distinction in the Group 1 sprints, raising hope for a competitive division again in 2020 as the ones who stay in training reach full maturity.

Battle-hardened five-year-olds Battaash and Blue Point were no doubt the standout stars of the sprint season but for a long time – until the six-year-old Donjuan Triumphant caused a 33-1 upset on heavy ground in the British Champions Sprint in October – they were the only older winners at the top level.

For much of the summer and autumn it was the three-year-olds who held sway as Ten Sovereigns and Advertise stepped up from Group 1 success as juveniles to bag more big prizes, while other less obvious talents blossomed as the season progressed.

The Commonwealth Cup, introduced to the Royal Ascot programme in 2015 as a way to allow three-year-olds to find their feet as sprinters before taking on their elders, again proved its worth with a high-class renewal. The Aidan O'Brien-trained Ten Sovereigns, beaten favourite when fifth in the 2,000 Guineas, headed the market again but was only fourth behind Martyn Meade's stable star Advertise, who was also dropping in trip after trailing home 15th in the Guineas.

The pair crossed swords again in the July Cup at Newmarket and this time Advertise was 3-1 favourite but there was another reversal of form as Ten Sovereigns, joint-second in the market on 9-2, left him two and three-quarter lengths back in second. The winner was given a Racing Post Rating of 125, a mark bettered only by Battaash and Blue Point in the European sprint campaign.

Advertise went to France next, justifying favouritism with a hard-fought neck victory over Brando in the Prix Maurice de Gheest, while Ten Sovereigns headed to York for a clash with Battaash in the Nunthorpe Stakes. He was favourite again but was firmly put in his place, finishing sixth behind the record-breaking winner.

Now it was the turn of some other three-year-olds to step up. The Haydock Sprint Cup went to the Kevin Ryan-trained Hello Youmzain, having his first run since finishing third in the Commonwealth Cup almost three months earlier. Khaadem, who had come out of the Royal Ascot race to win the Stewards' Cup, was one of the co-favourites with Hello Youmzain at Haydock but finished last.

O'Brien's Fairyland, third in the July Cup but tenth in the Nunthorpe and sixth in the Sprint Cup, bounced back only eight days after Haydock to take the Flying Five at the Curragh from stablemate So Perfect, becoming another Group 1-winning juvenile of 2018 to register a top-level sprint success.

Both the O'Brien fillies lined up in the Prix de l'Abbaye at Longchamp, where Battaash was hot favourite. The Nunthorpe winner failed to spark at all, however, and that opened the way for the Ryan-trained Glass Slippers to take the honours on her first venture into Group 1 company. She was the fifth different three-year-old to score in a top-level all-aged sprint in 2019, an impressive tally for the young guns.

▸ Young guns: Ten Sovereigns, winning the July Cup, and fellow three-year-old Advertise (right), who landed two Group 1 sprints

What are mycotoxins?

Mycotoxins are produced by moulds commonly found in grains, mixed feed, forages and bedding. They are generally referred to as being of either 'field' (Fusarium and Endophyte toxins) or 'storage' (Penicillium and Aspergillus) origin. They are implicated in a variety of acute equine health problems including colic, hypersensitivity, abortions and neurological disorders. Chronic cases can lead to cumulative effects such as damage to organ function, reduced growth, infertility and respiratory problems. Affected horses can appear agitated with possible head shaking, decreased feed intake and performance.

The mycotoxin dilemma

Mycotoxins are difficult to measure

- Many different mycotoxins can be present simultaneously in feed, making analysis difficult and expensive.
- Visible mould or spore counts are not definitive.
- Sampling of bulk feeds is difficult.

Mycotoxicosis is hard to diagnose

- Symptoms are usually non-specific.

Mycotoxin synergism

- Mould species coexist; and most can produce more than one mycotoxin.
- Mycotoxins are synergistic, meaning combinations have a greater impact than single toxins. As a result, seemingly low levels of individual mycotoxins can have a large impact on health.

Mycotoxin Forage Testing

The test is done within 10 days - to obtain a testing kit please email laboratory@rossdales.com. The test itself is £200 per sample. A full report is supplied with the major mycotoxin groups identified and the levels at which they have been found. Your referring vet will be able to discuss the results with you and any further steps that may need to be taken.

Each sample submitted needs to be from one common feed source ie hay or haylage, instructions are included in the testing kit.

What is the solution?

Visible and non-visible mould spores can occur naturally in forages and on pasture which can generate mycotoxins, products of mould metabolism, and are often hard to detect.

FORAGE GUARD® can help to maintain the normal performance of horses in the presence of mycotoxins in forage and feed. This broad spectrum mycotoxin binder is in powder form and can be directly added to feed.

FORAGE GUARD® can be purchased directly from Rossdales at £40/tub for a three month supply.

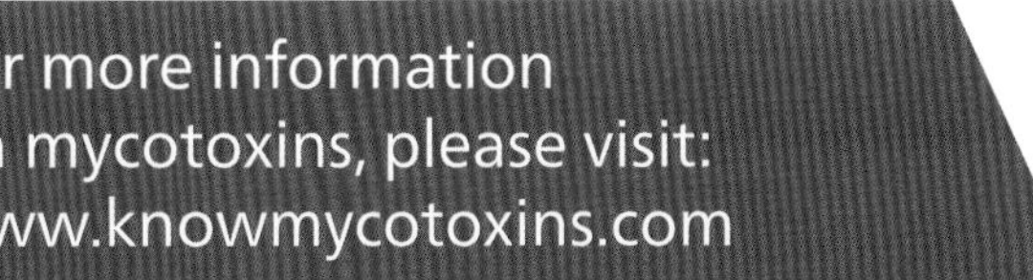

For more information
on mycotoxins, please visit:
www.knowmycotoxins.com

DOUBLE QUICK

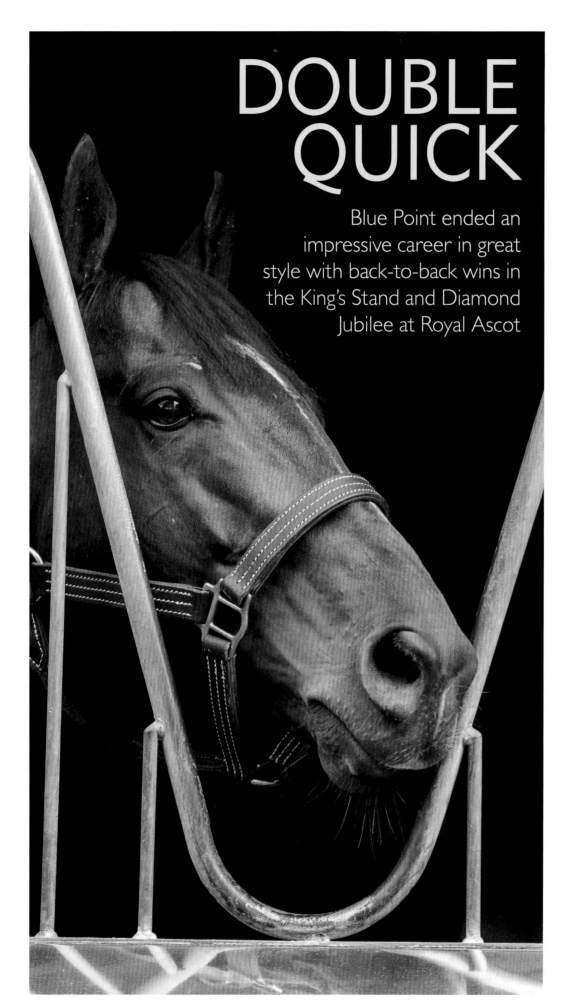

Blue Point ended an impressive career in great style with back-to-back wins in the King's Stand and Diamond Jubilee at Royal Ascot

By Nick Pulford

FOR a horse who departed the scene before halfway in the British Flat season, Blue Point achieved rather a lot at great speed. The Godolphin sprinter rounded out his career with five straight wins in 2019, culminating in a fabulous twin strike at Royal Ascot, before heading off to start a new life at stud. It was some finish.

Blue Point was already a Royal Ascot winner, having taken the scalp of Battaash in the 2018 King's Stand Stakes, but the Godolphin team and trainer Charlie Appleby were confident he could add further gloss to his stallion adverts in a final campaign as a five-year-old. How right they were.

A winter stint in Dubai brought three wins in dominant fashion. The best of them on the figures was his three-length victory in a six-furlong Group 3 contest – matching his career-best 123 on Racing Post Ratings – but the most prestigious was the Group 1 Al Quoz Sprint on Dubai World Cup night. "It's great at the age of five he's showing everyone just how good he is," said jockey William Buick. "He's developed into a top-class sprinter now."

The main target was Royal Ascot and a momentous week started with a rematch against Battaash in the King's Stand. Once again his old rival was favourite at 2-1 but Blue Point was close behind at 5-2, with James Doyle taking over in the saddle from his great friend Buick, who had been on the sidelines for more than a month as he recovered from a head injury.

The chief concern was the rain-softened ground, officially good on the day, although Appleby was in confident mood. "It looks like it's going to be a great race, but we're very happy with Blue Point, who has matured into a proper sprinter over the winter," he said. "We've always felt the stiff five furlongs at Ascot is his best trip and he seems to bring his A-game to the course."

Twelve months earlier Appleby's speedster had overpowered Battaash by a length and three-

▲ Bullet Point: Godolphin's Blue Point (front right) powers home to land the Diamond Jubilee Stakes just four days after winning the King's Stand Stakes, bringing up a Royal Ascot double to the delight of trainer Charlie Appleby (inset)

quarters with his best performance to that point. This time he produced almost a carbon copy, except this was even better. Doyle was bold, sending Blue Point into the lead with two furlongs still to run, but he was soon challenged as Battaash hit top gear. The old rivals were almost level going into the final furlong but Blue Point was the stronger up the hill and close home he was going away to win by a length and a quarter. It was a career-best 127 on Racing Post Ratings, a sprint performance of the highest order.

★★★★

MISSION accomplished, or so it seemed. Appleby, though, had a Diamond Jubilee Stakes entry up his sleeve, ostensibly made in case anything went wrong in the King's Stand. Now that everything was going right, Godolphin principal Sheikh Mohammed gave the go-ahead to attempt the double famously achieved in 2003 by Choisir, the trailblazer who had opened the door to a period of Australian domination in the Royal Ascot sprints.

There was nothing to lose and everything to gain in terms of boosting the profile of Godolphin's stallion prospect, who had once held the six-furlong course record at Ascot and could not have finished the King's Stand in more encouraging fashion. Having confirmed Blue Point for the Diamond Jubilee on the Thursday morning of Royal Ascot, Appleby explained the thinking.

"It was in the back of our minds and he was always going to be left in the two races so if he were to win the option would be there," he said. "He's only got two more opportunities to run at Ascot before he retires at the end of the year and it was either this or wait for Champions Day when he could be taking on testing conditions. The way the forecast is, it's going to be drying out nicely towards Saturday. His Highness Sheikh Mohammed is very sporting and he felt the horse deserved to take his chance."

Hard and fast

Blue Point joined the list of horses who have completed the King's Stand/Diamond Jubilee double

Prince Charlie 1873
Lowlander 1876
Hackthorpe 1879
Geheimniss 1884
Delaunay 1905
Hornet's Beauty 1913
Diadem 1920
Choisir 2003 *(right)*
Blue Point 2019

Diamond Jubilee Stakes previously called the All-Aged Stakes (1868-1925), Cork and Orrery Stakes (1926-2001) and Golden Jubilee Stakes (2002-11)

The ground did indeed continue to dry and was at its quickest on the final day of the meeting, officially good to firm. With nothing of the calibre of Battaash among his 16 rivals, Blue Point was a hot favourite at 6-4 with French raider City Light, a short-head runner-up to Merchant Navy 12 months earlier, next best at 6-1.

The Diamond Jubilee would have a tight finish again but the threat to Blue Point came from much closer to home. Dream Of Dreams, trained in Newmarket by Sir Michael Stoute, was a 12-1 shot who had a lot to prove at Group 1 level but he gave the favourite a serious fright.

At the furlong pole it looked as if Blue Point would win more emphatically than he had in the King's Stand, having gone past the pacesetting Kachy into a clear lead. Dream Of Dreams came out of the pack seemingly too late but, with Blue Point appearing to be feeling his double exertions, the gap closed with every stride. In truth it always seemed as if Blue Point had enough of a buffer to hold on, and so it proved as he got home by a head. Mission accomplished for the second time.

★★★★

THERE was nothing left to prove and two days later came the announcement that Blue Point would take up stallion duty at Dalham Hall Stud for the 2020 breeding season, joining his sire Shamardal on the Darley roster. "To do what he did within five days was the pinnacle of his career and he couldn't have done any more," Appleby said.

"The one thing we talk about all winter is Ascot, Ascot, Ascot," Appleby had said during the royal meeting, regarding the close attention Sheikh Mohammed pays to plans for his horses.

Blue Point, now a three-time winner on the stage that means so much, had been the star of the show. For him, it will always be Royal Ascot, Royal Ascot, Royal Ascot.

SPARKLING CRYSTAL

Crystal Ocean was a central player in three of the year's top races and landed a first Group 1 at Royal Ascot before injury cut short his career

By Andrew Dietz

ONE of the great anomalies at the start of the racing year was that Crystal Ocean had still to register a top-level success. His class was undisputed, his resolution never questioned. Yet as with a poker player bemoaning their luck, the cards had not fallen right when it mattered most. On the three occasions he had been to the big table, he had found one to beat him each time.

In driving rain on the second day of Royal Ascot, Crystal Ocean washed away any fears that a deserved Group 1 win would always elude him when he scored a gallant victory in the Prince of Wales's Stakes. The length-and-a-quarter defeat of high-class filly Magical not only filled the gaping hole on Crystal Ocean's CV, it resulted in Sir Michael Stoute's stable star being anointed as the world's best racehorse.

The rarefied distinction did not weigh heavy on his shoulders as the following month he lost out by just a neck when attempting to give 3lb to Enable in a momentous duel in the King George VI and Queen Elizabeth Stakes at Ascot. If that was the Rumble in the Jungle, the Thrilla in Manila took place at York in August. Crystal Ocean again showed his heavyweight qualities, going down by only a head to Japan in the Juddmonte International.

Sadly that would be the last time the son of Sea The Stars was seen in the heat of battle. He was retired in September following a career-ending injury on the gallops. Not for the first time, fate had conspired against Crystal Ocean, but his legacy as a tough and talented performer had already been secured in three of the signature races of 2019.

****

AS HE had done the previous year, Crystal Ocean started his campaign in April by winning Sandown's Gordon Richards Stakes. However, unlike 12 months earlier when he scrambled home, the five-year-old brushed aside his Group 3 rivals with contempt. He was a better horse now, the finished article physically and battle-hardened by the events of the past.

After the race Stoute declared he wanted to win a Group 1 with his warrior, who had finished second behind Capri in the 2017 St Leger, Poet's Word in the 2018 King George and Cracksman in the 2018 Champion Stakes.

Following a warm-up win at Newbury in May, again following the same path as the year before, Stoute nominated the Prince of Wales's as the Royal Ascot target for Crystal Ocean. Defending his Hardwicke Stakes crown over a mile and a half – the distance at which he had shown his best form – was another option, but Stoute and owner Sir Evelyn de Rothschild stuck to the plan even though the mile-and-a quarter contest was developing into the race of the week.

Main rivals Magical, Waldgeist

▸▸ *Continues page 130*

and Sea Of Class had all scaled heights out of Crystal Ocean's reach, gaining a total of seven Group 1 wins between them. The size of the task was reflected in Crystal Ocean's overnight odds of 9-2, but the rain-softened ground at Ascot was less of an inconvenience to him than some of his rivals and he was sent off the 3-1 second favourite.

With Ryan Moore on market leader Magical, Frankie Dettori came in for the ride on Crystal Ocean and delivered a masterclass in the gruelling conditions by making his move a good three furlongs out while keeping enough in reserve for the finish.

The driving rain throughout the race added to the drama as Crystal Ocean showed all his battling qualities to fight off Magical. "He was very tough," said Dettori, who asked for everything and received even more when the favourite threw down what looked like a winning challenge.

Stoute had his 80th Royal Ascot winner and his skill and patience in taking Crystal Ocean to the top had provided yet another example of the trainer's mastery with older horses, such as the likes of Singspiel and Pilsudski from bygone days. "He's a high-class horse. I'm delighted to have won a Group 1 with him," Stoute said. It was a notable success for Crystal Ocean not only in terms of achievement but on the ratings too, as he moved to the top of the Longines World's Best Racehorse Rankings for 2019 with a mark of 127.

'In all my career that was the hardest fought big race I've had, with two champions fighting it out. Give credit to Crystal Ocean, he put it out there and it was an amazing race'

★★★★

IT WAS back to a mile and a half in the following month's King George, a race in which Crystal Ocean had been beaten a neck by stablemate Poet's Word the previous year.

Arriving at Ascot unbeaten in three starts during the season and on the back of a merited first Group 1 success, he could not have been in better shape as he attempted to topple the mighty Enable, who had opened her campaign by winning the Eclipse.

As the stalls broke open, no-one could have predicted quite what a race he was about to give the great mare. James Doyle, another new jockey on Crystal Ocean, managed to get a good early position behind the leaders – in stark contrast to Dettori, who was trapped wide on Enable from the highest draw.

Doyle allowed his mount to drift back a little to sit well off the pace before winding up his challenge on the turn into the home straight. Dettori tracked the move and, although Crystal Ocean led approaching the two-furlong pole and appeared to be travelling better than Enable, it quickly became clear the race could go either way.

A shaken-up Enable responded to claim a narrow lead but Crystal Ocean would not go quietly and the pair fought out the most dramatic of finishes. Crystal Ocean briefly looked like he might get back up entering the last furlong, but try as he might he could not overhaul Enable, ultimately going down by a neck for the second year running.

Given his connection to Crystal Ocean, Dettori was ideally placed to comment on a battle royal that drew comparisons, including from Stoute,

▼ Battle royal: Crystal Ocean (left) pushes Enable all the way in a pulsating duel for the King George VI and Queen Elizabeth Stakes

with the famous 'race of the century' between Grundy and Bustino in the 1975 King George.

"In all my career that was the hardest fought big race I've had, with two champions fighting it out," the exhausted jockey said. "Give credit to Crystal Ocean, he put it out there and it was an amazing race."

★★★★

WITH Enable prepping for the Arc in the Yorkshire Oaks, the Juddmonte International appeared to be at Crystal Ocean's mercy. Having conceded 3lb to Enable at Ascot, he was still ranked the highest in the world and was sent off the 11-10 favourite to gain compensation for his heroic King George effort.

Again the race panned out smoothly for Crystal Ocean with Doyle breezing into contention and taking over the lead from Circus Maximus in the straight. Asked to put the race to bed two furlongs out, he was unable to forge decisively clear and the chasing pack began to close. The distress signals were noticeable in Doyle's demeanour and worries that the race had come too soon after Ascot rose to the surface.

Japan, confirming his reputation as the best of Aidan O'Brien's Classic crop, took up the lead inside the final furlong, but after all his scraps and skirmishes Crystal Ocean's default setting was to fight and he momentarily snatched back the advantage before Japan prised victory away by a head.

The heart bled for Crystal Ocean at the end of another thriller. In the space of 25 days, he went deep into the mire in two of the world's best races and emerged with nothing to show for it, aside from his dignity. "It's heartbreaking," Doyle said. "But I couldn't be more proud of my horse. He always brings his A-game. Even in conditions that are a little bit difficult for him he still gives his all. We're lucky to have him."

★★★★

YORK was always going to be one of Crystal Ocean's last races as stud duties at the end of the year had been mentioned as far back as the Prince of Wales's in June but injury intervened to make it the last. On September 12, during routine exercise in Newmarket, he had to be pulled up and dismounted halfway up the Warren Hill Polytrack canter. He was taken away in a horse ambulance and underwent surgery to have two screws inserted in a hind cannon bone.

One saving grace is that a life at stud awaits a horse whose ability and toughness shone through a career in which he won eight of his 17 starts and was never out of the first three. He won only one of his six Group 1 races but was second in all the others and was involved in some of the greatest battles of recent years.

"He was an absolute gentleman to have anything to do with," said Doyle in tribute to the retiring hero. "He looked after you every step of the way and he was a jockey's dream to ride."

Perhaps there was still some sense of what might have been had he carried on to the Arc or Champion Stakes, but he left nobody in any doubt he was a Group 1 performer of the highest order.

▲ Ocean wave: Frankie Dettori salutes the crowd after winning the Prince of Wales's Stakes at Royal Ascot on Crystal Ocean

▲ Japan (nearside) just gets the better of Crystal Ocean in the Juddmonte International at York

By Scott Burton

HISTORY is never written ahead of time and for all the yearning that built up around Enable's bid for a historic hat-trick in the Prix de l'Arc de Triomphe, 11 other sets of hopes and dreams went to post for the 98th running of Longchamp's great race.

For those intimately involved with the 'other runners' there could be no more beautiful chapter waiting to be written in the Arc's storybook than the one they imagined ending with them standing in the winner's enclosure. And indeed there was another belle histoire out there, if only we had known where to look. One that featured persistence, belief and above all a touch of genius on the part of the man preparing this particular challenger.

"We'll win the Arc." It's a simple enough phrase to utter but the first we heard of it was when, moments after his eighth triumph in Europe's greatest race, Andre Fabre recounted the words of jockey Pierre-Charles Boudot upon dismounting from Waldgeist at Ascot in July.

The pair had just finished a running-on third to Enable in the King George VI and Queen Elizabeth Stakes, an occasion that marked – at least in the minds of many British and Irish observers – the moment when the prospect of Waldgeist ever overhauling Enable seemed to vanish. The score then was 3-0 to the mare, but Boudot and Fabre were in complete agreement that the gallant chestnut had shown them something to keep them warm through the autumn until the climactic fourth meeting with Enable.

"I really thought he was eating the ground at Ascot and he had a pretty easy race, so it gave me confidence," said Fabre in those frenzied few moments after the impossible had just become a matter of historical record.

Reflecting on the two races a few days after Waldgeist had seemingly come from nowhere to deny Enable at Longchamp, Boudot said: "That day [in the King

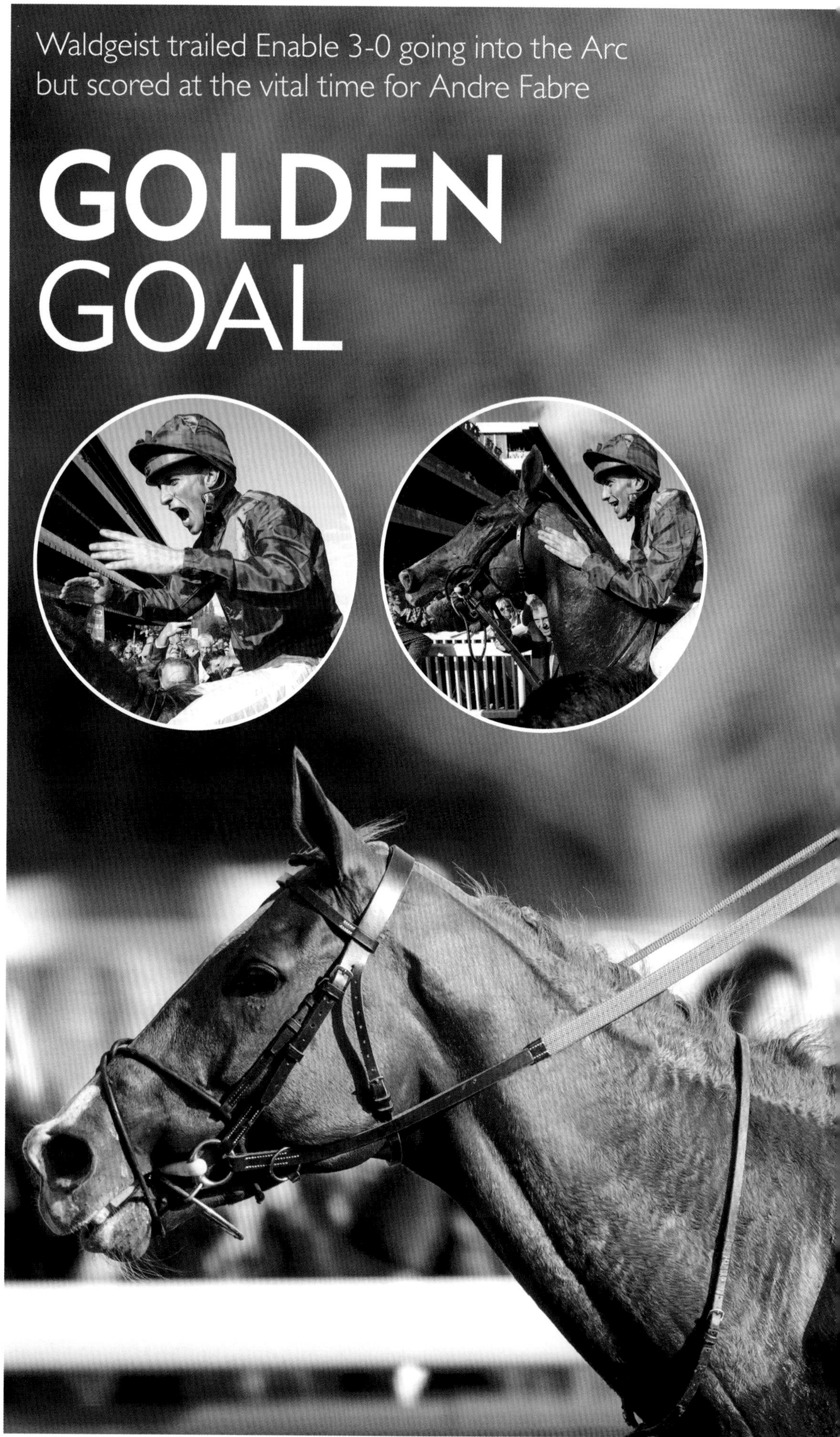

Waldgeist trailed Enable 3-0 going into the Arc but scored at the vital time for Andre Fabre

GOLDEN GOAL

George] the ground was pretty testing and he ran a lot better than on his previous visit to Ascot. I was really enthusiastic about his performance and we finished right on the heels of Enable and Crystal Ocean. It really left me feeling Waldgeist was capable of beating her one day."

****

IF THAT were all there was to the Waldgeist story, a simple reversal of racing fortunes, then he might be allowed to slip off into the darker recesses of Arc history: a five-year-old who proved tougher than the rest on a day when the Bois de Boulogne served up a severe test of stamina. But that would be to miss out on plenty of twists and turns, with multiple chances for a different story to unfold where the son of Galileo was not among the dozen to face the starter.

As a two-year-old the colt was an easy winner of the Criterium de Saint-Cloud and it seemed obvious he would be suited by a test of stamina and that deep conditions would show him to best effect. Arguably his best performance at three was when just failing to reel in Brametot in the Prix du Jockey Club over 1m2½f, with three subsequent attempts at a mile and a half ending in defeat. He did not win that season and more than 18 months had elapsed since his Criterium victory before he was successful again.

Waldgeist translates as 'woodland spirit' and his two German co-breeders – Gestut Ammerland's Dietrich von Boetticher and Andreas Jacobs of Hertfordshire-based Newsells Park Stud – remained convinced of his worth.

The third partner in breeding Waldgeist was the group of men who stand Galileo and at the end of his three-year-old career they took the rather less romantic decision to let their interest go.

Jacobs explains: "We were racing together, first in a partnership with Coolmore, based on a foal share. When he was three years old we felt he was going to get better and Coolmore felt he was probably not going to get better. So we were

▸▸ *Continues page 134*

lucky and here we are, we won the Arc."

There is no hint of malice in the retelling. Coolmore have dozens if not hundreds of such decisions to make at the end of each season. Given their efforts to find a way of beating Enable over the last three years, there is some irony in having sold their share in her eventual conqueror, though every single member of the Coolmore clan present at Longchamp warmly congratulated Fabre, who had trained Pour Moi to win the Derby in the all-navy of Susan Magnier.

Stamina looked to be Waldgeist's suit at four with a second Group 1 success at Saint-Cloud in the Grand Prix and the build-up to the Arc casting him as France's leading hope. After a sumptuous win in his trial, Waldgeist could do no better than fourth on the big day on ground that had little moisture but also lacked purchase after a difficult first season following the redevelopment of the track.

Waldgeist's 2018 season petered out at Churchill Downs and Sha Tin and, while Von Boetticher and Jacobs might have considered a truly tempting offer to stand him at stud had one arrived, the aim was set: win the Arc at five.

With the benefit of hindsight, his record in 2019 bears out what Fabre has said ahead of each race: Waldgeist is stronger at five and can be trained harder. The earlier versions of him would not have withstood two tough assignments at Ascot after his scintillating reappearance success in the Prix Ganay over 1m2½f, one which Fabre freely admits changed his thinking about Waldgeist.

"He's run a lot of races on soft ground but in the Ganay I suddenly found he was a different horse, you know. He handles anything."

****

THERE is no Waldgeist story without the broader sweep of Fabre and the Arc. While six of his seven previous winners were three-year-olds – indeed the likes of Carnegie, Sagamix and Rail Link did much to popularise the notion of a Fabre horse coming from relative obscurity to snatch the prize from more

▸▸ *Continues page 136*

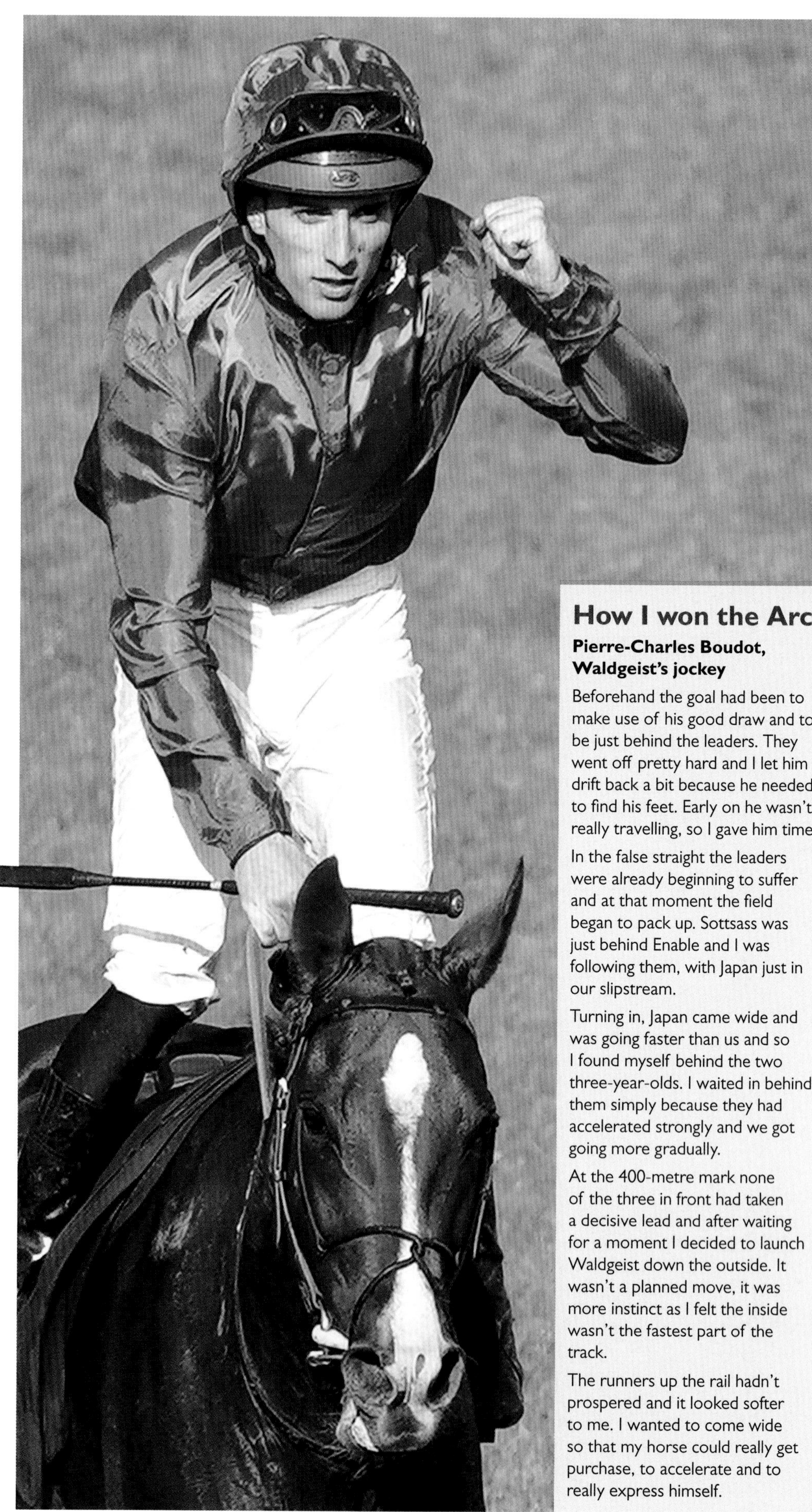

How I won the Arc

Pierre-Charles Boudot, Waldgeist's jockey

Beforehand the goal had been to make use of his good draw and to be just behind the leaders. They went off pretty hard and I let him drift back a bit because he needed to find his feet. Early on he wasn't really travelling, so I gave him time.

In the false straight the leaders were already beginning to suffer and at that moment the field began to pack up. Sottsass was just behind Enable and I was following them, with Japan just in our slipstream.

Turning in, Japan came wide and was going faster than us and so I found myself behind the two three-year-olds. I waited in behind them simply because they had accelerated strongly and we got going more gradually.

At the 400-metre mark none of the three in front had taken a decisive lead and after waiting for a moment I decided to launch Waldgeist down the outside. It wasn't a planned move, it was more instinct as I felt the inside wasn't the fastest part of the track.

The runners up the rail hadn't prospered and it looked softer to me. I wanted to come wide so that my horse could really get purchase, to accelerate and to really express himself.

ambitiously campaigned British and Irish contenders – he has shown down the years that he has a great many ways of winning big races.

If there is one, then Subotica might have been the prototype for Waldgeist: a winner of the Ganay early on in the year but then beaten at Epsom in the Coronation Cup and again in the Grand Prix de Saint-Cloud; the four-year-old even found one too good in the Prix Foy. But Fabre had him cherry ripe on the day that mattered most, getting the better of User Friendly by a neck.

It had been 13 long years since Rail Link extended Fabre's own record in the race to seven wins but in the intervening years he had hit the board a further eight times. And Boudot suggested afterwards that the master trainer had learned his lesson with Waldgeist from 2018.

"Last year he ran really well in the Prix Foy – perhaps too well – and then a little below that in the Arc," the jockey said. "This year we turned things around and he was not at his best in the Foy but really came on for that race. Andre Fabre prepared him beautifully [for the Arc]."

Like all those who work closely with Fabre, Boudot doesn't give too much away but when pressed as to what makes his boss the complete trainer, the jockey offered one simple recipe: "He finds all the quality and all the faults in his horses and he is very rarely wrong about them."

****

TO STAND in the paddock at Longchamp in the Waldgeist clan was to be among horsemen who knew both the form their runner was in, but also the magnitude of the task. As Waldgeist circled before them, they had everything you could want in an Arc challenger and he was about to go out and prove it.

Three-quarters of an hour later Von Boetticher related those last few moments and what then unfolded as Boudot launched Waldgeist down the centre of the track and into sporting legend. "Waldgeist looked well, Andre was positive. And Andre is a man you'd never, never doubt. So we all believed in him and we are sitting here today because he was right in what he was doing."

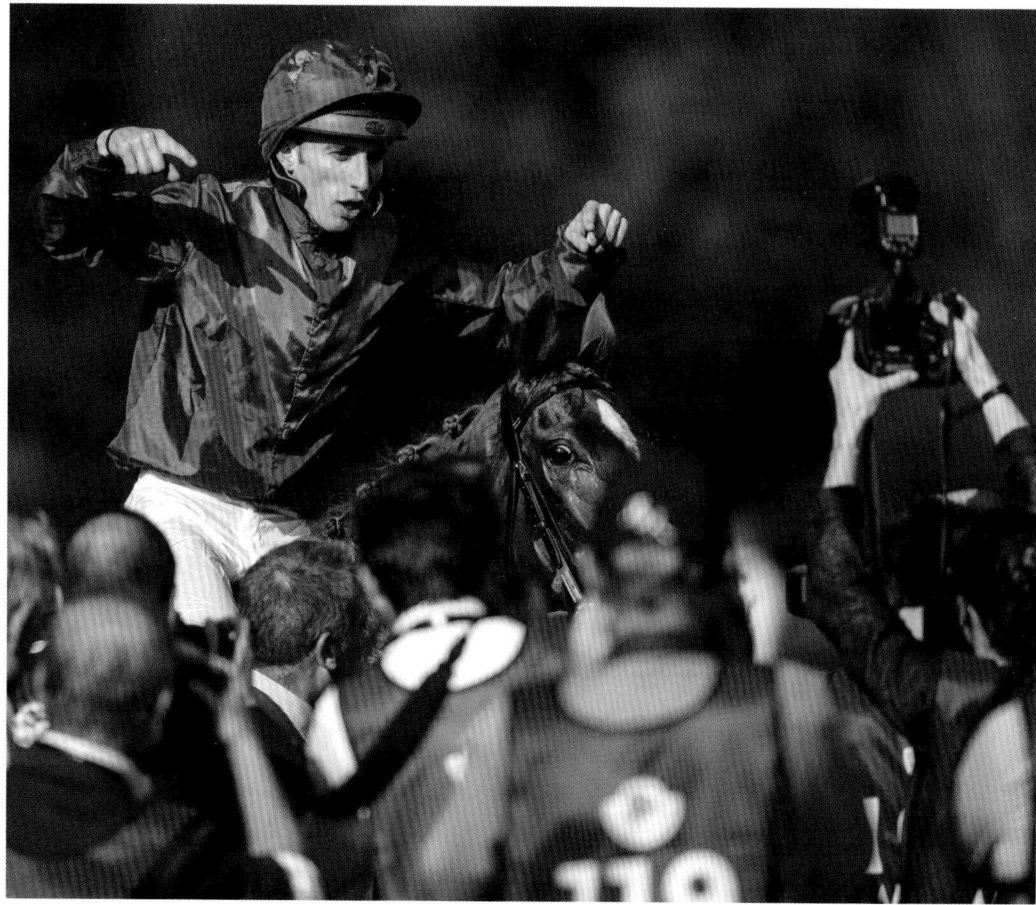

Von Boetticher continued: "Whether it's dry ground or good ground or wet ground, I'm always worried. But I also think the horse has become stronger over time. I didn't expect him to accelerate in the finish the way he did. I mean, he exploded."

In doing so Waldgeist and Boudot blew apart the dreams of so many fans who had travelled or tuned in to cheer Enable home. But hers was a story we already knew. Now we had the fresh and unusual tale of the 'woodland spirit' and his band of happy believers.

Super eight for Fabre

Andre Fabre, 73, has been France's champion Flat trainer on 29 occasions and, as well as a host of international triumphs, is the acknowledged master of his country's biggest race. He extended his own record of Prix de l'Arc de Triomphe wins to eight with Waldgeist's success, his first for 13 years.

Fabre's Arc winners

Year	*Horse*	*Jockey*
1987	Trempolino	Pat Eddery
1992	Subotica	Thierry Jarnet
1994	Carnegie	Thierry Jarnet
1997	Peintre Celebre	Olivier Peslier
1998	Sagamix	Olivier Peslier
2005	Hurricane Run	Kieren Fallon
2006	Rail Link	Stephane Pasquier
2019	Waldgeist	Pierre-Charles Boudot

▲ Stars of the show: Pierre-Charles Boudot and Waldgeist arrive in the winner's enclosure at Longchamp; left, trainer Andre Fabre

The new British champion Flat jockey has the personality and confidence to make a big name for himself on and off the track

OISIN

By David Carr

AS THIS year showed, you can tell you have made it when the world knows you by your first name alone – and we are not talking about the man who became Britain's prime minister in the summer.

Occasionally a personality comes along whose profile transcends racing, who is recognised even by those who wouldn't know a fetlock from a furlong. 'Lester' still scores highly in those vox pops asking people to name a jockey, even 37 years after Piggott was last champion, 36 since he won the last of his nine Derbys and 24 since his last ride.

'Frankie' has not won the title for 15 years yet he has had that same recognition factor since his Magnificent Seven in 1996 and

would be a familiar face to plenty of folk who could not begin to recall one of Dettori's countless Group 1 winners in 2019.

Now 'Oisin' looks on the way to joining that select group, with a profile that means the general public may well follow racing people in learning that young Murphy from Killarney is 'uh-sheen', not 'oy-zin' or any other mangled anglicisation.

That is not to say the new British champion Flat jockey is about to become a team captain on A Question of Sport or open a chain of restaurants bearing his name. But he offers a ray of hope for racing's marketing people, who are all too aware that Dettori cannot go on forever and worry about who could become the face of the sport when he has made his final flying dismount.

Enter an open and extremely personable 24-year-old who made time for interviews in seemingly every media outlet in the days leading up to his coronation in October. Each feature revealed him as a confident young man, keen to eschew platitudes and happy to engage with any subject no matter how personally embarrassing.

How many other jockeys, past or present, would hold their hands up after making headlines by failing a breath test at Salisbury in the summer and say in a Racing Post interview: "I broke the rules and deserved the publicity"? Who else would happily accept an invitation from a racing-mad headmaster and find himself addressing 240 schoolchildren, telling them about life as a jockey and not shying from questions about the whip?

Nor is that persona the product of media training, knocking the sport's rising star into shape so that he becomes as adept in front of a microphone as atop a horse. Even in his early days in Britain one could smell the nascent charisma of a youngster who had left a background in pony racing in Ireland – plus a stint with Aidan O'Brien at Ballydoyle – to join Andrew Balding's Kingsclere academy for young riding talent.

There was no mistaking the inner confidence with which he handled the day that put him on

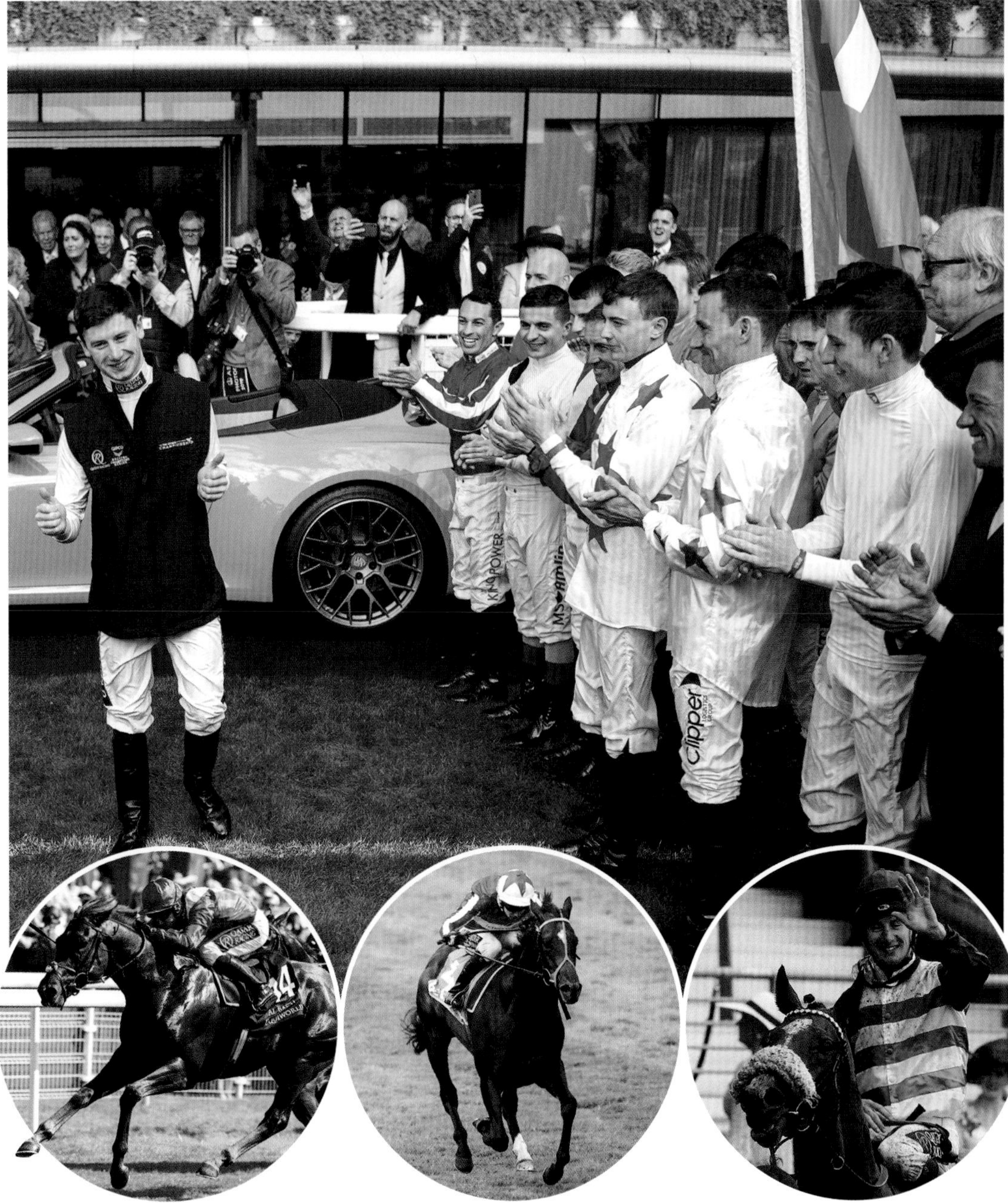

▲ Leader of the pack: Oisin Murphy is hailed as champion jockey at Ascot in October after a season that saw his Group-race winners include (from left) Threat, Mystery Power and Dashing Willoughby

the map as a teenage sensation, winning the 2013 Ayr Gold Cup as a 5lb claimer on Highland Colori and giving a succession of matter-of-fact interviews as he completed a double, treble and then a 9,260-1 four-timer. That was only six years ago and this is a man who has come a long way in a short time.

Champion apprentice in 2014, he rode his first Royal Ascot winner only in 2017 and announced his arrival at the top table with a stunning 2018. Having started the year without a British Group 1 win to his name, he ended it with more than many jockeys land in a career thanks to the likes of Lightning Spear, The Tin Man and the outstanding Roaring Lion, who took the Irish Champion Stakes at Leopardstown on a personally significant day when Murphy rode his first winners in the country of his birth.

Even so, he had still finished 27 winners adrift of Silvestre de Sousa in the jockeys' table and Paddy Power were not knocked over in the rush to grab the 5-1 they offered against his title chances last Christmas behind a champion who was a 1-2 shot to retain the crown.

Yet Murphy was a driven man – "I wanted it really badly," he admitted later – and knew what he had to do to close the gap. He felt riding out four mornings a week was not compatible with riding more horses than anyone else in the afternoons, so he cut that out. He restricted his trips north, where he lacked the network to pick up the rides that his support closer to home could provide, even with most of the big names also competing for mounts. And, most significantly, Murphy did his darnedest to make sure he was always available for those mounts by keeping his nose squeaky clean.

Reflecting on his bid for the title in a fascinating interview you can still see on the Racing Post's YouTube channel, he pointed to

▸▸ *Continues page 140*

▼ Pushing on: Oisin Murphy keeps up his title momentum on Benbatl (left) in the Joel Stakes at Newmarket

the 20-odd days he spent forced on to the sidelines as De Sousa surged clear and the lesson he learned for 2019. "I set my stall out not to get suspended and I haven't had any suspensions," he said. "I know that going one over the whip or letting my horse drift under pressure might win me the race but a few days' suspension could cost me four or five winners. It's difficult to maintain that frame of mind but it's vital."

****

DE SOUSA turned out not to be his main rival. The Brazilian's new retainer with King Power Racing restricted his freedom of movement, although not as much as the fall at Chelmsford in August that fractured his collarbone and chipped a bone in his neck, sidelining him for six weeks.

Instead it was the Scot Danny Tudhope, a 25-1 shot at the start of the season and ten years Murphy's senior, who emerged as the main danger to the early pacesetter. David O'Meara's stable jockey, who also had the backing of William Haggas's powerful string, rode four winners at Royal Ascot at a time when Murphy recalled: "My percentages were bad in June and I was getting beaten on lots of favourites for whatever reason."

At one point in July, Tudhope led Murphy by nine winners and was odds-on for the title. "When I went behind I was really under pressure. I couldn't believe I'd allowed myself to go so far in front and then give it all away," said Murphy, whose self-denial, inner drive and Saturday nights at Wolverhampton gradually began to pay off again.

He put his nose back in front at the Qatar Goodwood Festival, where his two-month stint in Japan the previous winter was rewarded with Nassau Stakes success on that country's flagbearer Deirdre. Murphy continued to fire in the winners, including Threat in the Gimcrack Stakes and old friend Benbatl in the Joel Stakes.

Paddy Power stopped taking bets with nearly a month of the season to go and he ended the campaign 35 winners clear of Tudhope. The youngest champion since Ryan Moore in 2006 was the fifth Irishman to come out on top in the last quarter of a century following Pat Eddery, Kieren Fallon, Jamie Spencer and Richard Hughes.

Each of those jockeys took the crown at least twice and one-off title winners are rare – Joe Mercer, Michael Roberts, Kevin Darley, Seb Sanders and Jim Crowley are the only ones since World War Two.

Which suggests Murphy could well be at the top for a while. As does the ambition revealed in the fact that he told one interviewer in the build-up to British Champions Day: "It will be lovely to look at Wikipedia and see Oisin Murphy as champion jockey but then you'll look down and see Kieren Fallon was champion jockey six times. I've only done it once."

You have been warned.

'What he did only spurs me on'

Escaping the shadow of a famous father is never easy, especially when you have virtually identical names, but Cieren Fallon has not made a bad start by winning the British apprentice jockeys' championship.

Kieren Fallon's career mixed three Derby wins and six British Flat jockeys' championships with enough controversy to fill a particularly sensational Dick Francis novel.

None of that mattered for much of the life of his son Cieren, who played rugby league and football while growing up in Wigan with his mother Julie, another ex-jockey. Horses were the last thing on his mind as he quietly qualified as a gym instructor. Until one morning at 17 he woke up and decided to give racing a go. "It was just seeing a few pictures on the wall in the house that made me think I wanted to try that," he recalled.

Cue a stint at the British Racing School and a start with Newmarket trainer William Haggas, riding four winners from barely more than two dozen rides in 2018 and looking an obvious candidate for the apprentice title in a couple of seasons.

But Fallon snr often reached goals quicker than anyone imagined and it was the same with his son, who thrust himself into the title reckoning a year early by riding 16 winners in July. He kept up the pace under the guidance of agent Phil Shea, who had steered Josephine Gordon to the crown in 2016, and the man who had not even sat on a horse two years ago ended up comfortably clear of Sean Davis at the top of the table.

So well did the second half of the season go that he rode more than 40 of his eventual 50 winners, including Time To Study in the Old Borough Cup and Oxted in the Portland Handicap, after the beginning of July.

Many an ex-jockey's offspring has taken the apprentice crown, including Ryan Moore, William Buick, Amy Ryan and David Egan in recent years, and Fallon jnr is not daunted by his father's achievements.

Asked about following in his father's footsteps, the 20-year-old said: "What he did only spurs me on. We're competitive in whatever we do together, so I really want to beat him, whether it's badminton or table tennis. I've got big goals. Hopefully I can achieve what he achieved."

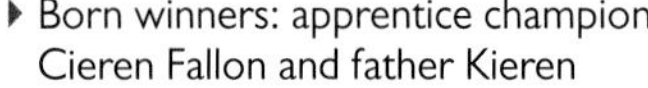

▶ Born winners: apprentice champion Cieren Fallon and father Kieren

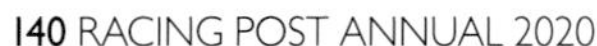

STAR QUALITY

Chris Hughes has gone from Love Island to a breakout role with ITV Racing that has won over a new audience

By Robbie Wilders

FEW people manage to change opinions on Twitter, the modern soapbox for anyone with a gripe, a grudge or worse, but Chris Hughes reckons he has managed to pull off the seemingly impossible. By dint of his personality and professionalism, the former Love Island contestant has turned around criticism of his early appearances on ITV Racing and can look back on a successful year as a regular on the sport's most high-profile presenting team.

Love Island alumni can head in various directions upon returning to reality but swapping the plush Spanish villa for British racecourses in all weathers is surely one of the most unusual. For Hughes, though, the ITV job was an ideal opportunity to develop his broadcasting career and follow his long-held passion for racing. They have been good for each other: Hughes has been able to prove himself outside the usual celebrity circuit and ITV has taken the opportunity to tap into a different, younger demographic.

Reflecting on where the journey began, Hughes, 26, says: "My first interaction with ITV was when I rode in the Macmillan charity race at York in June 2018 for Coral. I appeared on The Opening Show on the morning of the race and from there I just kept in touch via one person or another.

"I was on The Opening Show again at Cheltenham on the Thursday of festival week and joined the Social Stable in the afternoon for the first time, and it kind of worked really well. Me and Chappers [Matt Chapman] just bounced off each other from the get-go and I really enjoyed the day. I remember Chappers saying to me afterwards: 'That was brilliant, I wouldn't be surprised if we used you again.'"

Chapman proved to be spot on in his assessment. Hughes showed enough natural flair, combined with racing knowledge and passion, to prompt ITV bosses to deploy his services on a more frequent basis. Reaction to the newcomer was not so favourable on Twitter, however.

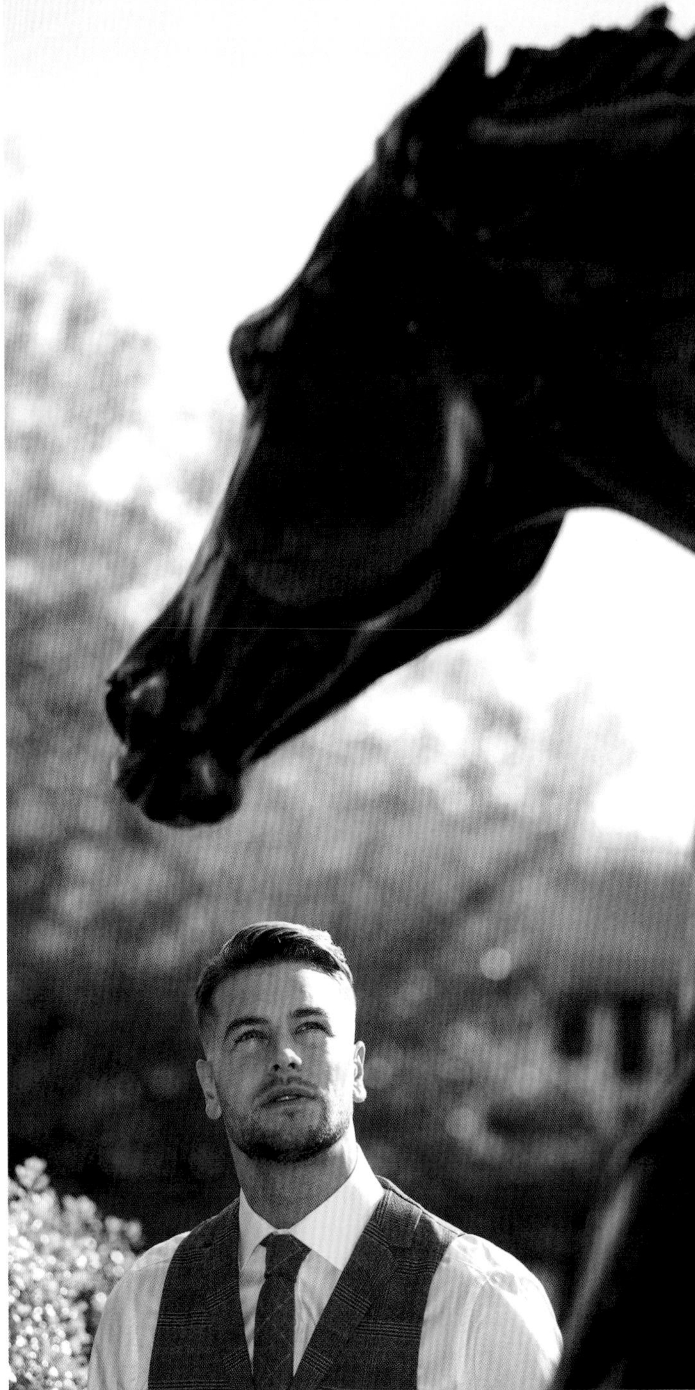

"Twitter is a very opinionated platform and the amount of abuse I used to get over the first three, four or five times I was broadcasting was ridiculous, whether that was from punters or whoever," Hughes says. "They just thought I was a kid from Love Island going in blindly to present horseracing."

Many of the critics would not have realised Hughes, who grew up in the Cotswolds, had a long-time link with the sport. "I've been involved in racing since I was 11 in terms of riding racehorses, whether it was point-to-pointers or Earth Summit, who was kept with Marcella Bayliss just down the road from Nigel Twiston-Davies in his retirement. It was at Marcella's point-to-point yard that I developed myself riding out. My dad has owned horses with Jonjo O'Neill and for me it was just something I was passionate about. I know about racing and it was about breaking that mould."

Hughes shrugged off the negative comments, kept working hard and has proved himself in

▸▸ *Continues page 144*

front of camera. "I now hold up the Social Stable on my own, present live on my own, and that's a skill set. It's something I'm happy to do and something I want to continue to develop. I don't receive those Twitter remarks anymore and it's all very positive now. I feel like people have started to understand my involvement in horseracing throughout my life and that has helped switch opinion. It took a while for perceptions to change in that respect."

The dark side of social media has touched Hughes in other ways too. His partner is Jesy Nelson, a member of chart-topping girl group Little Mix whose battles with online trolling and abuse featured in the hard-hitting BBC documentary Odd One Out in September.

Hughes has also teamed up with the BBC to film a documentary that aims to shed light on the delicate issue of male fertility. "It's in relation to my brother's testicular cancer, but 90 per cent of the focus is on male fertility. It's a stigmatised subject and hopefully we can help create awareness so that people can seek guidance and help if it affects them. It's a really exciting project that should be out in December or January."

****

WITH more than 500,000 followers of his own on Twitter and 2.1 million on Instagram, Hughes has helped racing reach a wider audience. "I've had tweets from all sorts of people," he says. "One guy tweeted me saying 'My daughter would never sit and watch horseracing with me, but now she's seen Chris from Love Island she's sat watching the whole coverage'.

"That makes it all worthwhile, seeing a younger audience take an interest in racing, because it's an unbelievable sport, we know that. It's great that it opens up that demographic of viewers with people tuning in to watch ITV Racing and if I can have an influence, that's brilliant. I think with sports like racing so many people are stuck in their ways and they don't want to see change. You want to increase participation and we want everyone to love the sport. A lot of racecourses are using the incentive of letting kids go for free now because it gets families involved, which is a superb initiative."

Hughes comes from a predominantly jumping background, having grown up with the likes of Sam Twiston-Davies and Jonathan England, but is a keen follower of Flat racing as well. He cites York's Ebor festival in August as a particular high point from his work with ITV.

"I really enjoyed the Ebor meeting," he says. "I've ridden around York [in the Macmillan charity race] and it's got a place in my heart. For me, York is the most beautiful racecourse in the country and it's such a friendly and hospitable environment. It's just fun. I also loved Oaks day at Epsom and I tipped up Anapurna live on air, which always helps."

▲ Winning team: Chris Hughes with Matt Chapman on ITV's Social Stable at Aintree on Grand National day. "Me and Chappers just bounced off each other from the get-go," Hughes says

He feels he has found a television home with ITV Racing. "It's a proper close-knit family from everyone you see in front of the camera to those behind the scenes. We all go out together as a team during big meetings for food and for a few drinks. It's very chilled out and that's why it works so well. The best thing is that every time we go on air, we try to improve. Whether that be with more

▸▸ *Continues page 146*

cameras, looking at alternative areas of interest, they're always doing more and that's why viewing figures have increased.

"I've really found my niche and it gives me stability amid a ridiculously hectic lifestyle, because every day I'm somewhere else. It's nice to have ITV Racing there for me. It's something I know I can focus on and something I can put my keen interest into."

★★★★

HUGHES is also an ambassador for Coral and is the face of the Coral Champions Club, the syndicate responsible for the Jonjo O'Neill-trained Annie Mc, who won twice as a novice hurdler last season but was denied a crack at the Grade 1 Mares Novice Hurdle Championship Final at Fairyhouse in April due to a vaccination error. Honeysuckle was an impressive winner on the day but Hughes felt Annie Mc would have gone close. "That race was run to suit with a strong pace and a good gallop and I think she'd have been first or second. In fairness, though, I'm just one of those people who is supremely optimistic. If my team Sunderland were playing Man City, I'd think we'd win."

Looking ahead to Annie Mc's bright future, he adds: "She's made for chasing and I think next year is her oyster. She's grown tremendously over the summer and she's a real size. She looked magnificent anyway but she looks unbelievable now."

On his own career path, Hughes says: "I have to be busy to get enjoyment out of life and I just want to better myself and be more successful than I am now. I probably thought people needed me at one stage when I first came out of Love Island, but that was never the case. You're in demand but you've got to get your head down, work, find your niche and do what makes you happy."

That's not a bad recipe for life and it certainly seems to be serving Hughes well.

▸ At ease: Chris Hughes at Jonjo O'Neill's yard in the build-up to his ride in the Macmillan charity race at York

THE BIGGER PICTURE

Trainer William Knight's N Over J and rider Rosie Tester walk through the bluebells in Angmering Park, West Sussex in April

EDWARD WHITAKER (RACINGPOST.COM/PHOTOS)

10

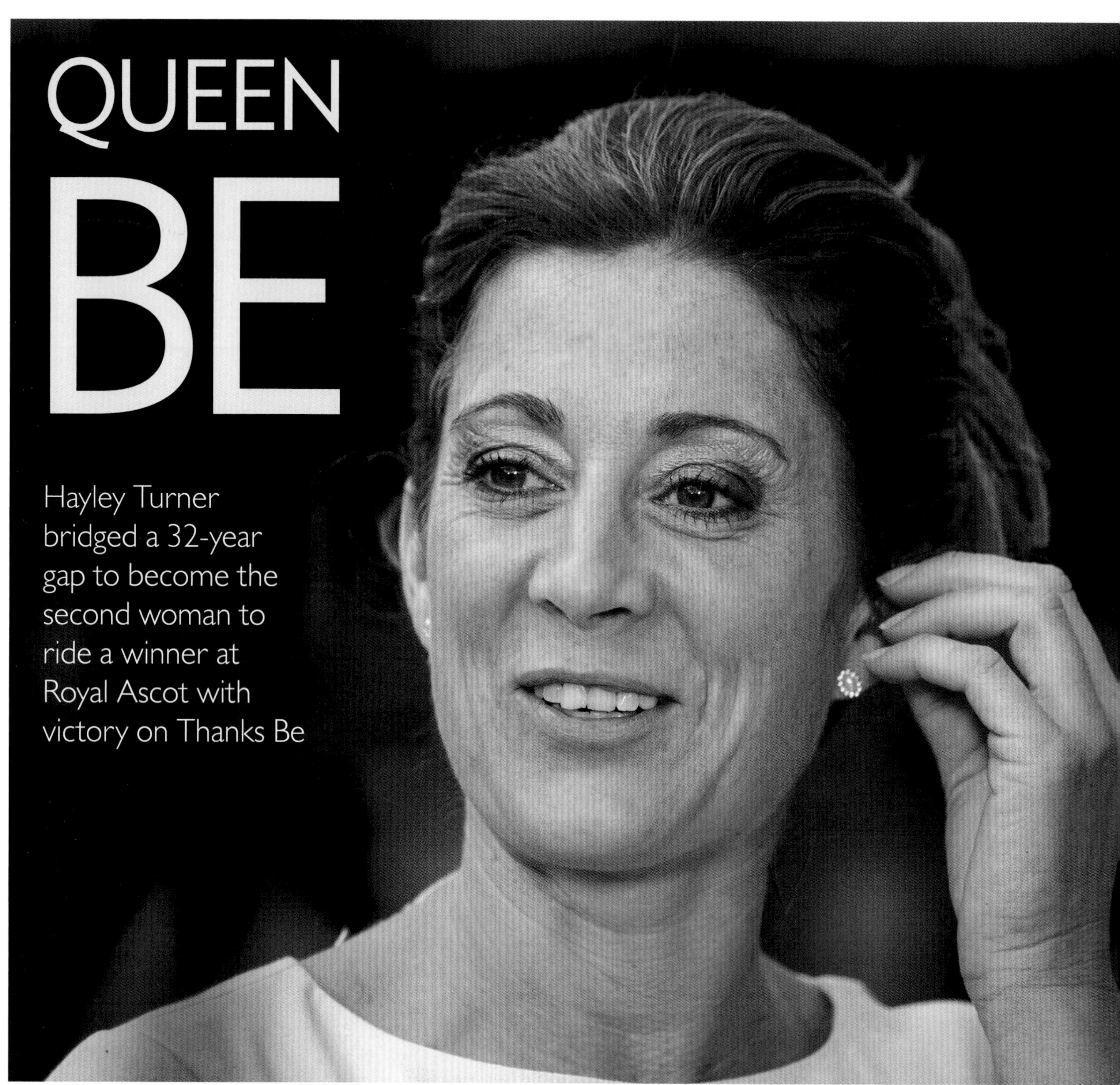

QUEEN BE

Hayley Turner bridged a 32-year gap to become the second woman to ride a winner at Royal Ascot with victory on Thanks Be

By Lewis Porteous

HAYLEY TURNER is something of a reluctant pioneer and mould-breaker but she has made rather a habit of being in the first place at the right time and she was at it again in 2019. Her victory on Thanks Be in the Sandringham Handicap was not the first time a female jockey had triumphed at Royal Ascot, and we can say with a fair degree of confidence that she will not be the last, but if anyone was going to bridge the 32-year gap from Gay Kelleway and Sprowston Boy winning the 1987 Queen Alexandra Stakes, it had to be Turner.

The first woman to ride 100 winners in a year in Britain and the first to win a Group 1 race outright, she has set herself apart through her spectacular achievements. Thanks Be was not expected to triumph but there is always hope when Turner is in the saddle and there was a rare magnitude to the moment as the 33-1 shot and her rider scythed through the heart of the pack before fending off royal runner Magnetic Charm to land the Sandringham.

Unpretentious and understated, Turner did not want to make the moment about her gender, rather the realisation of a dream every jockey harbours to ride a winner at the most famous race meeting in the world. There was, however, little that could be done to underplay the scale of her achievement.

"It means quite a lot because we have to listen to Gay every year – fair play to her, but I can take those bragging rights off her now," she joked, before adding more seriously: "Well done to her because it's a great achievement and it was nice to have that goal to aim for as well. I was always going to persevere, if it wasn't this year then I'd have another go next year. I've been second in the Albany and third in one of the handicaps, so I've been knocking on the door before."

On the wider development of female riders, with Josephine Gordon, Nicola Currie and Hollie Doyle among the others who have shone on the Flat in recent years, Turner said: "Hopefully the standard of girls has risen so much that they'll just keep coming and coming now. The numbers are rising and in ten years' time, the girls will be having winners more often and it won't be a big thing. It's just going to snowball but it'll take time."

Turner has proved she operates on a level playing field during a career spanning nearly 20 years and more than 800 winners, but success at the royal meeting was the one she craved above the rest. "Just to be part of it is wonderful. I feel bad for beating Her Majesty but I'm sure she'll understand," she said. "Royal Ascot is hard, but it's hard for everybody, not just the girls. I'm in disbelief."

The facts agree with Turner's every word. It does not get more competitive than Royal Ascot and there are only 30 races in which to pick up a ride each year, never mind a winner. Dozens of jockeys leave empty-handed each and every June. But of course Turner's success had extra significance, especially considering women were not allowed to race-ride on professional courses until the 1970s, a decade after Royal Ascot first permitted female trainers.

It is also a somewhat harsh reality that, in contrast to the big jumps festivals like Cheltenham, Ascot does not give female riders the same opportunity to make an early mark as conditionals or amateurs, nor do they ride as many short-priced runners – the odds of Thanks Be a perfect case in point. There had been near-misses since Kelleway's breakthrough in 1987 but it took something and someone out of the ordinary to make it happen again.

"This is a really important moment for the sport and it just shows if the horse is good enough the girls are good enough," said Kelleway, now a trainer and who had watched history being repeated 50 miles away at Goodwood. "Hayley has always said to me she's going to ride a Royal Ascot winner and now she's done it. I hope it's not another 32 years until the next one."

★★★★

THANKS to Turner it seems unlikely the wait for a third name to join hers and Kelleway's will be anything like as arduous. As Turner pointed out, the women's changing room is occupied every day on racecourses now and the level of professionalism and raw talent among the current generation of female riders is undeniable. That is as much down to Turner's achievements on a racecourse as it is any other factor, as she has made race-riding an aspirational profession for any novice starting out on racing's road.

Champion apprentice in 2005, she reached 100 winners in 2008 and is the only face that comes to mind when the Shergar Cup is mentioned. Her first Group 1 win arrived in 2011 when Dream Ahead put her on cloud nine in the July Cup and the following month she was at it again with Margot Did in the Nunthorpe. The following year she won the Grade 1 Beverly D Stakes in the United States.

Yet her legacy could have been so different, having decided to walk away from race-riding at the end of the 2015 season. She had already achieved plenty at that stage but she was only 32 and there was more to do. She spent some time on the ITV Racing team but the lure of the racecourse was too strong and she decided to make a full-time comeback in 2018, although it has been tough at times to climb back to something approaching a prominent position in a profession that waits for no man or woman.

"I think I needed the break to recharge," she explained at Royal Ascot. "I've come back keener than ever and I'm enjoying it more than ever." Ripp Orf's win in the 2018 Victoria Cup and the way she entertained at the Shergar Cup were instrumental in her reincarnation and, along with a band of loyal supporters headed by old ally Michael Bell, she managed to put herself in a position where she was at least in consideration when the Royal Ascot rides were

▸▸ *Continues page 152*

being dispensed in June. That was all she needed.

Amid the fanfare of her historic victory, there was the unsatisfactory realisation that she had used her whip beyond what the rules deem is an acceptable level in the Sandringham finish. Turner received no special dispensation from the authorities, who slapped her with a nine-day ban and a £1,600 fine. She took it on the chin and admitted she was wrong, but that was only the start.

Thanks Be's trainer Charlie Fellowes seized the opportunity to take umbrage with the current punishments for whip misdemeanours, going as far as to claim his horse should have been disqualified because Turner had gone over the permitted level of strikes, something that would have wiped his as well as Turner's first success at the royal meeting from the record books.

Turner conceded that allowing jockeys to keep a race after they have broken the rules makes little sense and admitted if she had been facing the prospect of a two- or three-month suspension, she would never have broken the whip rules in the first place.

The furore surrounding her ban turned into something of an unwanted sideshow when the sport should have been basking in a momentous occasion, although it will not be the last discussion on the whip, just as it is unlikely to be the last time a female rider strikes gold at Ascot.

So who will be the next to join Kelleway and Turner? Perhaps it will not be a new name, rather Turner creating her next slice of history.

"I just want to keep enjoying it," said the rider after the dust had settled on her historic success. "I love my job and the bigger the winner, the better it is. I'm not a magician, but I can take the opportunities I'm given. I'm getting a good number of rides and people realise now that I'm riding full-time again."

Turner might not possess supernatural powers but the magic moments keep coming.

▲ Happy day: Hayley Turner drives Thanks Be home in the Sandringham Handicap

▶ The delighted jockey high-fives ITV Racing presenter Ed Chamberlin

▼ Trainer Charlie Fellowes celebrates his first Royal Ascot winner with Turner

Hollie Doyle jumped to the forefront of the new generation of female Flat riders with a breakthrough season

FORCING THE PACE

By Lewis Porteous

HAYLEY TURNER has pointed the way for female riders on the Flat in Britain over the past decade and 2019 proved a memorable year for Hollie Doyle, one of the new generation who have followed her lead in an expanding women's jockeys' room.

In her seventh season with a riding licence, Doyle, 22, enjoyed a glorious campaign that saw her dwarf her previous best of 59 winners in Britain from 2017 and move into the top ten riders based on victories. Far and away the leading female jockey in the standings, Doyle was inspired by Turner and Irish pioneers Cathy Gannon and Nina Carberry in her formative years and would like to play her part as a role model too.

"I'd love to be as good as Hayley and Cathy in the long run and I'd love to inspire other girls to get into it and show they can do it, just like they inspired me," Doyle said in the autumn as she reflected on her breakthrough season.

By her own admission, Doyle's career was a slow burn at the beginning. Following her father Mark by becoming a jockey was always the dream and, after cutting her teeth on the pony and Arabian racing circuits, she joined David Evans as an apprentice but struggled to find her feet. "At one stage, I must have been only 18, things weren't really happening for me and I didn't have much confidence in myself. I thought I wasn't good enough," she admitted. "So I moved to Richard Hannon's and thought 'if you can't do well here, you can't do well anywhere' and luckily it just snowballed."

Doyle has topped 50 winners for three years in a row now but there is no doubt why the past 12 months have been by far the most prolific of her career. Of more than 600 rides in Britain in 2019, close to a third were from the prolific yard of Archie Watson, with the Lambourn trainer supplying the lion's share of her winners.

Young and fiercely ambitious, the pair have plenty in common and it is a partnership that clearly works well. "I had a few rides for him as an apprentice and he asked me to go and ride out," Doyle recalled. "I didn't think much of it at the time and it was just one day a week to start with when I was still claiming 3lb. When I lost my claim he asked me if I could come over more regularly and I've managed to slide into a little position."

While there is no official title to her role at Watson's burgeoning operation, she rides out there four times a week and it is a working relationship both are enjoying. "He's very fair and very easy to ride for," she said. "He knows how good or bad his horses are and they're placed very well. Every horse, no matter their ability, has a plan for the whole season. I tell him what I think and he listens. He has a lot of trust in his jockeys, which is a big deal."

While Watson has helped to take Doyle to the next level, it was Hannon who put her on the map and he continues to be a supporter despite her decision to fly the nest. "I had a great few years there when

▸▸ *Continues page 156*

I was an apprentice and he got me to where I was. The last thing I wanted to do was leave. It was my comfort zone and I loved it but I had to look at the bigger picture and, as a professional jockey, was I going to get to the next level there?

"I was competing on level terms with Sean Levey, Tom Marquand, James Doyle and Frankie [Dettori] even, and when I got an offer from Archie it was a bit of a no-brainer and something I couldn't turn down at that stage of my career."

****

WHILE Marquand, her partner and weighing-room colleague, would be horizontal if he were any more laid back, Doyle is something of a worrier. She admits she would like to mute that side of her personality at times, although the fear that her ascent could hit the buffers at any time is the motivation she uses to keep her foot firmly to the floor.

"It's weird but I don't feel established at all," she reflected. "I still feel like an apprentice and in my mind I don't feel any different to three years ago. I ride a lot better now but mentally I don't feel like I've made it."

Laying bare her innermost fears, she continued: "We're all self-employed, so the moment you start getting fewer rides and fewer winners it's your livelihood that's impacted. I think about it the whole time – I'd like to be able to switch that off but it's taken so much hard graft to get to where I am, I don't want to let it slip."

Barring injury, there is no logical reason why she would suddenly sink down the pecking order. Instead, she is heading quickly in the opposite direction. If she were to consistently match this season's success, she has a realistic chance of going down as one of the most successful female riders of any generation, although she is not one to get wrapped up in trying to quantify her achievements.

In that regard, she is very much like Turner and Josephine Gordon, another trailblazer with her apprentices' title win in 2016. They have left it to others to evaluate their impact in a sport dominated by men for so long, while quietly going about their business with professionalism.

"I'm aware of it but only because people talk about it," Doyle said of her standing. "If it wasn't spoken about I wouldn't even really know. I don't think 'I'm the leading female rider'. Being in the top ten riders is more important to me."

****

NO DOUBT it has been a big year for female riders on the Flat, with Turner becoming the first in more than three decades to ride a winner at Royal Ascot, while Nicola Currie, Doyle and Turner bagged three of the first four places in a £150,000 handicap on King George day to mark another watershed moment.

Yet the statistics for 2019 tell a different tale. Doyle and Currie are the only women in the top 50 riders based on winners and the debate rumbles on as to whether female jockeys are getting the same opportunities as the men.

▲ Job share: Hollie Doyle at Doncaster with her partner and fellow rider Tom Marquand

"The ratio of female riders to male riders in the first place is quite low, so for only two of us to be in the top 50 doesn't surprise me," Doyle said. "You can count only ten who have lost their claim and it's hard for an apprentice to be in the top 50, and I'm not really surprised or worried by it.

"Over the years I've been riding, the number of girls in the weighing room has doubled and I think there are enough coming through the ranks. I think if they want it that badly and they're good enough they'll break through the barrier."

As for herself, she is keen to cement her standing as one of the best riders in the country, regardless of gender. "I want to keep on learning. There's so much out there to learn and I want to keep on improving and building my network of connections. I'm in a happy place at the moment and I hope I can keep it up."

Rachael Blackmore has accelerated from 0 to 90 and her talent shone last season with a title challenge and a string of festival winners from Cheltenham to Punchestown

By David Jennings

TO FULLY understand the breakthrough of Rachael Blackmore, we must do some number crunching. She rode one winner during the 2010-2011 Irish jumps season. There was just the solitary success the following campaign too. None whatsoever in 2012-2013. There were two winners in each of the next two campaigns and six during the 2015-2016 season. That amounted to just 12 winners in five and a half years. Those are not the sort of numbers you would usually associate with a championship contender.

Blackmore, however, was in the thick of the battle last season and her 90-winner haul made Paul Townend pull out all the stops to claim his second title. She rode seven more winners than Davy Russell and 42 more than Ruby Walsh. Ninety winners would have been enough to finish top of the pile in 2011 and 2015.

It was about more than simply numbers last season, though. There was a first Cheltenham Festival success on A Plus Tard in the Close Brothers Novices' Handicap Chase and she doubled that account three days later when Minella Indo landed the Albert Bartlett Novices' Hurdle. It was her first Grade 1 victory, and only the second for a woman over jumps at the festival – just 24 hours after Bryony Frost had been the first on Frodon. Perhaps Blackmore's popularity is best summed up by the fact she had 17 rides at the festival.

"I did think to myself in the build-up that I had some book of rides," says Blackmore, 30, reflecting in the summer on her memorable campaign. "I had a lot of rides that had good, solid each-way chances and I knew if there was ever a year it was going to happen, it would be this year. That's why there was more relief than anything when I did actually ride a winner.

"People expected me to ride a winner, that was the vibe I was getting before Cheltenham. But people forget there are only 28 races at Cheltenham, and some of them I can't even ride in, so it really isn't that easy. Monalee and A Plus Tard were the two I fancied most, but I really fancied A Plus Tard."

She might have fancied A Plus Tard but there was no way she could have known the Henry de Bromhead-trained five-year-old

would win by 16 lengths. "When I gave him a squeeze after the last, he absolutely accelerated. I knew we'd done it. He just took off with me. I did think turning in that this could be the day, but we still had to get over the last two fences. When he accelerated after the last, I knew I'd stretched quite a distance clear. I've never felt a horse take off in the way he did. He flew."

★★★★

THE monkey was now off Blackmore's back; she had ridden a Cheltenham Festival winner. There were still some decent rides to come, but when Monalee could finish only fourth behind Frodon in the Ryanair Chase it looked like one winner was her lot for the week. Then the Albert Bartlett came along.

"I definitely thought he might be in the first five and I was surprised how big a price he was," says Blackmore of 50-1 outsider Minella Indo, also trained by De Bromhead. "In saying that, I couldn't believe he had actually won. The difference between riding a favourite who wins and a 50-1 shot who wins is massive. When A Plus Tard won, the whole way down the chute people were cheering and clapping and roaring at me. It was an unbelievably magical walk. It wasn't like that when Minello Indo won. It was a lot more subdued.

"You're just completely caught up in the moment, though. People tell you what it's like to ride a Cheltenham winner but I find it very hard to explain it right. I don't really know what words to use. You really have to experience it yourself. It's a phenomenal feeling and, waking up the next morning, you know that split-second when you remember what happened yesterday, now that's some feeling. It's class.

"What's different about the winners at Cheltenham is that you can enjoy them properly afterwards. With winners everywhere else it's almost like they must happen. You get to the point where people are expecting you to ride winners and you have to be doing it.

"You ride a winner on a Thursday but there's racing on Saturday and Sunday, so your winner on Thursday is already gone and it's all about Saturday and Sunday. There's no time to reflect. You don't have time to say 'Jesus, that was a great winner on Thursday'. You're just on to the

▸▸ *Continues page 160*

next day. Cheltenham is a bit more special and people are still talking about it the next week.

"I remember on Minella Indo I made a half-hearted attempt at punching the air when I got back to the winner's enclosure, but it didn't really turn out the way I wanted. I'll need to work on that just in case it ever happens again. It was poor, very poor."

****

IT WAS about the only thing Blackmore did poorly last season. Everything else seemed to come off and the hot streak did not cool down after Cheltenham either. She had a first winner at the Aintree Grand National meeting when Moon Over Germany took the Close Brothers Red Rum Handicap Chase and there was more Grade 1 glory when Honeysuckle won the Irish Stallion Farms EBF Mares Novice Hurdle Championship Final at the Fairyhouse Easter festival and Minella Indo supplemented his Cheltenham success by digging deep to land the Irish Daily Mirror Novice Hurdle at Punchestown. That was Blackmore's third Grade 1 in six weeks.

This is supposed to be the same Rachael Blackmore who took five and a half years to ride 12 winners.

"Since I turned professional, I'm riding a lot more. That's huge. If you're not riding, it's very hard to improve. You can do whatever you want in the gym, and you can run as far as you like, but you really have to be riding to get better. Turning pro meant I got more rides and the snowball effect of that was natural improvement in that practice makes you better," she explains.

One of her biggest fans is Gigginstown racing manager Eddie O'Leary, hardly surprising given she rode 38 winners for the operation last season. "Rachael works extremely hard, harder than anyone else, and she needs to in order to play off a level playing field and get the chances she is getting," O'Leary says. "What people might not know is that she does an hour of weight training every night. She has a terrific attitude, she really does, and wants to get better all the time.

"She's very positive and suits our horses. Horses run for her. The biggest compliment I can pay her is that we don't regard her as a lady rider, we simply regard her as a rider and right now she's as good as anyone, male or female."

▲ Pleased as Punch: Rachael Blackmore celebrates her first Grade 1 win with Minella Indo in the Albert Bartlett Novices' Hurdle; previous page, the 50-1 shot lands the race by two lengths

▼ Minella Indo's owners Mike and Barry Maloney

****

BLACKMORE only joined the professional ranks in 2015 after a shove from Shark Hanlon. "I turned professional because I was going badly as an amateur. I needed to try something different, I needed to get more rides and better rides," she says. "For other jockeys, the career path is to do really well as an amateur, move up the ranks and turn professional. For me, I wasn't doing well as an amateur, so it was a case of trying something different or giving it up altogether.

"A lot of people said it wouldn't be the right thing to do, but I didn't have anything to lose. It wasn't like I was leaving behind a fantastic career as an amateur."

Blackmore has more than made up for lost time since turning professional. She broke new ground as Ireland's first female champion conditional jockey in the 2016-17 season and has moved the bar higher still. "The future used to worry me," she says. "I have a degree in equine science, but I had no idea what I wanted to do, and then I got this lifeline of turning professional and I'm absolutely living in this amazing dream now. I'm not even going to think about where I'll be in ten years as I feel so privileged to be living this life right now."

We are the privileged ones. Watching Blackmore's numbers go from nought to ninety in the space of six years has been one of the most heartwarming chapters in Irish racing for some time. She is not finished rewriting the history books yet either. The best might be yet to come.

Five runners jump off for the Hollymount Nursing Home Chase at Ballinrobe in August. The race was won by the Henry de Bromhead-trained favourite Moon Over Germany (second right), ridden by Rachael Blackmore

PATRICK McCANN (RACINGPOST.COM/PHOTOS)

THE

BIGGER

PICTURE

HUNGER GAME

Richard Johnson won his fourth successive jump jockeys' title in the 2018-19 season and has the appetite for more

By Graham Dench

RICHARD JOHNSON, for so long the perennial runner-up to Sir Anthony McCoy, has turned into a serial winner with four successive British jump jockeys' titles of his own, and waiting so long to fulfil what had been a burning ambition has clearly made the reward all the sweeter. He is still hungry for more and won't be retiring any time soon. Not of his own accord anyway.

Johnson has already gone on two years longer than McCoy, who retired at 40 in April 2015, but he is inclined to dismiss any talk of challenging the record 4,348 winners over jumps that his great rival accumulated in 20 successive championships, in 16 of which he came second. A fifth title is Johnson's immediate priority and he insists he would still carry on if he was beaten, as long as he was getting as much enjoyment from race-riding.

Johnson, who turned 42 in July, completed the second double century of his career with just a day to spare in the 2018-19 campaign and ended the season with a career total of 3,623 winners – 725 behind McCoy.

"At my age it's a question of taking it year by year and seeing what happens," he told the Racing Post Annual in the autumn. "Being champion jockey is the thing I'm trying hardest for again and some people think if I get beat then that'll be it. But if it doesn't happen it doesn't mean I'll throw in the towel and strop off like a schoolkid.

"This is all I ever wanted to do and it took me a long time to be champion, so I want to make the most of it now. I want to do what I enjoy doing for as long as possible. None of us knows what's around the corner, but I've got lots of potentially very nice horses to ride and if I'm still enjoying it there's no reason why I wouldn't carry on."

****

WHEN McCoy retired it seemed unthinkable that anyone might ever challenge his record, yet as Johnson lifted his fourth championship trophy aloft at the end of the season, one bookmaker was offering just 2-1 that he would get there one day. Johnson would not be tempted by those odds, even if he were allowed to bet, and not just because he has the reputation – deserved or not – of knowing the value of a pound.

"People started talking about AP's record last season but at the moment I'm just taking it season by season. It would be lovely just to get to 4,000 winners, and that's still some way off, so I think they're getting a bit ahead of themselves."

Johnson took his first title by a clear 106 winners, but his winning margin has been narrower every time and last season he ended just 22 clear of Harry Skelton. Brian Hughes was giving him a good run for his money in the early months of the current season and the reigning champion does not regard his continuing dominance as any sort of formality.

"I've had four good years, but they've got closer and closer by the year. Brian has a particularly strong team behind him nowadays and, like me, he's not reliant upon one main yard. Riding for lots of different people gives you that consistency through the season which is so important. Anyone who wants it has to work hard to get those winners on the board and I'm sure Brian would love to be champion just as much as I would.

"He isn't the only challenger either. The likes of Harry Skelton, Sam Twiston-Davies, Aidan Coleman and Harry Cobden all have powerful support systems and they're all very competitive. We all love winning, so there are a lot of lads pushing me along. Competition keeps us all working harder, but the main thing for me is to stay in one piece and to hope that the stables I ride for stay in good form."

Last season was not Johnson's best in terms of major prizes, with his only Grade 1 wins coming courtesy of La Bague Au Roi at Kempton and Leopardstown. However, there will always be horses with the potential to reach that level coming through and that helps to sustain his longevity.

"Grade 1 winners aren't easy to find and there were only two for me last season, but the nice horses in the pipeline are a massive part of what keeps you going," he said. "Philip [Hobbs] has had a couple of quiet seasons as far as those top horses are concerned, but it was great for him to win another Grade 1 at Cheltenham in March [the JP McManus-owned Defi Du Seuil, partnered by retained rider Barry Geraghty] and he's got some really nice young horses coming through.

"Olly Murphy had some near misses with horses like Brewin'upastorm and Thomas Darby in the big novice hurdles, and there's La Bague Au Roi to look forward to again with Warren Greatrex. My other main stables all have nice horses too."

****

SOME top jockeys seem lost when the time comes to hang up their boots, but Johnson will never be short of something to do, whether he stays in racing in some capacity or not. His future after riding is not mapped out for him, he insists, but farming and raising horses is going to play a big part, along with spending time with the family.

"When the time comes it'll be interesting to see what's available and what I can do, but I'm lucky to have the farm and I've also got a wife and three young children. I want to make sure I don't miss the children growing up, and we're already breeding horses at home, which is something I really enjoy. There are cattle on the farm too, and on the horse side there are mares, foals, yearlings and two-year-olds. We've sold a couple of three-year-olds this year. We also still have Looks Like Trouble and Menorah at home, as well as a group of ponies.

"We never have a quiet day and I can't remember the last time there was nothing for me to do. There's plenty to get on with, but keeping busy is what I'm used to."

Mainly that means keeping busy riding winners.

Special day at the Palace

Richard Johnson's best day of the year came towards the end of February, not on the racecourse but at Buckingham Palace.

The news that he was to receive an OBE in the Queen's New Year's Honours crowned a fantastic 2018, in which he had won his third jockeys' title and enjoyed a hugely popular second Cheltenham Gold Cup victory on Native River after a terrific battle with Might Bite.

There were no wins of quite that calibre in 2019, but receiving the OBE from the Queen herself for his services to racing made for as special a day as any he has enjoyed on the racecourse.

"It's very special to be recognised by the Queen on a national level," he said. "I suspect it was for my duration in racing rather than anything else but it was a massive honour and also a bit of a shock.

"Obviously Her Majesty does not do all of these ceremonies, so to get there and discover she was doing this one left me feeling I couldn't be more pleased."

The ceremony took place when the festival was just around the corner and in their brief exchange the Queen talked about Cheltenham and asked how his championship bid was going.

Johnson said: "Going to Buckingham Palace with Fiona and the children was a very special day. It's something I will always be very proud of."

By Joe Tuffin

LUCK played its part in the end as Dan Skelton landed his first Grade 1 triumph with Roksana at the Cheltenham Festival but the journey there owed nothing to fortune and everything to meticulous planning, skilful training and a steely focus on the main goal.

Roksana's dramatic victory in the Mares' Hurdle, following the final-flight fall of Benie Des Dieux, was the most high-profile illustration of Skelton's relentless rise as a top-level jumps trainer, but it was far from the only one in a season that brought him a double century of winners. In just his sixth campaign, Skelton achieved the remarkable feat of becoming the only trainer apart from 15-time champion Martin Pipe to reach the 200 mark in a British jumps season.

Roksana's victory on racing's biggest stage was the icing on the cake and, despite the huge slice of luck that changed the complexion of the race in her favour, her success was testament to the confidence Skelton has in his ability to make a plan and carry it out. When Roksana was injured the previous autumn while being prepared for the Long Walk Hurdle, Skelton was not scared to be bold. "I said to rip up the plans and have one race before the Mares' Hurdle at Cheltenham," he explained.

****

THAT prep run came when she was third behind Buveur D'Air in the Listed Contenders Hurdle over two miles at Sandown in early February, almost ten months after Roksana's last race. It was her first run outside novice company and, at the age of seven, only her seventh start under rules. She had shown distinct promise when a close second to Santini in a Grade 1 at Aintree the previous spring and Skelton was keen to have another go at the top level, even though Benie Des Dieux was a formidable obstacle in the Mares' Hurdle.

For weeks before Cheltenham, Ruby Walsh had made plain his belief that Benie Des Dieux was his

Dan Skelton continued his rapid rise with a memorable season featuring his first Grade 1 winner and a double century

THE ASCENT OF DAN

best chance from a typically strong book of rides and the festival's most successful jockey looked set to be proved right as he powered towards the final flight with a commanding three-length lead over Roksana. Everything changed, however, when the 10-11 favourite, having hit 1.03 in running, clipped the top of the hurdle and knuckled on landing, sending Walsh to the ground.

It was an unfortunate carbon copy of the 2015 Mares' Hurdle in which Walsh, in the same colours of Rich and Susannah Ricci, had fallen on red-hot favourite Annie Power at the last with the race at his mercy. On that occasion victory had gone to a Willie Mullins stablemate, Glens Melody, but this time Skelton's mare picked up the pieces. Having been left in front, Roksana drifted from the far side of the track to the stands' rail but had the stamina to hold off Stormy Ireland, the Mullins second-string, by two and a quarter lengths.

In the saddle was Harry Skelton, the trainer's younger brother and trusty lieutenant, who was on his way to a career-best 178 winners for the season and second place behind Richard Johnson in the championship.

"You're never home until you jump the last and luck has been on our side," the rider said. "You have to take days like these. It means the world to have a winner here. These are the four days when it really matters."

The trainer echoed his brother's thoughts. "It's an amazing feeling. I thought I was past all that youthful stupidity and excitement, but last night I honestly felt like a kid at Christmas. I got that warm feeling you don't often get, that buzz. It's a magic day – to win on Tuesday just sets your week up."

There was no denying the luck involved, but equally so Skelton's

⏩ *Continues page 168*

skill in getting Roksana in position to benefit on just her eighth outing in owner Sarah Faulks' colours. "We got her unraced and started in bumpers – it's been a full team effort from the start," the trainer said. "We planned this race. I said to Sarah this was the race we wanted to be going for. One run and go there. What gave me a lot of confidence was Native River – one run and he wins the Gold Cup [the previous year], so it can be done."

Faulks saluted the trainer, saying: "Dan found her for me as a broodmare, but he said, 'I've found you a broodmare, but the trouble is she hasn't run yet.' He said, 'I guarantee you I'll get black type.' It's a fantastic tribute to Dan and the team who have done such a good job. They leave no stone unturned and it has all come together."

Skelton was right about Roksana's win setting up his week because on the final day of the festival he doubled up with Ch'tibello in the County Handicap Hurdle, his third success in that race in four years and his fourth festival winner overall. The previous year Harry had been fifth when the yard won with Mohaayed, ridden by the jockey's fiancee Bridget Andrews, but this time he was on the right one as Ch'tibello scored by a length and a half.

The trainer, who said the County had been the plan with Ch'tibello for 18 months, was confident enough to take the eight-year-old there fresh after a three-month break and to send Harry out for the race with the words: "You've got 10lb in hand, go and do what you want to do."

The festival double meant a lot, especially considering the way the first leg had been secured with Roksana. "To have one you work hard and everyone says 'great, you did it, you've got a winner', but to have two means you've probably not just been lucky," said the trainer, who learned from a master during nine years as assistant to Paul Nicholls in the golden era of Kauto Star, Denman, Master Minded and Big Buck's that brought so many festival highs.

★★★★

HAVING taken out his trainer's licence in 2013 at the age of 27, Skelton has forged a jumping powerhouse at Lodge Hill Stables – developed near Alcester in Warwickshire by his father Nick, the double Olympic show jumping gold medallist – and there was further confirmation in April when Aux Ptits Soins became his first Aintree festival winner and the family operation reached 200 winners for the season.

The milestone was achieved in style with the yard sending out six winners on Easter Sunday, capped by Montego Grey's victory under Harry at Market Rasen to bring up the double century. "We spotted we had a chance of 200 at the end of February or early March and brought the summer horses forward a bit," the trainer said. "As we got closer to the target we wanted to make sure for everyone's sanity that we got over the line. To get so close and not achieve it would have been very annoying."

Pipe had been the only previous trainer to reach 200 winners in a British jumps season, achieving the feat eight times, headed by his record of 243. It is a measure of Skelton's achievement in reaching a final total of 205 that Nicholls' seasonal best is 171, although the erstwhile boss had a cheeky message for his star pupil. "I rang him and said, 'What took you so long considering how many winners you've had since October?" Nicholls said. "But seriously, it's a great effort. Dan's a winning machine and I'm proud of what he's done."

▲ That winning feeling: Harry Skelton has a kiss for Ch'tibello after their victory in the County Hurdle at Cheltenham; previous page, Skelton celebrates as he crosses the line on Roksana in the Mares' Hurdle, kickstarting a festival double for the rider and his brother Dan (previous page, right)

Skelton has had four consecutive top-ten finishes in the jumps trainers' championship and over the past three seasons has moved up from seventh to fifth to third, with only the titans Nicholls and Nicky Henderson ahead of him.

The next jump is the hardest but it is one Skelton is determined to attempt. "My ambition is to close the gap on Nicky and Paul. I'm not going to catch them just yet but I hope to get closer to them in the coming years."

With the Skeltons' focus set to switch more towards the core winter season and with better quality coming into the yard – including £620,000 record sales purchase Interconnected and Grand National contenders Blaklion and Don Poli – nobody would bet against it.

Noel Fehily closed his glittering riding career with memorable days at Cheltenham and Newbury

END PRODUCT

THE final emotional act on an unforgettable Thursday of Cheltenham came towards the end after Noel Fehily had produced a full-blooded winning drive on 50-1 shot Eglantine Du Seuil in the Tattersalls Mares' Novices' Hurdle. The short-head victory was unexpected and so was the jockey's post-race announcement that he would soon be retiring.

Wiping away tears, Fehily said: "This will be my last festival. I've enjoyed every minute of riding horses and I'm going to miss it. It's going to be tough walking away. I've loved doing it but it's a great way to bow out. To ride a winner for Jared Sullivan [Eglantine Du Seuil's owner] is very important for me. He's been a great supporter and it's great to do it for him."

It was obvious Fehily was getting near the end – "I'm 43, which is too old to be in this game," he wisecracked – but his decision to stop had not been long in the planning. "I spoke to my agent Chris Broad, my wife and kids about it a couple of weeks ago – you can't go on forever."

Fehily did not go on much beyond Cheltenham. Nine days after his longshot success on Eglantine Du Seuil, he was at the other end of the scale for the last ride of his career on 1-3 chance Get In The Queue at Newbury. The perfect ending was almost assured and Fehily made no mistake, scoring by a comfortable four and a half lengths. "I think my career would have been deemed a failure if I'd got beat on a 1-3 shot in the last," Fehily said. "Fantastic that it came off. It's a very special day and one that I won't be forgetting for a long time."

Fehily had been given the traditional guard of honour by his fellow

▼ Going out on a high: Noel Fehily celebrates a final win at the Cheltenham Festival

jockeys and there was a presentation and autograph signing for one of the most respected members of the jumps weighing room. Broad spoke for many when he said: "Every young jockey should aspire to be Noel Fehily. The way he rides, the way he conducts himself, the way he looks after himself – everything. He's the way a jockey should be."

****

THE farmer's son from Dunmanway, County Cork, cut his teeth as a point-to-point rider in Ireland before moving to Charlie Mann's Lambourn yard in 1998. He was champion conditional within three years but big-race success came late to him, with all bar two of his 27 Grade 1 wins packed into the last seven years of his career.

The first major winner in Fehily's golden autumn was Rock On Ruby in the 2012 Champion Hurdle – officially trained by Paul Nicholls but prepared by his then assistant Harry Fry, who became a close ally of Fehily as a trainer and, fittingly, provided Get In The Queue for that last hurrah. Fry said he had "never known pressure like it" in the days leading up to Fehily's Newbury farewell.

Other memorable moments came on the Sullivan-owned Silviniaco Conti, who won back-to-back King George VI Chases in 2013 and 2014 among six Grade 1 successes under Fehily, and in 2017 he had a rare double at Cheltenham on Buveur D'Air in the Champion Hurdle and Special Tiara in the Queen Mother Champion Chase. He was only the second jockey to land those two big prizes in the same year.

At the time of his retirement Fehily stood ninth on the all-time list of jump jockeys in Britain and Ireland with 1,352 winners and the man at the top, Sir Anthony McCoy, gave a glowing tribute. "The best thing I can say about Noel Fehily is thank God he wasn't really discovered earlier because that would have meant fewer winners for me," he said. "I'm not sure why it took so long because he's always been a great rider. His strength is he has no weakness. He's an all-round, complete rider. Technically and tactically he's brilliant, and he's strong and horses jump for him."

Retirement first entered Fehily's thoughts after he broke his neck at Punchestown on the last day of the 2017-18 season and re-emerged when he was sidelined by appendicitis early in 2019. "That was the one that got me thinking. I knew if I didn't get back then, it'd be difficult to get going again through the summer and kick on the next season, having missed so much time already. I managed to get back in time for Cheltenham and it seemed like the ideal scenario – getting a winner there had to be the right time to go."

In its own way, the 50-1 Cheltenham shocker was a neat tailpiece to a high-class career. Festival success eluded Fehily until 2008, when he broke his duck on the 50-1 shot Silver Jaro in the County Hurdle, and in the same year he landed his first Grade 1 on the Mann-trained Air Force One at Punchestown.

From there on, it was onwards and upwards for a working life that perhaps earned more critical acclaim than public fanfare. In his last five full seasons he managed four centuries – including a career-best 127 in 2013-14 – and passed the £1m mark in all five of those campaigns, the £2m mark in one of them, propelled by that welcome burst of quality in his final years as a jockey.

"I thought about it long and hard and I'm sure I'm doing the right thing at the right time," he said at the end. There was little left to achieve, and certainly nothing to prove, after a career streaked by class in and out of the saddle.

▲ Rousing sendoff: Noel Fehily walks through a guard of honour before his final ride on Get In The Queue at Newbury; top, he celebrates victory after the race

IN THE PICTURE

One Cool Poet writes record-breaking legend at Galway festival

ONE win in five years and then three in five days. That summed up the unlikely transformation of lowly handicapper One Cool Poet from almost zero to Galway festival hero in an unforgettable week for trainer Matthew Smith and owners Ollie Ryan, Paul Devery, John Flanagan and Shay Gillen.

The remarkable story began on July 30, the second day of the festival, when One Cool Poet lined up in a 17-runner 1m½f handicap for horses rated 55-70, worth a little over €10,000 to the winner. He was second favourite, having been knocking on the door with two close seconds earlier in the month (one in a 1m4½f handicap and the other in a 2m3½f chase), but his only win in 29 previous starts had been way back in April 2015.

Smith had tried the roguish seven-year-old in various combinations of headgear and on this occasion opted for blinkers and a tongue-tie, with the most significant change being that Billy Lee was in the saddle for the first time.

This time the narrow verdict went One Cool Poet's way as he won by a neck, with much praise heaped on Lee for a perfectly timed run. "Matthew said not to get there until the last 50 yards. He's a clever old boy but thank God he won," the jockey said.

Smith turned out One Cool Poet again two days later in a 1m4f handicap with similar race conditions, but with a 6lb penalty for his win. Lee delivered him late again and this time the winning margin was a more emphatic length and a half.

With the old rogue in the form of his life, Smith backed him up again two days later in another 1m4f handicap and this time One Cool Poet shrugged off a double penalty of 12lb to score by five lengths.

That made him the first horse to win three Flat races in the same week at Galway. Since it became a seven-day affair in 1999, Busted Tycoon in 2013 had been the only horse to win three races at the Galway festival with victories in two Flat handicaps and a handicap hurdle.

Explaining the transformation, Smith said: "It's a confidence thing, it definitely is. He always had the ability but didn't know how to get his head in front. I could see after he won on Tuesday he was more confident in himself and he improved for the second day. It was the same story after he won for the second time and his best run of all was on the Saturday. It has just been an unbelievable week."

Nor did it stop there. On Irish Champions Weekend in September, One Cool Poet landed a premier handicap worth almost €90,000 to the winner. That was one cool pot for this belated success story.

Pictures: PATRICK McCANN (RACINGPOST.COM/PHOTOS)

Winner

MARK IN HISTORY

Mark Johnston set more records in another relentless and remarkable campaign

By David Carr

FOR a man who claims to have little interest in records, Mark Johnston is awfully good at breaking them. Time and again as history has beckoned in recent seasons, he has stressed he would not dream of one extra horse just to secure a place in the record books. Yet the trainer who is 'always trying', according to his yard's famous motto, seems always to be beating the achievements of those who have gone before.

The master of Kingsley House in Middleham is driven simply by the desire to get the best out of every horse and that has been his aim since he started training in 1987, perched slightly perilously next to a bombing range in Lincolnshire, but the numbers have stacked up to unprecedented heights.

In 2009 he became the first British Flat trainer to send out 200 winners in a season and, uniquely, he has reached three figures in each of the last 26 years. In 2018 he passed Richard Hannon snr's total to become the most successful trainer in British racing history when Poet's Society struck at the Ebor meeting to give him his 4,194th winner.

So successful has he been that it is sometimes his own records he is breaking now, such as in a remarkable July of 2019 when he sent out an astonishing 50 winners, having struck four times in a day on three separate occasions. Not only had he bettered his own mark for the most successful month in history, he is now responsible for eight of the top 11.

After that high summer jamboree, Johnston was at it again just before the clocks went back in autumn. All season long he had looked on course to smash the record number of winners in a year on the Flat in Britain, set by Hannon snr with 235 in 2013 and equalled by Richard Fahey two years later, and the existing record-holders must have realised the game was up long before he caught them in late October.

Of course, quality means as much as quantity – if not more so – to a trainer who has won Classics with Attraction and Mister Baileys and whose list of Group 1 winners runs from the juvenile Awzaan to the ten-year-old Zavana's Pace.

In that respect 2019 was a slightly frustrating year, whatever the record books may say, with no top-level success in the core months, extending a surprising drought that stretches back to The Last Lion's win in the Middle Park Stakes in 2016.

That is despite sending out a dozen winners in Group 2 or Group 3 company in 2019 and going close time and again in the highest grade. Dee Ex Bee was perhaps the unluckiest contender at the top level, suffering the misfortune of being around in the same era as dominant stayer Stradivarius, whom he chased home in the Gold Cup and Goodwood Cup.

Walk In Marrakesh, Communique and Raffle Prize (twice) were others to finish a galling second in Group or Grade 1 events and Sir Ron Priestley and Nayef Road gave him second and third behind Logician in the St Leger, making it five horses in total that Johnston has now had placed in a Classic that plays to his strength with three-year-old stayers and that he would dearly love to win.

Had Sir Ron Priestley gone one place better he would also have been a first Classic winner for Franny Norton. The veteran jockey has become an important part of the team – proving Johnston's eye for human as well as equine talent – and the trainer was effusive in his praise after the Liverpudlian fulfilled a lifetime ambition by defying a wide draw to win a muddy Chester Cup with a masterful effort on the aptly named Making Miracles.

Norton burst quickly out of stall 16, darting across and grabbing the lead while most onlookers were still wiping the rain from their eyes, and was never headed thereafter. "We discovered Franny Norton by using him at Chester, but he's actually the same on any track in the country," Johnston said. "He brims with confidence, he never worries about the opposition, never worries about the other jockeys. He believes he's as good as anybody and he comes into his own on a very difficult track like Chester."

****

BUT no jockey demonstrates more what Johnston is all about than long-serving Joe Fanning, a self-effacing, loyal team player who is extraordinarily effective in the saddle. It was probably no coincidence that he returned from a broken collarbone just in time to play his part in the yard's record-breaking July and it is a measure of his ability and longevity that he rode his 2,500th British Flat winner the following month – Frankie Dettori is the only other active rider to have reached that landmark.

Through the season Fanning was associated with a couple of horses whose exploits illustrate exactly why their trainer now has his own chapter in the record books.

The jockey warned "there should be more to come" after winning on new recruit King's Advice over a mile and a half at Lingfield in March and rarely can a prediction ever have been proved more right. The five-year-old improved in a way that was extraordinary even by the standards of the yard's middle-distance handicappers, so that five months later he scored his eighth win of the season off a BHA mark fully 37lb higher, landing a £100,000 race at Glorious Goodwood where Johnston was top trainer for the 13th time since 1998.

Fanning also won Scotland's only Group race for one of the country's greatest racing sons, with a filly who embodies the stable's approach. Rose Of Kildare was a €3,000 yearling who thrived on a busy season and showed tenacity typical of her trainer's runners as she rewarded enterprising placing to land the Group 3 Firth of Clyde Stakes, looking better than ever on her 11th appearance of the year.

Just to prove how much her yard's horses thrive on racing, she then defied a penalty to beat a field of bluebloods in the Oh So Sharp Stakes at Newmarket in October.

'Braveheart' may be a slightly jokey nickname for Glasgow-born Johnston but there is many a southern trainer nowadays who probably understands how the English felt when William Wallace came raiding.

2019: another record-breaking year

- With his relentless charge in 2019, Mark Johnston made it to the trainers' record for the most Flat wins in a calendar year in Britain – previously held jointly on 235 by Richard Hannon snr (2013) and Richard Fahey (2015)
- This is the second time Johnston has held the record. His previous record was 216 in 2009, when he became the first British trainer to win 200 Flat races in a year
- King's Advice *(right)* was the biggest contributor to his record – the five-year-old's victory at Glorious Goodwood was his eighth handicap win of the year
- Johnston set a new mark for the most wins in a month in Britain by winning 50 races in July, breaking his own record of 47 in July 2015
- He scored his ninth double century, breaking the British trainers' record of eight he had previously shared with Martin Pipe. This is also the record 26th consecutive year in which he has scored a century of wins
- He had become Britain's winningmost trainer of all time in 2018 and his career score now stands at nearly 4,500
- Winners abroad do not count towards a British record but the German 1,000 Guineas with Main Edition was the eighth Classic of his career (2 in Britain, 2 in Ireland, 3 in Germany, 1 in Italy)

Compiled by John Randall

INSPIRATIONAL

Pat Smullen was forced to retire in May after a brilliant career but still had another big winner up his sleeve

By Alan Sweetman

IRISH Champions Weekend is a showpiece occasion with two days of top-class action featuring six Group 1s and a host of valuable supporting races. And yet, as a wealth of drama unfolded at Leopardstown and the Curragh over those two days, all else at the 2019 edition was overshadowed by a contest valued at a token €59.10.

The Pat Smullen Champions Race for Cancer Trials Ireland, contested over a mile at the Curragh by an elite group of nine retired former champion jockeys, was a remarkable and unique occasion.

As the racing world united to support a project initiated by nine-time Irish champion Smullen, the Curragh witnessed an afternoon of profound emotion, at times heartrendingly poignant but ultimately richly inspirational. In excess of €2.5m was raised by the venture, a tribute to the respect and affection inspired by Smullen, who announced his retirement from the saddle in May, just two weeks before his 42nd birthday.

Smullen's diagnosis with pancreatic cancer in March 2018, ten days after partnering his final winner on Togoville for Anthony McCann at Dundalk, cast a pall over the subsequent Irish season. By the end of 2018 there was better news when the jockey recounted a successful spell of chemotherapy, the removal of a tumour and a hard-fought recovery from complications arising from surgery.

Smullen clung to the hope of returning to the saddle. By early May he was forced to concede to medical advice. "I'm almost 14lb heavier than when I was riding and when I explained to my doctors what would be involved in getting down to a riding weight they strongly advised it would not be wise to go down that road. They told me it would be very foolish, as it could compromise my immune system," he said.

****

SMULLEN, from Rhode in County Offaly, obtained early experience with Joanna Morgan and with local trainer Tom Lacy, who provided his first win on Vicosa at the old Dundalk track in 1993. He spent two years with John Oxx and was champion apprentice in 1995 and 1996. The following year he enjoyed a first Group 1 success on Tarascon for Tommy Stack in the Moyglare Stud Stakes.

After joining Dermot Weld as understudy to Mick Kinane, Smullen became stable jockey at Rosewell House in 1999 when Kinane left to team up with Aidan O'Brien. Reflecting on a 20-year

▸ Pulling power: Pat Smullen (left) put together a star-studded line-up for his Champions Race for Cancer Trials Ireland

▲ Champions united: Pat Smullen with race winner Sir Anthony McCoy (left) and Ruby Walsh, the runner-up; Smullen and all nine riders before the race

association with Weld, Smullen said: "Dermot is a great trainer, always has been. It wasn't easy in the early years. He could be very strict, but he was the making of me and we developed a very successful association over the years."

Smullen's alliance with Weld was responsible for 11 of his 12 European Classic wins, the first achieved in the 2001 Irish St Leger with Vinnie Roe, who quickly followed up in the Prix Royal-Oak. Smullen rode Vinnie Roe to four consecutive Irish St Leger victories and the pair finished second behind the great Makybe Diva in the 2004 Melbourne Cup.

Refuse To Bend became his first British Classic winner when landing the 2,000 Guineas in 2003. The following year he won the Irish Derby on Grey Swallow.

On account of his commitments to Weld, Smullen never enjoyed the same degree of opportunity on the international circuit as Kinane and Johnny Murtagh, the first two Flat jockeys in Irish racing history to carve a global reputation from a domestic base.

However, he made the best of the chances, such as when landing the 2007 Prix de l'Abbaye on Benbaun for British-based Tipperary native Mark Wallace, and taking the 2008 Breeders' Cup Marathon at Santa Anita on Muhannak for Ralph Beckett. In all, he won six Pattern races on Benbaun, though that was small beer relative to his record of 20 stakes-race wins on Famous Name for Weld.

Smullen enjoyed a golden season in 2015 when his big-race haul included the Irish Oaks and the Prix de l'Opera on Covert Love for Hugo Palmer, Royal Ascot success for Weld on Free Eagle in the Prince of Wales's Stakes and on Snow Sky for Sir Michael Stoute in the Hardwicke Stakes, the Champion Stakes on the Weld-trained Fascinating Rock, as well as the Tattersalls Millions Trophy on Gifted Master for Palmer.

In 2016 he set the seal on his career with a Derby/Irish Derby double on Harzand for Weld and the Aga Khan, and compiled his highest annual domestic total, 129, of which 21 came at Listed level or above.

****

SMULLEN'S fitness and mental strength, key weapons in his armoury as a rider, served him well during the battle to regain health after being diagnosed with a notoriously aggressive cancer. In May, when announcing his retirement, he looked strong and healthy, exuding a characteristic positivity and determination. At the same time, he was aware of what the future could hold. "My treatment has been completed and I will be having regular check-ups to keep on top of the situation, as there is always the chance the cancer could return," he said.

During the summer Smullen formulated plans for a fund-raising race involving fellow retired jockeys. Legendary figures of the sport were quick to volunteer. This was no ordinary charity race. From the world of jump racing came Paul Carberry, Sir Anthony McCoy, Charlie Swan and Ruby Walsh, joining forces with Flat champions Ted Durcan, Kieren Fallon, Richard Hughes, Johnny Murtagh and Joseph O'Brien.

Smullen was set to join the nine for a one-off comeback until a setback to his health in August ruled him out. He never wavered from the task he had set himself and showed relentless energy in bringing the plan to fruition.

When the day came around, Pinatubo produced an electrifying performance in the National Stakes, his old boss rose to the occasion by saddling Search For A Song to win the Irish St Leger in the Moyglare Stud colours Smullen had so often worn with distinction, and his brother-in-law Aidan O'Brien won the other two Group 1 contests.

But the imposing new Curragh roof was really raised when McCoy guided Quizical to beat Walsh on Aussie Valentine. Wonderful stuff. "It's not about me, it's about raising awareness and vital funds," Smullen said.

A modest man by nature, he would never have made it about himself. Yet it was to Smullen that the racing world responded with a rare solidarity of purpose and generosity of spirit on an unforgettable day.

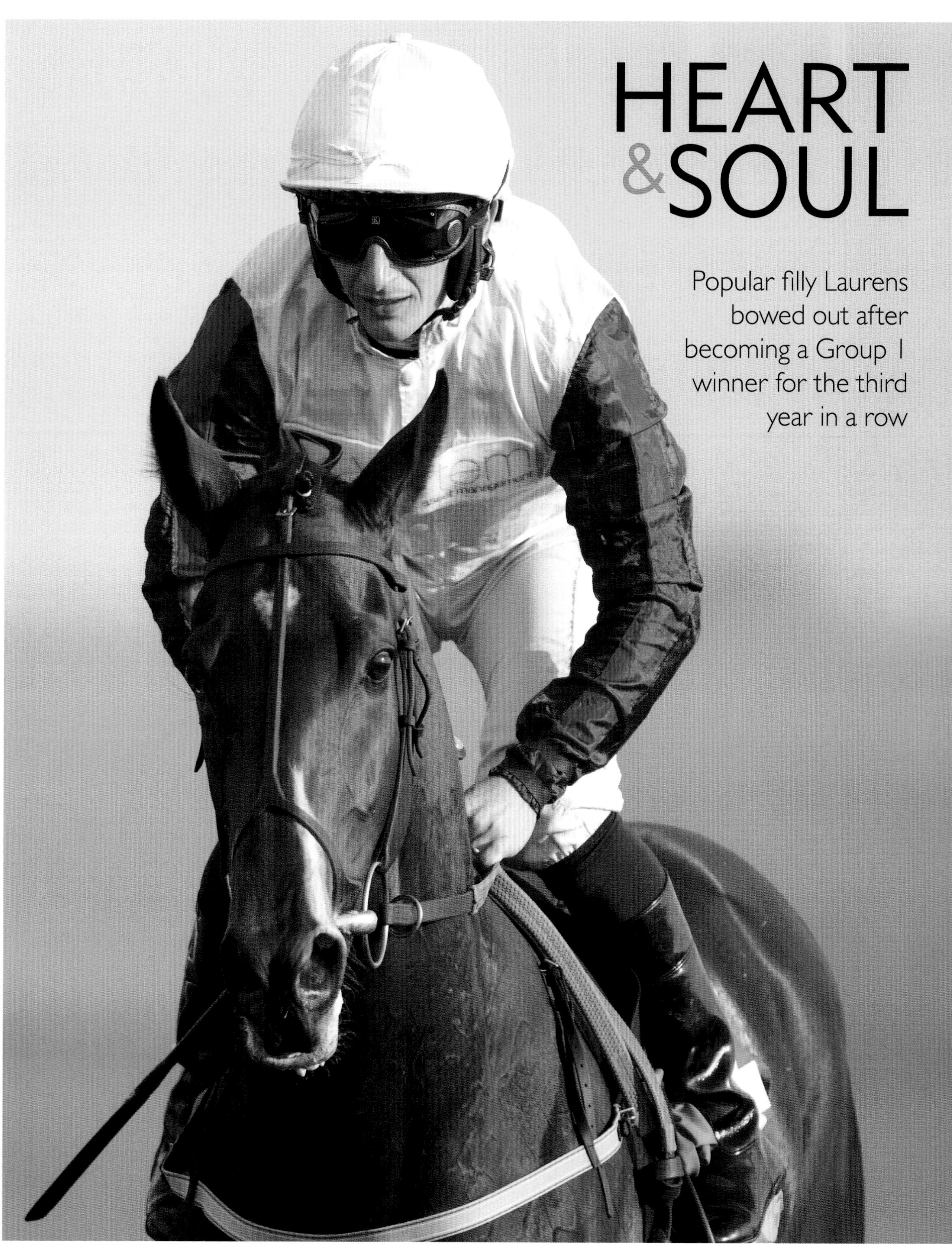

HEART &SOUL

Popular filly Laurens bowed out after becoming a Group 1 winner for the third year in a row

By David Carr

A THING of beauty may indeed be a joy forever but that doesn't mean it will remain a racehorse forever. Laurens, the stunning filly whose talent, toughness and tenacity lit up the last three seasons, was retired from racing in October and headed off for a new lead role in owner John Dance's budding broodmare band.

Her offspring will be well worth looking out for if they are anything like their dam, a pin-up girl of a thoroughbred who turned heads from the day she was bought for £220,000 at Doncaster as a yearling in 2016 and had a racing spirit to match.

Three years and six Group 1 wins later, trainer Karl Burke was still bursting with pride at the fine physical specimen who said farewell to her fans in the Sun Chariot Stakes. "Luke Harvey came up to me as they were exiting the paddock. He was working for ITV and said he couldn't believe how well she looked," he recalled of that Newmarket Saturday. "He'd seen her every race in England this season and he thought she looked better than ever."

Burke could not have agreed more. "She was a beautiful yearling and she kept getting better-looking as she grew older. She was a credit to the whole team, especially to my daughter Lucy who looked after her the whole time."

Looks are not everything and Laurens trailed in seventh behind Billesdon Brook that afternoon, confirming the impression created by her previous Matron Stakes fourth that her racing days were over. Yet it would be perverse to focus on two low points in a career packed with soaring highs, even though there was a slight feeling of what might have been at the end of her final season.

Her reappearance second in the Lockinge Stakes at Newbury, beaten only by the race-fit Mustashry, certainly augured well for the year. And she ran better than her finishing position suggests in the Queen Anne Stakes at Royal Ascot, leading inside the final quarter-mile only to be swamped for speed and end up sixth. That disappointment was then compounded by the minor setback Laurens suffered as she was being prepared for the Falmouth Stakes, which would have been her first race of the year restricted to her own sex and a clear winning opportunity.

But it takes more than a tiny sprain in a hind leg to keep a tough filly out of action for long and a return to winning ways was delayed rather than cancelled. She was rerouted to another Group 1 for fillies and mares, the Prix Rothschild at Deauville in late July, and regular rider PJ McDonald had the race under control for most of the way, having virtually all the field off the bridle fully three furlongs from home.

Although Laurens held on by just half a length at the line, she never really looked like being caught and delighted Burke and Dance, who had said at the start of the season that landing one more Group 1 would fully justify holding off retirement for another year. The Rothschild victory meant she had been a Group 1 winner in each of her three racing seasons and it was her third top-level success in France, where her only defeat came against subsequent Prix Maurice de Gheest winner Polydream in the Prix du Calvados at Deauville on her Pattern-race debut at two.

★★★★

"I HAVE no regrets about keeping her in training this year," Burke reflected after she had run her final race. "How can you when she landed another Group 1 win? It's just a shame she didn't get two this season and maybe I could have turned the screw a bit more at home going into the Lockinge.

"We were thinking of the way she'd petered out slightly at the backend of the previous season and we'd given her a nice break through the winter as she'd been on the go for a long time. We'll never know whether she'd have improved on her second place at Newbury had we done more with her.

"Ascot doesn't play to her strengths and the niggles after the Queen Anne cost her the chance of running in the Falmouth Stakes, which could have been a good race for her."

Laurens' blitzing Rothschild performance, as well as her home work, convinced Burke and Dance she had become faster as she got older, so much so they felt it was worth trying a drop to seven furlongs at the Ebor meeting. Carrying a Group 1 penalty in the City of York Stakes and going down by just a nose to Shine So Bright, a specialist at the distance, did nothing to disprove their theory and the seven-furlong Prix de la Foret was actively considered for her farewell appearance.

Which makes it all the more intriguing that analysis of her stride pattern suggested she ought to have been running over longer trips, not shorter ones. Her cadence was measured at an average of 2.16 strides per second, which is the sort of figure you would expect of a filly racing over a mile and a half.

On that basis it is astonishing that she should have come out on top so often at shorter distances. Those renowned battling qualities were the hallmark of a remarkable filly doing her darnedest to fight off rivals who threatened to outspeed her.

That toughness, plus her durability and consistency, helps to explain the appeal of a filly who was 10lb inferior to Enable on Racing Post Ratings yet would probably have given the wondermare a run for her money in any popularity poll among punters.

As Burke said: "She was fantastic for us, pure quality. She wore her heart on her sleeve and she loved a battle."

▼ Super six: Laurens adds to her tally of Group 1 wins in the Prix Rothschild at Deauville in July

Carroll

IN THE PICTURE

Pour La Victoire does like to be beside the seaside

BRIGHTON is renowned as a track for specialists and there is none better than Pour La Victoire, who notched a modern-day record with his tenth success at the idiosyncratic seaside course in September.

The Tony Carroll-trained nine-year-old, in his eighth season of racing and making his 96th start, moved into double figures at Brighton with victory in a Class 5 seven-furlong handicap by one and a half lengths under Hollie Doyle. Overall he has won 15 races and had 33 other top-three finishes in an admirably consistent career but by far his favourite track is Brighton, where his record stands at ten wins, six seconds and four thirds from 29 runs.

Pour La Victoire was locked in a rivalry with Roy Rocket, a nine-time Brighton winner who ran the same day but without success, allowing Carroll's gelding to move ahead. Pour La Victoire has accrued more than £54,000 for connections at the Sussex track, where he hit the mark in August 2013 on his first visit and has scored in every year since except 2017.

Naturally he is a favourite at Carroll's Worcestershire stable, which he joined as a three-year-old after failing to win in seven starts for Nigel Tinkler. "He keeps me on my toes as a trainer as he goes about things in his own way, but as long as he's happy that's all that matters," Carroll said. "He's just lovely and an incredible character. He's a good old horse."

Carroll, whose dark suit had white splodges after he was 'seagulled' ("it was lucky!" he said), added: "He deserved to win again and he deserved the record, although he's one of my children, so I would say that. We've had a lot of fun with him and he loves this place. I don't know why but our horses perform well here, and the owners love it as well."

Pour La Victoire's owner James Lawrence said: "We've been trying all season to get the record. For any horse to win ten times at any track is impressive. Hollie rode him exactly as we asked. This just shows the fun you can have with a handicapper who tries. It shows you the importance of horses for courses as well."

Doyle, riding the crest of a wave in a breakthrough season, was delighted to win on her first ride aboard Pour La Victoire. "He's a legend," she said. "He travelled so nicely and everything dropped away, so we got there way too soon. He knew he'd done enough and he's a wise old fox – that's partly why he's been able to hold his form for so long."

Picture: CONNORS BRIGHTON

FOND FAREWELL

Australia's wondermare Winx bowed out in style in April with her 33rd straight win

By Lee Mottershead

SHE won again and then it was over. Had she not kept winning it would have been over much sooner, which might have pleased some curmudgeons. It certainly would not have pleased the 43,844 people who sold out Royal Randwick, nor the men, women, boys and girls of Australia to whom she became a national icon, nor the racing fans all over the world who agreed she was a horse like no other. After that day at Randwick it was indeed all over, but only after a last hurrah fitting for the glorious wonder that was Winx.

On April's first Saturday, Aintree staged what is very possibly the most famous horserace in the world. On April's second Saturday, more than 10,000 miles away on the other side of the world, a racecourse in Sydney's eastern suburbs played host to the mare who was indisputably the most famous racehorse in the world.

She had been the most famous for some time. As her winning spree grew bigger, so did her fame. There were those who questioned what she was beating, but she was beating them, all of them, every time, in every race on every different sort of ground and over plenty of different trips. Invariably she beat them easily, although there were days, such nerve-racking days, when she beat them most dramatically.

Racing is showbiz on hooves. Winx seemed to know that. She was an entertainer, probably also a bit of a diva, and this was her final curtain call. The farewell tour had reached its final stage. Time to bow out.

It would have come as no surprise had she bowed out six months earlier at Moonee Valley after she had achieved the defining moment of her life, becoming the first horse to win the Cox Plate, Australia's weight-for-age championship, for a fourth time. By that point she was already a southern hemisphere seven-year-old, a grande dame of the turf by top-level Flat racing standards. To those who raced her and those who watched her there was no race bigger than the one she had just won. It had been her date with destiny and destiny had been fulfilled. They could so easily have stopped right there.

****

YET they carried on. They seemed reluctant to say the final stopping point would be Randwick on April 13 but increasingly a date was being carved in stone. By the time she had won the three build-up races of her autumn preparation everyone knew the end was in sight. We knew and they knew, so for them, particularly for trainer Chris Waller and his staff, the weight of expectation was colossal.

Winx seemed not to realise the enormity of what was unfolding when she was paid a visit on the Tuesday morning of race week. At Waller's main Sydney base, set within the large training complex at Rosehill Gardens racecourse, one of her two personal assistants, Candice Persijn, was attending to the great lady in stable 51. Outside the Winx residence there was a sign indicating she should undergo both front and hind stretches in the morning and afternoon, core stability exercises and receive treatment from a massage ball. Waller and his young British assistant Charlie Duckworth had absolutely no time for massage-ball treatment, given that their working days begin in the middle of the night and seldom allow much time for relaxation.

"I know I'll get emotional on Saturday and I'll definitely shed a tear," Duckworth said that morning. "I've got choked up for every one of her last five runs. It doesn't help that I watch her races with Chris. When you see someone else cry it rubs off on you."

He had seen Chris cry on numerous occasions, as had we all. Going into the Longines Queen Elizabeth Stakes, a prize Winx had already won twice, the joint-world champion of 2018 had captured her last 32 races, 24 of which were in Group 1 company. In the interviews that followed so many of those races, Waller had spoken with a voice breaking with emotion. He did not own her – that was the pleasure of Debbie Kepitis, Peter Tighe and Richard Treweeke – but he treated her like one of his own. Like a member of the family, in fact.

"A horse should not win 32 races in a row," he said later that Tuesday in between buying yearlings at the Inglis Sales complex by Warwick Farm racecourse. "Luck might get you to win ten in a row. Winx has only got to 32 because of her exceptional ability."

Now she was trying to turn 32 into 33. The world was watching. Australia was expecting. "On Saturday I'll try in my mind to put into perspective what is pressure," Waller said. "Is pressure really training a champion racehorse? Pressure is going to war or fighting a health battle. To be part of an amazing horse's career is a privilege. The pressure is more self-built than anything. Telling myself all that is what will keep me sane."

Waller's sanity was tested even before sunrise on the Thursday when Winx became irritable during a seriously early Rosehill media call that followed her final racecourse gallop. She kicked out

▸▸ *Continues page 184*

and struck a metal fence. We gasped. Waller rued his decision to remove the earmuffs Winx usually wore at such a function. "As you all saw, she's showing no signs of quietening down," he said, adding: "She's cherry ripe." Speaking two days earlier he had been even bolder. "She's ready to explode," he said.

★★★★

ON EXPLOSION day Randwick was bathed in warm sunshine that turned into hot sunshine as the day went on. The citizens of Sydney are not so obsessed with sport as their southern counterparts in Melbourne but they love a star and they love a major event, so they flocked from the city, in which a wall on Wynyard Street had been adorned with a Winx mural, and they descended on what became known for the day as Royal Rand-Winx.

Many of them will not have been ardent racing fans but they were Winx fans and they wanted to be at a racecourse that was flying a Winx flag next to Australia's. "Sydney farewells Winx" proclaimed a huge sign. The world was farewelling her too, as evidenced by the presence of international racegoers among the excited throng.

A sizeable percentage of that throng made a point of visiting Winx during the countdown to the 3.05pm off time of the Queen Elizabeth Stakes. At any one point you could have seen hundreds of people, young and old, packed deep around a rail in the racecourse stables, all of them hungry to get a glimpse of the champion in box 114.

When it was time to work Winx came out of stall nine. Under regular partner Hugh Bowman she began from a wide berth and was still four horses off the fence turning for home. Once in sight of the winning line she knuckled down in characteristically determined fashion, drawing clear of Japanese challenger Kluger to rapturous applause and cheers. This was her 33rd straight win and her 25th Group 1. For Waller, it was the 100th top-flight triumph of his remarkable career.

"We came here as confident as we've ever been," Bowman said. "What a journey it's been. I can't believe this is

▸▸ *Continues page 186*

▾ Pride and joy: Winx and Hugh Bowman parade in front of the sellout crowd at Randwick after her final outing

Wonderful Winx in numbers

37 wins

25 Group 1 wins (world record)

33 consecutive wins

89.85 total number of lengths by which she won during her 33-race streak

£14,564,743 career earnings (world record)

130 rating in 2018 Longines World Rankings when equal world champion with Cracksman

43 fastest recorded speed in miles per hour in 2018 Winx Stakes (equalling Frankel in 2012 Queen Anne Stakes)

the end." But it was the end. For Waller that meant it was a relief and, in some ways, a release. There was no longer any need to hide the happy but heavy burden he and many others had been carrying.

"So many people have been under so much pressure," he said. "The farrier, the vet, my foreperson, my racing manager, my business manager, my PA and my wife, not to mention the owners. We've all felt the pressure. It hasn't just been today. It has been four years."

Do not for a second think he was complaining. Waller would not have foregone any of it, for the pressure was more than matched by the pleasure. You could see it on his face as he stood alongside Winx and Bowman on Randwick's turf, both men saluting the enormous and joyful crowd. Pride poured out of their faces.

****

WALLER insisted he had not envisaged how the day might go. "I didn't think about it," he said, fighting back the tears and all but losing the fight. "I thought about everything except winning. It's as simple as that. You don't set yourself up for these big wins. You just do your job."

The trainer did that job superbly, as was made clear by the owners of Winx, whose final victory made her the highest-earning horse of all time with a haul of £14,564,743. The owners won the biggest share of that enormous sum but this really was not about money.

"Winx is the most amazing supreme athlete I've ever seen, handled by the best coach," said Kepitis, while Tighe broke down when expressing gratitude to racing fans in Australia and beyond.

▲ Fighting fit: Winx shows her wellbeing during a trackwork session before her final outing

▼ Celebrations after the wondermare brought down the curtain on her illustrious career

"We love her to bits," he said. "I want to say a big thank you to everyone right around the world. It has been a great journey and I'm glad everyone has enjoyed it as much as we have."

If you did not enjoy it, you follow the wrong sport.

As Winx was paraded by Bowman past the Randwick grandstands, Tina Turner's Simply The Best was played loudly across the racecourse. Truth be told, we can never know whether Winx was the best, of her own era, let alone any other, although she very likely is the best racehorse ever trained in Australia.

On this day, as on so many others, when thousands and thousands of people came to honour an incredible racehorse, when their affection and admiration for that horse was obvious, when the horse brought a nation together and gave those who watched a real sense of happiness, it mattered not a jot where Winx might sit in the pantheon of the greats.

What mattered most then, and still does now, was that happiness, the admiration, the affection, the capacity to unite and the power of one horse not just to be good, but to do good.

Winx may or may not have been the best, yet possibly more than any other horse ever has, she made people feel better. Not a bad way to go out.

Famous Flat winning runs

54 Kincsem 1876-79

33 Winx 2015-19

25 Black Caviar 2010-13

19 Zenyatta 2007-10

14 Frankel 2010-12

Kentucky Derby victory was taken away from Maximum Security, leaving a trail of acrimony and argument surrounding America's greatest race

MAXIMUM CONTROVERSY

THE Kentucky Derby is acclaimed as "the greatest two minutes in sport". In 2019, those two minutes were only the start of it as the 145th running of America's most famous race was swept up in a swirl of controversy involving disqualification, argument, legal action and even one of Donald Trump's tweets.

The day seemed ripe for an upset when heavy rain turned the Churchill Downs track into a sloppy mudbath but nobody could have foreseen how events would play out, nor how the ramifications

◂ Winner to sinner: Maximum Security (pink) comes home in front by a length and three-quarters from Country House (yellow) but the result was soon to be overturned by the stewards

would rumble on. The portentously named Improbable – one of three runners for Bob Baffert, seeking to join Ben Jones on a record six Derby wins – took over late as favourite at 4-1 just ahead of 9-2 shot Maximum Security, who would go on to win and then lose the race. Among the relatively unconsidered longshots were Country House, Long Range Toddy and Bodexpress, but they too were to play significant roles.

The race seemed to go pretty well for Maximum Security and his jockey Luis Saez, who was able to assume control of the pace and keep enough in reserve to cross the line a length and three-quarters clear of Country House in a time of 2:03.93. Cue wild celebrations for Saez, trainer Jason Servis and owners Gary and Mary West. But not for long.

Objections were lodged by the riders of Country House and Long Range Toddy and the stewards started to examine a chain reaction of events on the home turn, where Maximum Security lugged out from a rail-hugging position towards the centre of the track, taking three horses wider with him, allowing Code Of Honor to slip through on the inside to lead briefly. Maximum Security fought back bravely to come out on top in the stretch duel from Country House, Code Of Honor and Tacitus – with the win seemingly secured on merit – but the stewards' focus was on what happened around the turn. While the 157,729 spectators watched the big screens for the outcome of the stewards' deliberations and TV analysts debated the incident, it was clear Maximum Security's connections were becoming increasingly concerned. Elation had turned to alarm.

Finally, more than 20 minutes after the race finish, the stewards' sensational verdict was announced on track. "There's been a disqualification. Maximum Security disqualified from first." Nine words that turned the result on its head as 65-1 longshot Country House was moved up to first place, becoming the second-biggest-priced winner in the race's history. It was the first time a Derby winner had been disqualified because of an infringement on the track. In 1968, Dancer's Image won but failed a drug test and was disqualified.

"We had a lengthy review of the race," said chief steward Barbara Borden, reading a statement but taking no questions from the media contingent. "We interviewed affected riders. We determined that the seven horse [Maximum Security] drifted out and impacted the progress of number one [War Of Will], in turn interfering with the 18 [Long Range Toddy] and 21 [Bodexpress]. Those horses were all affected by the interference. Therefore we unanimously determined to disqualify number seven and place him behind 18, the lowest-placed horse that he bothered."

★★★★

COUNTRY HOUSE'S veteran trainer Bill Mott, having been handed his first Kentucky Derby win at the age of 65, said "it feels pretty darn good" but added: "It was an odd way to do it and we hate to back into any of these things. It's a bittersweet victory. I know the stewards had a very, very difficult decision and I'm glad I wasn't in their shoes."

On the other side, the stewards' decision brought a furious response

▸▸ *Continues page 190*

from Maximum Security's owner Gary West. "I think this is the most egregious disqualification in the history of horse racing, and not just because it's our horse," he said. "When you're leg weary, you're not going to run straight all the time. Horses don't either."

"I never put anybody in danger," maintained Saez, the Panamanian rider who had seen a first Derby victory snatched away from him, with the bitter pill soured further a few days later by a 15-day suspension "for failure to control his mount and make the proper effort to maintain a straight course". Servis agreed with his jockey's view, saying: "He straightened him up right away and I didn't think it affected the outcome of the race."

The US president waded into the controversy, tweeting: "The Kentuky [sic] Derby decision was not a good one. It was a rough and tumble race on a wet and sloppy track, actually, a beautiful thing to watch. Only in these days of political correctness could such an overturn occur. The best horse did NOT win the Kentucky Derby – not even close!"

The Wests wanted to appeal to the Kentucky Horse Race Commission, with their lawyer arguing the actions of the stewards at Churchill Downs were "arbitrary and capricious and did not comply with applicable administrative regulations", but it was denied because Kentucky regulations do not allow appeals of stewards' decisions.

Within a fortnight, the Wests filed a lawsuit in the US District Court seeking the reinstatement of the original order of finish. The suit questioned the stewards' actions and claimed the disqualification violated the plaintiffs' right to due process because they could not appeal. "Despite the fact that no objection had been lodged by the owner, trainer, or jockey of War Of Will or Bodexpress, the stewards unilaterally determined that Maximum Security had committed a foul and then lied to the public that they interviewed the 'affected riders' when they knew they did not interview War Of Will's jockey, Tyler Gaffalione, nor Chris Landeros, Bodexpress's rider," the lawsuit said. It added that Maximum Security was the "leading horse", meaning he was "entitled to any part of the track".

In response the Kentucky Horse Racing Commission asked for the case to be dismissed on the grounds that the litigation "fails to state a claim for which relief can be granted" and that the plaintiffs were attempting "to claim legal rights to which they are not entitled". Months after the race, the case was still open.

****

'This is the most egregious disqualification in the history of horse racing, and not just because it's our horse'

AMID all the legal wrangling, more racing went on. The Preakness Stakes, the second leg of the Triple Crown, went by without Maximum Security – "There's no Triple Crown on the line for us and there's no reason to run a horse back in two weeks when you don't have to," Gary West reasoned – or Country House, who was ruled out with a cough. Victory went to the Mark Casse-trained War Of Will, who had been one of the sufferers in the Derby and had finished eighth (placed seventh). Improbable was favourite again but finished sixth, two places worse than his final position at Churchill Downs.

War Of Will tried to follow up in the Belmont Stakes, the third leg, but was ninth of ten behind stablemate Sir Winston, a newcomer to the series. Tacitus, promoted to third in the Derby, was second in the Belmont having missed the Preakness.

Country House was out for the whole summer but Maximum

Security returned to action in mid-June and suffered another sensational defeat. Faced by only five rivals in a Listed race at Monmouth Park, one of which was his longshot stablemate Direct Order, Maximum Security was sent off at 1-20 but went down by a length to King For A Day.

"This is horse racing, anything can happen," said Saez, who by now knew that better than anyone. "He's a real good horse. That hasn't changed. I think the next time he will be okay."

When the next time came around, Maximum Security lined up against five rivals again, including King For A Day, in the Grade 1 Haskell Invitational at Monmouth Park and Saez was right, his mount would be okay, but not before there was more controversy. Amid a heatwave on the east coast of the United States, the New Jersey track called a halt to afternoon racing and moved the stakes races to the evening, with the Haskell going off more than two hours later than its scheduled post time and without being broadcast nationally by NBC Sports Network.

The delay did not appear to upset Maximum Security – "He got two lunches today," Servis said – and he came home in front, scoring by a length and a quarter from Mucho Gusto at odds of 4-5.

Soon after the finish, however, the inquiry sign flashed again as the stewards started to look at an incident involving Maximum Security and King For A Day at the three-eighths pole. "My heart skipped a beat," admitted Gary West but added: "After I saw a replay, I knew they wouldn't take him down. If they took him down today, I would know for sure that the racing gods had something against me."

The gods, the rules, the stewards, whatever, were all on Maximum Security's side this time and the Haskell was his. It was vindication of his high standing among the US three-year-olds but scant consolation for all the bitterness and hurt of Churchill Downs. "I'm so happy to see this horse back where he belongs, in the winner's circle," Gary West said. "But [the Derby] is just something that will always be there. You can't ever replace what we lost."

▲ Reversal of fortune: Original runner-up Country House (left) wears the winner's rug; media and connections gather on the track to hear the objection ruling (top); jockey Flavien Prat celebrates his first Derby victory following the change of order

THE BIGGER PICTURE

Maximum Security is washed after a morning workout in the build-up to the Kentucky Derby at Churchill Downs in May. Two days later the Jason Servis-trained colt would win the race, only to be demoted to 17th by the stewards

MICHAEL REAVES (GETTY IMAGES)

John McCririck, the betting pundit who became racing's most colourful TV personality, died on July 5, aged 79. His life and impact are remembered in this Racing Post obituary

'He knew his audience, knew what they wanted and knew how to give it to them'

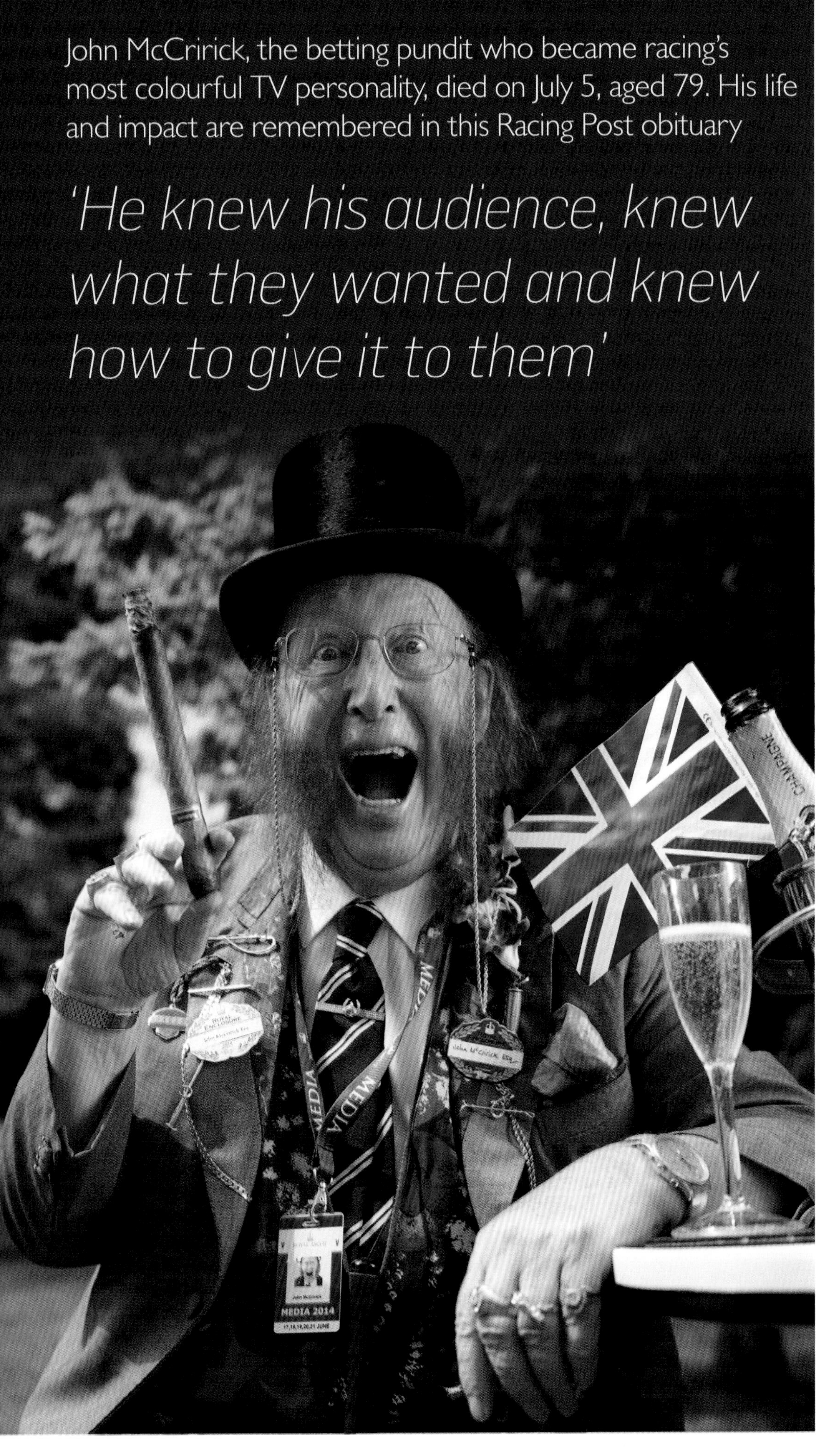

By Lee Mottershead

LARGE and loud, he was for many the improbable face and voice of horseracing. He was the one the public recognised, liked, loathed and stood alongside for a picture while he made a funny face. He was the one television, radio and newspaper folk turned to when a quote or interview was needed. John McCririck undoubtedly made his presence felt.

He called himself a failed bookmaker, a failed punter and a failed journalist. He may have been the first two but he was certainly not the third. Long before he became a figure known to millions, McCririck was a hugely respected award-winning journalist. He was brave and fearless, traits he carried into his television career, together with a not inconsiderable portion of intentional silliness. He largely knew what he was doing, and he did it supremely well.

McCririck was also many things you might not have expected him to be, not least somewhat insecure when away from the cameras, a person who would avoid gatherings and parties if he felt there would be nobody present with whom he felt comfortable. Those who knew him best have lost a man who was kind, thoughtful and exceptionally generous. The right-wing Tory views he espoused were sincerely held, yet many in his inner circle, past and present, lived at the other end of the political spectrum. They liked him enormously. Once you got to know him, he was easy to like. He was a man who was better for knowing.

John McCririck was born in Surbiton on April 17, 1940. He might not have been keen to confirm that, however, for McCririck never spoke about his age and despised birthdays, particularly his own. He also said little about his childhood, but it was unconventional, perhaps setting a trend for the person who lived it.

An only child, he spent much of his early life in Jersey, although there were regular visits to see two

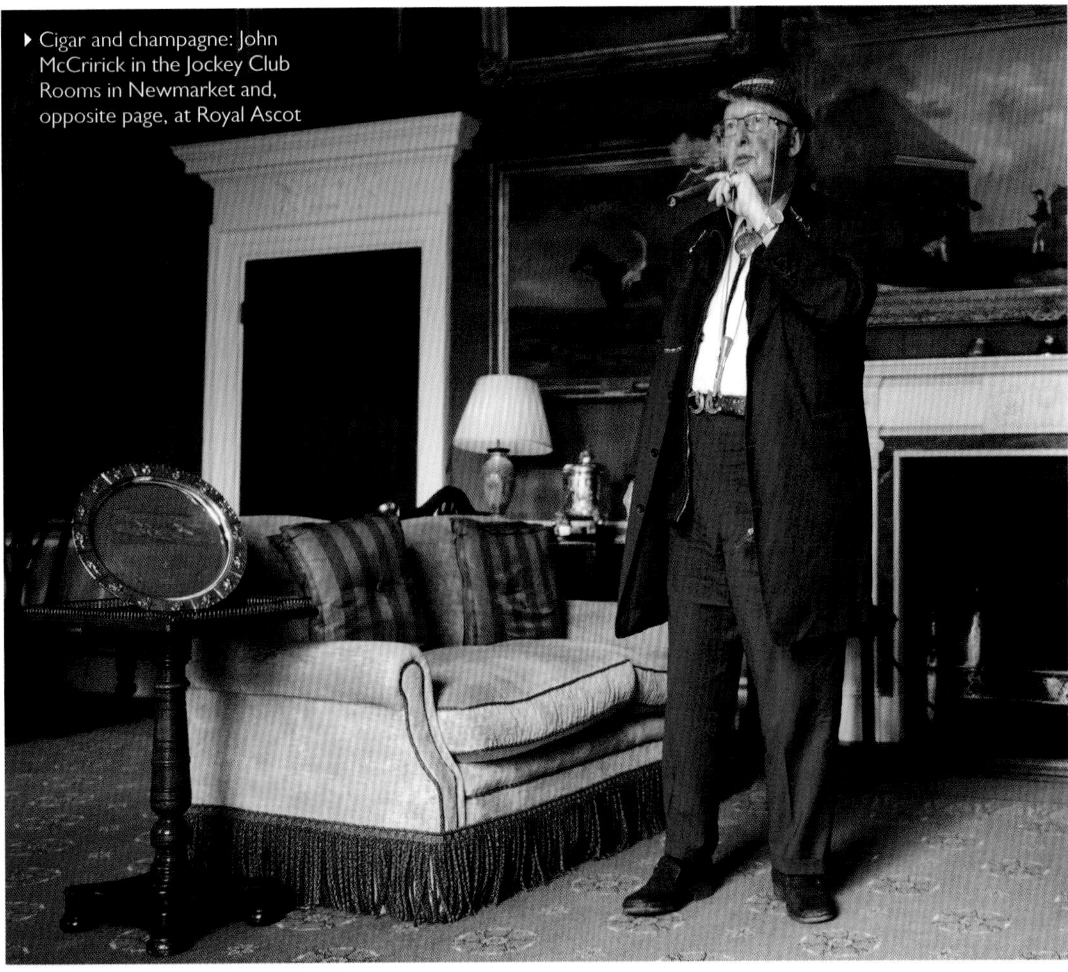

▸ Cigar and champagne: John McCririck in the Jockey Club Rooms in Newmarket and, opposite page, at Royal Ascot

aunts in Chichester, from where he made trips to Goodwood. His mother, a lady with a penchant for a fur coat, planned that her son would attend prep school and Harrow before entering the diplomatic corps. McCririck was not a huge loss to international diplomacy, but he did attend prep school and Harrow, leaving the latter with three O-Levels and a friendship with the BBC's future racing correspondent Julian Wilson.

Indeed, it was at Harrow that McCririck began to dabble in bookmaking, enduring one particularly bad day when laying Wilson £5 at 1-2 about the school's athletics captain winning the spring term cross-country race. He won.

From Harrow, McCririck went to The Dorchester, which would have delighted his mother, except for the fact his time there was largely spent in the kitchens. "That catering training was totally wasted as I can't boil an egg," he would say later. "My father never ever went in the kitchen. That was my mother's place. It's the same with the Booby. She's a great cook. I always say there's more of me now than when the Booby married me. That's her fault."

McCririck was never heard in public to call his wife of 48 years anything other than Booby, a nickname he gave Jenny due to what he believed were her similarities to a species of sea bird. He claimed he first saw her while she was out walking her dog. "The only reason the Booby got hold of me was through a labrador called Simon," he said. "I had never had a dog but always wanted one. It infuriated her mother that on the wedding invitation we wrote the wedding would be hosted by Simon the Dog."

The mother in question did not immediately warm to her son-in-law, although the feelings of hostility were initially reciprocated. Once, on returning to the couple's then Bolsover Street flat, McCririck was met by his mother-in-law. She took one look at her daughter's beau and said: "You had no idea I was here, did you?" Quick as a flash, McCririck replied: "Oh yes I did. There's a green slime all the way up the stairs." Despite that, they were reconciled.

★★★★

BEFORE the Booby and Simon the Dog there was Wingy the Bookie. After a spell working for Boots on London's Edgware Road, McCririck became involved with a one-armed street bookmaker he described as smelly and nasty. Among McCririck's roles was to guard Wingy's preferred telephone box. That paid the bills for a while, but as soon as betting shops first opened in May 1961, McCririck fell into their thrall and began working in them.

From 1965 to 1970 he was employed as a private handicapper for tipping services, while on Derby day in 1971 he took punters' money during a short and unsuccessful stint as a racecourse bookmaker. McCririck had yet to find his calling.

It turned out he had two callings. Both were soon to call him.

His entry into mainstream journalism came when he secured a job with The Sporting Life, for which he gained his first big break thanks to the publication's hare coursing correspondent taking his last breath during the Barbican Cup meeting. Editor Ossie Fletcher needed to find a replacement at short notice and duly dispatched McCririck to the event with a first-class rail ticket and a bicycle. From that lowest rung his star soared, principally because of his brilliance as an investigative journalist.

In 1978 he was named specialist writer of the year at the British Press Awards, blessed with a portfolio that included coverage of the Rochester greyhound coup – which would have bagged those behind it £350,000 had bookmakers paid out – and a scandal linked to betting-office commentary provider Extel, whose policy to give off times by the minute not the second meant criminals were able to back dogs after races had started if the commentaries were slightly delayed.

One year later McCririck was named campaigning journalist of the year, this time after persistence paid off and he proved the Tote was authorising bets following the off in order to reduce dividends. As a result of 'Totegate', home secretary Willie Whitelaw set up an independent inquiry that came close to forcing chairman Woodrow Wyatt – almost as famous a cigar chomper as McCririck – to quit the organisation.

By now McCririck's outward demeanour was well established. He was noisy, flashy, arrogant and prone to make sexist, vulgar, outlandish statements. He was therefore perfectly suited to television.

He spent ten years behind the scenes as a sub-editor on the BBC's iconic Saturday afternoon sports programme Grandstand. McCririck landed the position through what he called 'the old school tie', in his case a recommendation from Wilson. He adored Frank Bough but detested David Coleman.

▸▸ *Continues page 196*

A senior BBC executive who defected to ITV then asked McCririck – also a devoted follower of greyhound racing – to work on the London region's Friday evening sports programme. He now had a foothold in front of camera, but his time with The Sporting Life, which he viewed as the happiest of his life, was about to come to an end, linked to rumours he owed money to bookmakers.

By 1984, when the Daily Star printed a front-page story linked to his alleged gambling debts, McCririck was already an integral part of television racing coverage. His TV bosses stood by him. McCririck was way too valuable to lose.

The betting ring would be his home, first for ITV and then Channel 4, which assumed full control of racing output on commercial television in 1985. After being hired by Andrew Franklin, the man who became his boss for more than three decades, McCririck enjoyed his first high-profile gig as part of the ITV team for Shergar's Derby in 1981. More than one star was born that Wednesday afternoon.

Nobody had ever done what McCririck did – and he did it brilliantly. Not only did he possess a masterful understanding of his subject, he was a natural performer. His updates from the ring were accompanied by flamboyant tic-tac gesticulation and references like "Burlington Bertie, 100-30".

He would shout at punters who waved while he was broadcasting, bringing a sense of fun to the programmes. That was enhanced by him bestowing pet names upon his Channel 4 Racing team members. John Oaksey was The Noble Lord and John Francome became The Greatest Jockey. In later years Alice Plunkett and Emma Spencer were known as Saucy Minx and Pouting Heiress. They appeared not to mind, for although McCririck could seem disparaging towards women, addressing the ladies who worked in the Channel 4 gallery as "girlies", all those ladies loved him. They could see behind the act.

****

BUT it wasn't all knockabout humour. McCririck spent hours preparing for programmes, creating thick handwritten books filled with notes, facts and results of races compiled over decades. He placed the punter and viewer central to everything he did. When he was the first on screen after a commercial break, he would often say: "It's great to have you back with us." There was strong emphasis on the word "you".

McCririck was also the one selected when someone was needed to carry out a heavyweight interview, especially with a politician. Given he was a political junkie who once sat down with Margaret Thatcher for the Daily Mail, that played perfectly to his strengths.

McCririck's celebrity status grew and grew, even in his beloved America, where he often popped up on television during his annual holiday to the Breeders' Cup. They called him 'Mutton Chops' because of his wild whiskers. They probably also loved his colossal rings, flamboyant outfits and many hats. The monster cries of "Howay the Lads" – he was a massive Newcastle United fan – may have been lost on them.

Aside from the time McCririck's hat was blown off by the wind one racing afternoon, nobody ever saw the top of his head, with the possible exception of the Booby. That was until McCririck – who by now had formed a betting-ring double act with Tanya Stevenson, whom he dubbed The Female – became a housemate in Channel 4's 2005 series of Celebrity Big Brother. The millions watching saw not only McCririck's head but also his baggy white underpants. He was wearing nothing else at the time. McCririck unashamedly said he took the job for the money. He took more money when hired for Celebrity Wife Swap, during which he was required to live with Edwina Currie. The pair did not bond particularly well.

Come 2012 those programmes were in the mind of TV executives putting together the new-look Channel 4 Racing team. Having for years been paid to cover racing, Channel 4, motivated by bookmaker advertising, flashed the cash and gained an exclusive mainstream deal, forcing the BBC out of televised racing. Also forced out was Highflyer, the company that had produced Channel 4's coverage to that point. Among those dropped was McCririck. His appearances had already been reduced by Channel 4's sports boss Andrew Thompson and his successor Jamie Aitchison. The latter, together with the IMG team that replaced Highflyer, decided that from January 1, 2013, McCririck was not wanted at all.

The man who had been Channel 4 Racing's most famous employee was incensed. He launched a £3m age discrimination case against Channel 4. Had he simply sought to prove unfair dismissal he might conceivably have won. Instead he lost, the tribunal panel noting in its judgement: "All the evidence is that Mr McCririck's pantomime persona, as demonstrated on the celebrity television appearances, and his persona when appearing on Channel 4 Racing, together with his self-described bigoted and male chauvinist views, were clearly unpalatable to a wider audience."

At his side that day, and all days, was his wife. John and Jenny McCririck were the tightest of units. Quite how he wooed her in their courtship days one can only imagine, but it worked. He adored her. He also could not have lived without her. She organised his life, cooked for him, drove him everywhere and defended him to the hilt. They were inseparable.

She knew all his faults but also all his qualities, many of which were seen only by those in his inner circle. Her husband was fiercely loyal to his friends and unfailingly generous. He was kind, helpful and supportive. He also abhorred anything he considered to be the mistreatment of horses and campaigned to have the whip banned.

McCririck was educated at Harrow, dined regularly at The Ivy, quaffed Dom Perignon champagne, lived in a plush Primrose Hill home and spoke with horror at the mere thought of flying in what he referred to as "cattle class". He was not a man of the people, yet few racing broadcasters have been so blessed with the common touch. He knew his audience, he knew what they wanted and he knew how to give it to them.

John McCririck achieved much in his life but to most people he was the large, loud, eccentric man who talked about racing on the telly. He was probably very pleased about that.

This is an edited version of an article that appeared in the Racing Post on July 6

▸ Ring master: John McCririck was a brilliant television performer with his updates from the betting ring

INJURED JOCKEYS FUND
Injured Jockeys Fund

Our selection of the horses and people likely to be making headlines in 2020 starts with three Classic contenders for Godolphin

PINATUBO

BETTER than Frankel. That's a heavy tag for any horse to carry but at this stage of his career it's true for Pinatubo, who put up the juvenile performance not just of 2019 but for many years with his brilliant victory in the Group 1 National Stakes at the Curragh in September.

Racing Post Ratings gave Pinatubo a mark of 128 for his nine-length win, making it the best-ever juvenile performance in Ireland and behind only the electrifying displays by Arazi in 1991 and Celtic Swing in 1994 in RPR history. Frankel, who was quick to mature into a top-level performer, reached an RPR of 126 as a two-year-old with his Group 1 win in the Dewhurst Stakes.

Nicknamed Pinaturbo by the Racing Post after that extraordinary National win, Godolphin's star colt was not at the same level on his final start of the season in the Dewhurst but he was clearly on top as he pulled away towards the end for a two-length victory over Arizona, who had finished a distant third in the National but put up more of a challenge this time. Pinatubo's performance was worth 121 on RPRs, still a high mark for a two-year-old, and completed a perfect six-race campaign that also featured clear-cut wins at Royal Ascot in the Chesham Stakes and Glorious Goodwood in the Vintage Stakes.

The question with any brilliant juvenile is whether they will train on – Frankel improved to a staggering 143 on RPR while Celtic Swing, despite winning the French Derby, and Arazi regressed – but Godolphin owner Sheikh Mohammed, trainer Charlie Appleby and jockey William Buick can dream all winter of what might lie ahead for Pinatubo.

Sheikh Mohammed, who gave a little dance of delight on the winner's rostrum after the Dewhurst, said: "Every year you have a favourite horse. I have seen him many times and we all love him. I will be looking forward to seeing him next year."

Precocious two-year-olds can burn themselves out through over-exuberance but there seems little danger of that with Pinatubo. From early on Appleby pointed out the colt's laid-back nature at home and before races, and it was the same after the Dewhurst.

"You can't get excited about him in the mornings," Appleby said. "He just goes about his business. In the preliminaries he was just sauntering around and I said to Will [Buick] 'you'd think he was an old horse walking around in a handicap'. He doesn't exactly fill you full of confidence coming into Group 1s but, as long as he keeps turning up in the afternoons, I'm not too worried what he does in the mornings."

Another worry would be that Pinatubo had a long season, starting on May 10 with an all-weather debut at Wolverhampton and continuing for another five months. Appleby could have stopped a month earlier after the National but wanted him to have the extra run in the Dewhurst.

"People had asked why we were running again," the trainer said. "I want someone with experience and he's been there when it comes to a dogfight. He's been up hill and down dale and has brought a wealth of experience to the table as well as an engine."

Buick, who missed Pinatubo's first four runs as he was absent for 12 weeks of the season with a concussion-related injury, also felt the Dewhurst was important. "It was his best performance as he had to show different qualities," he said. "He had to be brilliant in a different way – only a good horse can adapt like that."

If the turbo is fired up and ready to go next season, exciting times lie ahead.

EARTHLIGHT

EARTHLIGHT has a lot in common with Pinatubo – same owner, same sire, same unbeaten record – even if he has a long way to go to match him on Racing Post Ratings.

Trained in France by Andre Fabre, this Godolphin son of Shamardal finished off a five-race winning run with a pair of Group 1 victories in the Prix Morny at Deauville and the Middle Park Stakes at Newmarket. Both of those wins were by a neck, which kept him down to a best RPR of 119, and over six furlongs, but Fabre sees him as a serious Classic contender.

"He'll go further and I'll aim him at the Newmarket 2,000 Guineas," the trainer said at Deauville, and there was a sure sign of that intent when Earthlight was sent across the Channel for the Middle Park. Fabre's three Newmarket Guineas winners – Zafonic and Pennekamp in the 2,000, Miss France in the 1,000 – were tested on the Rowley Mile as two-year-olds, and like them Earthlight passed the test in winning style.

The difference was that he was kept to six furlongs but again Fabre made clear his opinion in the Newmarket winner's enclosure. "I was a little concerned six furlongs might be a bit sharp for him, but I was confident of his ability and he won well," he said. "Hopefully he'll get a mile next year when he could come back here or maybe Longchamp, but those decisions are six months away."

Pinatubo's progress will have a bearing on those decisions but, wherever he goes, Earthlight should have his chance to shine.

VICTOR LUDORUM

FOR most other owners Victor Ludorum would be a rare asset, but in Godolphin's rich two-year-old crop he ended the season behind Pinatubo and Earthlight with a Racing Post Rating of 113. Like them, though, he is an unbeaten Group 1-winning son of Shamardal, having landed the Prix Jean-Luc Lagardere, and radiates Classic potential.

The Godolphin pecking order might change depending on how the trio progress over the winter and Andre Fabre, trainer of Victor Ludorum as well as Earthlight, certainly expects this one to improve.

"Victor Ludorum has a big heart, is a beautiful mover and goes on any ground," he said after the narrow victory in the Lagardere at Longchamp on Arc day. "I don't see him as a natural two-year-old, he is next year's horse. I don't know if he'll stay a mile and a half but definitely a mile and a quarter, which I think Earthlight will as well."

A winning margin of three-quarters of a length over Alson may well have underplayed Victor Ludorum's superiority in the Lagardere. With all three of his wins coming over a mile, the last of them on very soft ground, he is proven over further than the other Godolphin star juveniles and his strong suit may well be stamina.

Fabre's inclination was towards a French Classic campaign with Victor Ludorum and there is also a certain mile-and-a-half race at Longchamp next October that the trainer rather likes. Might Arc day 2019 have shown us a contender for next year's big race?

QUADRILATERAL

A SURE sign of the belief in Quadrilateral was the £40,000 supplementary fee paid by owner Khalid Abdullah to put her in the Group 1 Fillies' Mile at Newmarket in October. The money came back with interest when she won more than £320,000 with a narrow victory, consolidating her pre-race status as 1,000 Guineas favourite.

"The easier option was to go for the Oh So Sharp [the Group 3 the day before]," trainer Roger Charlton said. "I was thinking it's not often good fillies come along, we could go and win that and keep the dream open for May rather than taking on the best. Management encouraged me [to go for the Fillies' Mile] and the result was good."

Quadrilateral had won her first two starts at Newbury but for a long way it did not look like the result would be good at Newmarket as she was off the bridle heading into the Dip and then found herself short of room on the far rail. She produced an electrifying burst in the last 100 yards, however, to score a shade cosily from Powerful Breeze, even though the margin was just a head. "She's a very talented filly and she got me out of trouble," said winning rider Jason Watson, landing his first Group 1 victory at the age of 19.

With her flashes of brilliance and appetite for a battle, this attractive daughter of Frankel has plenty going for her.

CHACUN POUR SOI

FRENCH-BREDS have changed the face of jump racing in Britain and Ireland over the past quarter of a century but few have made an impact at the top level as quickly as Chacun Pour Soi.

Less than two months after a 31-length win at Naas on his Irish debut for Willie Mullins, the seven-year-old scored a stunning victory at the Punchestown festival in the Grade 1 Ryanair Novice Chase. Defi Du Seuil, impressive winner of the JLT Novices' Chase at Cheltenham, was four and a quarter lengths back in second and 20 lengths behind in third was the Mullins-trained Duc Des Genievres, who had run away with the Arkle Chase at Cheltenham.

In all, Chacun Pour Soi beat four Grade 1 winners at Punchestown and his decisive victory catapulted him to the top of the novice chase division in the Anglo-Irish Jumps Classifications on a mark of 167. He was 5lb clear in the two-mile category and 3lb ahead of Topofthegame, the RSA Chase winner who headed the three-mile-plus section.

Chacun Pour Soi's age should give a clue that his progress off the track had not been so quick and straightforward and a look at the form book confirms his last race in France before moving to Ireland was as a four-year-old chaser in March 2016. Rich and Susannah Ricci bought him shortly afterwards but what Mullins described as "niggling problems" meant they had to wait nearly three years before getting to see him race.

"I've been tipping him as my horse to follow for the last three seasons but we never saw him race until March," Rich Ricci said at Punchestown. "It has been so frustrating but we had to stay patient because we knew he was very good."

Confirmation of what they knew came in Mullins' pre-race words to Robbie Power, the lucky man on board at Punchestown. "I told Robbie we think he's a star and that if he's as good as we think he is, God knows what would happen," the trainer said. "To turn in with an Arkle winner one side of him, a JLT winner on the other side and to still be cantering marks him out as a special horse."

The Queen Mother Champion Chase is the obvious target as Chacun Pour Soi jumps straight into the senior ranks following his short novice campaign but Mullins hinted at versatility by saying "he'll gallop and stay all day" and that soft ground won't bother him. Connections are shooting for the stars and this exciting chaser looks capable of rocketing there.

ANTHONY HONEYBALL

WHILE most jumps trainers were gearing up for one of the busiest spells of last season, Anthony Honeyball was forced to shut his Dorset stable for nine weeks from December due to a virus in his yard and ended the troubled campaign with just 14 winners. That was 20 fewer than the previous season and a return to his earlier progressive form would make him a trainer to watch this winter.

Ms Parfois, Acey Milan and stable favourite Regal Encore all bagged Listed wins in the first two months of 2018, while Midnight Tune was a Grade 2 novice hurdle winner in the same period. Honeyball hopes the addition of some well-bred young horses can revive that momentum this season. "I'm really happy with the horses we've bought. They look great and I hope they can fly the flag for us this season," he said in the autumn.

Acey Milan was one of those hit by the virus, which meant he started the new season on a handicap mark of 126 over hurdles. "He could be very well handicapped," the trainer said. "He could be a 140 or 150 horse. He'll get three miles and handles heavy ground."

Kilconny Bridge, Bleue Away and Kid Commando are names to note out of the point-to-point field, according to Honeyball, who hopes Midnight Tune could be the one to fill the gap in high-quality chases left by Ms Parfois' departure for the breeding paddocks.

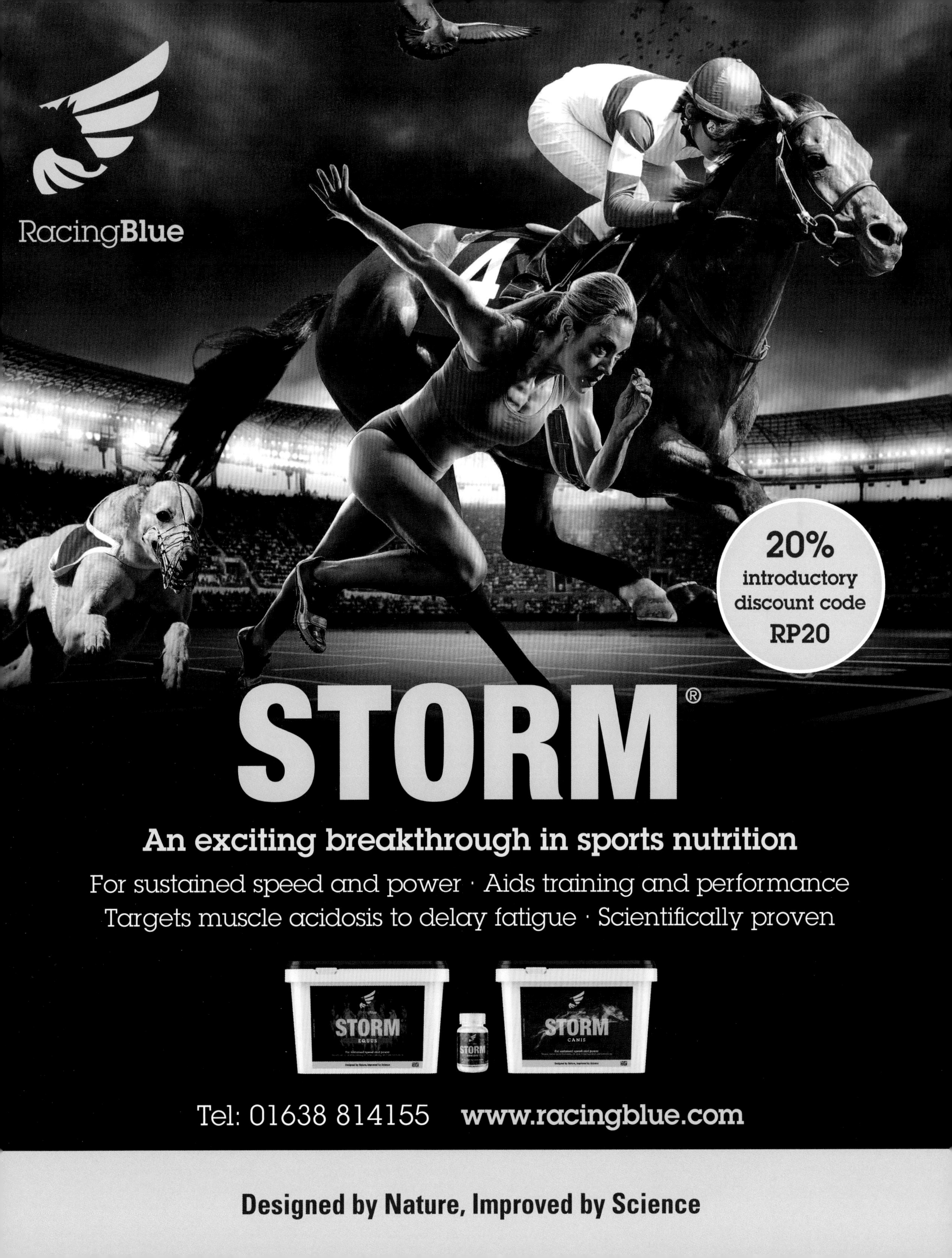
RacingBlue
4
20%
introductory
discount code
RP20
STORM®
An exciting breakthrough in sports nutrition
For sustained speed and power · Aids training and performance
Targets muscle acidosis to delay fatigue · Scientifically proven
STORM
EQUUS
STORM
STORM
CANIS
Tel: 01638 814155 www.racingblue.com
Designed by Nature, Improved by Science

LOGICIAN

WITH established superstars Enable and Stradivarius hogging the limelight, Logician started 2019 in the wings at John Gosden's yard but gradually took a more prominent role and next year he could be an even bigger star of the show.

In any normal stable, in any normal year, Logician might have taken top billing after completing a five-race winning run with a course-record victory in the St Leger, just four months after making his racecourse debut. He was favourite for all five starts and was in cruise control nearly all the way, most impressively when quickening clear to win the Leger by two and a quarter lengths.

The feeling was that the final Classic had been targeted because it was there to be won, rather than because Logician was seen as a stayer, and Gosden said afterwards this was a mile-and-a-half horse in the making.

Even more excitingly, after a few days' thought, the trainer was looking at dropping him back to a mile and a quarter. "The plan is to target the Coral-Eclipse next year with Logician, who is not short of speed and should handle the drop in trip," he said. "Something like the Group 3 Brigadier Gerard Stakes could be a warm-up race."

Gosden has won the Eclipse four times in the past eight years with Nathaniel (2012), Golden Horn (2015), Roaring Lion (2018) and Enable (2019) but even so it is a bold plan. Paddy Prendergast snr was the last to land the St Leger followed by the Eclipse, with Ragusa in 1963 and 1964, although at that time the great Irish trainer was the third to achieve the feat in seven years.

Logician won his first two starts over a mile and a quarter and a sign of how highly Gosden rated him came on his third outing, over a mile and a half at Newbury, as Dettori later related: "He made me go to Newbury one evening and ride him in a handicap – I thought it was a bit strange. Obviously he had big targets in mind."

The targets have become even bigger now but there is no disguising Gosden's regard for the son of Frankel. "He won in a course-record time with one flick of the stick," he said after the Leger. "He's a gorgeous horse, he's done nothing but improve through the year. He's amazing to be around, he's got this wonderful stride and this laid-back attitude. We'll put him away now. I don't want to be taking advantage of him in any way."

FUSIL RAFFLES

NICKY HENDERSON landed an unprecedented clean sweep of the three big juvenile hurdles with Pentland Hills taking the Triumph at Cheltenham and the Anniversary at Aintree before Fusil Raffles completed the hat-trick in the Champion Four Year Old Hurdle at Punchestown.

Both are top-quality prospects for Henderson but the more intriguing of the pair is Fusil Raffles, who had to miss Cheltenham and Aintree after suffering a nasty cut to his leg when winning the Adonis Hurdle at Kempton in February on his British debut. Before that he had been sick in the depths of winter following his move from France, and to come back and win a Grade 2 followed by a Grade 1 was an excellent achievement.

Henderson was certainly impressed by his resilience in securing Punchestown victory by two and three-quarter lengths over Fakir D'Oudairies, who had finished a neck behind Pentland Hills in the Anniversary. "I was nervous whether he'd be quite ready for a battle like that, mentally and fitness-wise, because we started training him again only three weeks ago," he said.

Daryl Jacob, the rider for owners Simon Munir and Isaac Souede, was already anticipating what Fusil Raffles might produce with a smoother preparation. "You'd definitely expect improvement – when he won the Adonis it surprised us a little bit," he said. "Hopefully he's got a big season ahead of him."

MARCO GHIANI

MARCO GHIANI followed in the famous footsteps of Frankie Dettori when he began his riding career in Britain with legendary trainer Luca Cumani and the young Italian jockey might yet emulate his illustrious countryman by landing the British apprentice title.

The association with Cumani was cut short by the trainer's retirement in 2018 but Ghiani, 20, has continued to build his reputation in Newmarket and gone on to form a prolific partnership with Stuart Williams. He made the perfect start with victory on his first ride for the trainer and an exceptional autumn helped him reach the notable 20-winner mark at a strike-rate of 16 per cent.

"He's worked hard to get where he is," Williams said. "We sit down and go through all the races and do our homework and it's paying dividends with the results he's getting and the opportunities he's being given.

"He's listening to me and his jockey coach, and Luca gives him insights as well."

Ghiani, who scored 100 per cent in the British Racing School's fitness test, had his claim reduced to 5lb when he hit 20 winners but looks well placed to use this year's success as a springboard to do even better in 2020.

"I always want to win more but this whole season is about becoming better and having more experience," he said. "It's important now to keep getting rides. Next year I'd like to be champion apprentice. It's the biggest goal I have."

PIERRE LAPIN

PIERRE LAPIN'S progress was held up as a juvenile, just as it was for his half-brother Harry Angel in 2016. If the Roger Varian-trained colt makes anything like the same strides as Harry Angel from now on, he will be competing at Group 1 level before long.

The son of Cappella Sansevero is already a Group 2 winner having landed the Mill Reef Stakes at Newbury on his second start, which came four months after an impressive winning debut at Haydock. He "fell away" after that first run according to Varian, who showed typical patience to bring Pierre Lapin back in top form.

Harry Angel also won the Mill Reef following a four-month break before going on to land the July Cup and Haydock Sprint Cup at three, and Pierre Lapin matched him with a Mill Reef-winning Racing Post Rating of 111.

"He's not a rock-and-roll two-year-old," Varian said. "He's a horse for next year and will have learned a lot. I think he's a six-furlong horse – when he's stronger I think he'll be faster."

JESSICA HARRINGTON

A 72-YEAR-OLD trainer with a bulging CV might seem an unlikely inclusion in a list of the precocious and the promising, but Jessica Harrington is finding new ways to excel and is definitely one to watch in 2020.

The County Kildare trainer, the most successful female trainer of all time at the Cheltenham Festival and one of the select group – man or woman – to have won the Cheltenham Gold Cup, Champion Hurdle and Queen Mother Champion Chase, has increasingly turned her attention to the Flat with eyecatching results.

First there was Alpha Centauri, the brilliant miler who won four Group 1 races in 2018, and now there are a whole host of exciting fillies following in her wake.

Chief among them are Cheveley Park Stakes winner Millisle and Albigna, who landed the Prix Marcel Boussac eight days later. There are only four Group 1 races in Europe restricted to two-year-old fillies and remarkably Harrington won two of them, with different horses.

If that was the whole story, Harrington would have had a memorable Flat season and have good reason to be excited about next year. But it wasn't. Overall 2019 was by some distance her best campaign on the Flat and all year her stable was the dominant force with two-year-old fillies in Ireland.

One of the other leading lights was Alpine Star, a half-sister to Alpha Centauri who won the Group 2 Debutante Stakes at the Curragh in August. Owned and bred by the Niarchos family, like Alpha Centauri and Albigna, she was pencilled in for the Marcel Boussac before being ruled out with a pulled muscle. The fact that Albigna could stand in successfully at Longchamp, only three weeks after she was found to be in season following a flat effort in the Moyglare Stud Stakes, was testament to Harrington's strength in depth.

Cayenne Pepper also had a Group 1 setback when only fourth to Quadrilateral in the Fillies' Mile at Newmarket, but stable jockey Shane Foley had picked her as his favourite of the group and she remains a promising prospect. So do potential middle-distance filly Silence Please and Valeria Messalina, who was beaten only a neck in the Group 3 Oh So Sharp Stakes at Newmarket in October.

Assessing her two Group 1 winners, Harrington said: "They've never worked together but Albigna has showed she stays a mile, so she looks more like a Classic filly." She is not the only one in Harrington's powerful string.

ANGUS VILLIERS

BRITISH pony racing has emerged as a good source of riding talent and Angus Villiers so impressed Richard Hughes at an event in Bath in 2018 that the former champion Flat jockey offered him a job at his Weathercock House yard in Lambourn.

"I was walking back to the weighing room and Mr Hughes came up to me to offer me a job," Villiers said. "I couldn't really believe it. That was probably one of the best days of my life."

Villiers, 17, has made the most of the opportunity in his first year, reaching double figures by the start of October, and could hardly have asked for a better mentor than the three-time champion. "Richard loves to keep it simple and he's great to work for," the rider said after his first win in May.

With more than 100 rides in 2019, he has caught the eye of a number of trainers and his high-profile rides have included Intisaab in the Ayr Gold Cup for David O'Meara and the Alan King-trained topweight Who Dares Wins in the Cesarewitch.

Villiers' 7lb claim makes him a good option for big handicaps in 2020 and gives him the platform for his stated ambition of a push for the apprentice title.

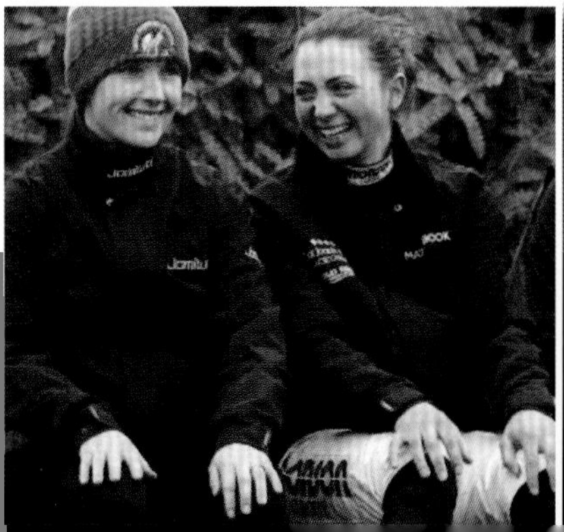

LOSTINTRANSLATION

COLIN TIZZARD has been in the thick of the Cheltenham Gold Cup action in recent seasons, notably with 2018 winner Native River and the unlucky Cue Card, and the Dorset trainer has another serious contender on his hands with Lostintranslation.

The majority of the exciting chaser's novice campaign was spent tackling intermediate distances, where he had a long-running rivalry with Defi Du Seuil that culminated with a courageous second in the 2m4f JLT Novices' Chase at the Cheltenham Festival, but it was on his first start beyond three miles that his true potential was revealed.

His six-length thrashing of RSA Chase winner Topofthegame in the Grade 1 Mildmay Novices' Chase at Aintree was one of the performances of the season by a novice and earned Lostintranslation a lofty Racing Post Rating of 165. That is the same as Native River achieved when winning the same race in 2016 and only 2lb below Cue Card's best RPR as a novice chaser.

Lostintranslation now has the honour of being in the same box Cue Card once occupied at Tizzard's star-studded yard and there is no hiding the expectation.

"The world's in front of him," said Tizzard of the seven-year-old. "I've had some great chasers and I hope he can be the next one. Everything we do is to try to make him into a Gold Cup horse. He was very competitive at two and a half miles and he stays well too. He has everything you need to be a Gold Cup contender and he's ready for the big time."

While the Paul Nicholls-trained Topofthegame has been ruled out for the season with injury, several other second-season chasers have excellent credentials and competition should be fierce as they step up to take on established stars such as Al Boum Photo and Kemboy.

Despite a troubled preparation, Santini pushed Topofthegame all the way in the RSA in March and has long been the apple of Nicky Henderson's eye, while RSA third Delta Work landed a third Grade 1 of the season in convincing style at Punchestown at the end of April. Tizzard has not ruled out Mister Malarky, who was fourth in that high-quality RSA, making his presence felt in the big league this season either.

It takes a good horse to bridge the gap to the top in their second season over fences but this crop looks well above average and Lostintranslation could easily be the leader of the pack.

JONJO O'NEILL JNR

IF PEDIGREE has anything to do with it, Jonjo O'Neill jnr is a shoo-in for the British conditional jockeys' championship. Following family tradition as he carves a career in the saddle over jumps, he is out to emulate his dad, who won the conditionals' title in his youth before a record-breaking riding career that included two champion jockey crowns and countless big-race wins.

The achievements of O'Neill snr, now a Cheltenham Gold Cup and Grand National-winning trainer, inspire rather than stifle his 21-year-old son. He is determined to succeed on his own terms and the signs were positive last season when his 30 winners included a first Cheltenham Festival victory on the Joseph O'Brien-trained Early Doors in the Martin Pipe Conditional Jockeys' Handicap Hurdle.

That was in the colours of JP McManus, owner of the Jackdaws Castle establishment where O'Neill

snr trains, but equally as important for the young rider's career was his Lanzarote Handicap Hurdle success aboard the Jennie Candlish-trained Big Time Dancer in January.

"It was a turning point," he said. "It was in different colours for different people and you need the Saturday winners on ITV. That's what gets you noticed. There was no better time to get the message out there that I'm my own man."

The conditionals' title is in his sights – "You can't think about it until December time really but it's something I'd like to do" – and along the way O'Neill jnr could well get more chances to make his own name in some of the bigger races.

CHAMP

BEING named in homage to 20-time champion jockey Sir Anthony McCoy brought a high degree of expectation even before Champ started his racing career and, while he did not quite live up to the tag last season, he still has time to prove he is the equine real McCoy over fences.

A champ he was not as a novice hurdler, falling 1lb short of Minella Indo in the three-mile-plus division of the Anglo-Irish Jumps Classifications, but he was a high-class performer.

The Nicky Henderson-trained seven-year-old won everywhere in his first full season over hurdles except possibly when it mattered most at the Cheltenham Festival, where he could manage only second behind City Island in the Ballymore Novices' Hurdle. He was successful in his other five races, notably at Grade 1 level in the Challow Novices' Hurdle at Newbury before Cheltenham and in the Sefton Novices' Hurdle at Aintree afterwards.

He raced at around 2m5f until being stepped up to 3m½f in the Sefton, where he proved a point to Henderson. "With next season in mind, we wanted to find out whether he'd be a three-miler," he said. "He's starting to live up to his name and has a lovely nature."

As well as Champ, owner JP McManus has Birchdale as another potential top novice chaser in the yard. "It could easily be the strongest bunch of novice chasers I've had," Henderson said.

If Champ emerges as the best of them, he could well be a champion.

HARRY BENTLEY

HARRY BENTLEY improved his personal-best tally of winners for the fifth year in a row in 2019 and looks well placed to continue on the upward curve.

Best known for his association with top sprinter Limato, Bentley made his mark as the gatecrasher to the party on Gold Cup day at Royal Ascot 2019 when he halted the Frankie Dettori juggernaut with victory on Biometric in the Britannia Handicap. Dettori looked set to complete a five-timer as he went for home on Turgenev but, in a fevered atmosphere, Bentley held his nerve with a well-timed run.

It was a first Royal Ascot success for Bentley, 27, who is benefiting from a solid relationship with Biometric's trainer Ralph Beckett. He is not stable jockey but takes most of the rides and the team had another red-letter day in October when Bentley rode four winners on the Future Champions card at Newmarket, part of a five-timer on the day for Beckett.

One of the Newmarket wins came in the Group 3 Zetland Stakes on Max Vega, who will be in Beckett's team of promising three-year-olds for 2020 along with Kinross, Mascat, Wyclif and Tomfre, another from the Newmarket four-timer.

Beckett is known for bringing his horses to a peak as their careers develop and the same might be said of his influence on Bentley. "He's ridden plenty for us over the past year and he's coming of age now," the trainer said.

With strong backing, more big days surely lie ahead for Bentley.

McFABULOUS

PART-OWNER Chris Welch has an exciting first horse in McFabulous, widely seen as the best novice hurdle prospect in Paul Nicholls' yard after capping a fine season in bumpers with victory in the 2m1f Grade 2 contest at Aintree's Grand National meeting in April.

Welch heads the five-strong Giraffa Racing syndicate and, while he may have been caught up in the moment at Aintree, he was entitled to dream big with the half-brother to Grade 1-winning chaser Waiting Patiently. "He's some horse and will win the Gold Cup as well in a few years!" the euphoric owner said. "He's a beautiful horse and Paul has done a great job with him. It was terrifying to watch but he's decent, I think."

Bought for €88,000 as a three-year-old, McFabulous won three of his four bumpers – returning with sore shins from his only defeat at Cheltenham in November 2018 – and his form looks strong. Thebannerkingrebel, the one-length runner-up at Aintree, won his first two novice hurdles in the summer and the well-regarded Faustinovick (trained by Colin Tizzard) and Silver Hallmark (Fergal O'Brien) were second and third to McFabulous in another good race at Newbury in March.

Nicholls, who had schooled McFabulous even before his bumper debut, is clearly excited. "He's got a huge engine," he said. "He jumps really well and is very much one to look forward to in novice hurdles."

ENVOI ALLEN

CHEVELEY PARK STUD is better known for its Flat horses but owners David and Patricia Thompson, who enjoyed Grand National success with Party Politics in 1992, have recently increased their involvement over jumps and their diversification reaped a quick reward at the 2019 Cheltenham Festival when the Gordon Elliott-trained Envoi Allen landed the Grade 1 Champion Bumper and A Plus Tard took the Close Brothers Novices' Handicap Chase for Henry de Bromhead.

Envoi Allen came with a Flat price tag at £400,000 following a ten-length Irish point-to-point win in February 2018 and quickly proved himself one of the best young prospects with a four-race winning run in bumpers, culminating in his Cheltenham victory by three-quarters of a length from Blue Sari. Such rapid development surprised and delighted connections, with jockey Jamie Codd saying: "He's an incredible horse, 17 hands and a big baby, and now he's won a point and four bumpers."

Chris Richardson, managing director of Cheveley Park, explained the owners' thinking for the jumps move. "They obviously love what goes on at the stud and on the Flat, but David felt the winters were a bit slow. He wanted to have some fun and some entertainment during the winter. He wanted to have runners at Cheltenham and now two have won," he said.

With Envoi Allen, who is "going to end up being a three-mile chaser one day" according to Elliott, the fun could be only just starting.

KLASSICAL DREAM

AFTER four Champion Hurdle triumphs in six years, Willie Mullins has been denied the crown in the past three seasons but it might not be long before he is back on the throne if Klassical Dream continues his impressive progress.

That was certainly the way Mullins was thinking in late summer when he looked ahead to another exciting season with his team. "Klassical Dream has done well over the last few months," he reported. "He didn't do anything wrong last season and you'd like to think he looks as good as some of our past champion hurdlers."

The signs are auspicious. Klassical Dream hit a Racing Post Rating of 158 when he won the Supreme Novices' Hurdle at the Cheltenham Festival and then went even higher to 160 with his Champion Novice Hurdle victory at Punchestown. By comparison, the best of Mullins' Champion Hurdle winners as a novice was Faugheen with an RPR of 161, while Hurricane Fly was on 158 and Annie Power on 155.

In the Anglo-Irish Jumps Classifications, Klassical Dream was champion novice hurdler on a mark of 160, 5lb ahead of Getaway Trump. That clear advantage over his peers reflected his superiority by four and a half lengths over Thomas Darby at Cheltenham and by five and a half lengths against Felix Desjy at Punchestown.

Going into Cheltenham, Mullins was confident in what he had. "[After] his work at the Curragh [the previous weekend] we came away thinking here was one who would take a lot of beating, no matter what he came up against," he said.

That view only strengthened at Closutton over the summer, but there is more to Klassical Dream's story than pure ability. Plenty of emotion is wrapped up in there too.

The five-year-old runs in the colours of Joanne Coleman, whose late husband John dreamed of a Cheltenham winner but sadly never got to see it. His widow carried his ashes in her handbag at the festival.

"It's a very poignant victory for us," Mullins said at Cheltenham. "John had a lot of cheaper horses with me and then he retired and sold his business two years ago and said, 'here's a few quid, go and buy me a Cheltenham horse', and this is the horse. Jo and family will be invited over for a few beers to celebrate this winner. I'm delighted it happened for the family."

There will be double delight if it happens again at the 2020 festival.

ARIZONA

ARIZONA became Aidan O'Brien's ninth winner of the Coventry Stakes in June, which in itself marked him out as a top prospect. Two of the trainer's previous eight winners did not make it to the track after their juvenile season but the other six included three Classic winners, a top sprinter and a Group 1-placed miler, with just one flop.

O'Brien was already looking well ahead after Arizona's Royal Ascot success, describing him as "a fine, big horse for next year", and the form was boosted when three others from the first seven later joined the Ballydoyle colt as Group 2 winners.

The problem for Arizona afterwards was that he kept bumping into one or other of Godolphin's crack team of juveniles. He was only fourth behind Earthlight in the Prix Morny, with heavy ground a legitimate excuse, and then was beaten twice by Pinatubo.

He was a distant third in the National Stakes at the Curragh but put up much more of a fight in the Dewhurst, finishing two lengths behind as Pinatubo forged ahead on Newmarket's uphill finish. A Racing Post Rating of 116 puts him in the Classic/Group 1 picture for 2020 and, even if Pinatubo remains out of reach, there should be plenty of options with him.

O'Brien kept saying he needed good ground, which he got only once after Royal Ascot. In the right conditions, he looks set to be a major player at the top level.

Reporting by Nick Pulford, Lewis Porteous and Jonathan Harding

IN THE PICTURE

Top effort at Aintree as Worsley completes incredible comeback

WINNING on your first ride over the challenging Grand National fences is an impressive achievement and even more so if it is gained after relinquishing and then regaining the lead against one of your most formidable rivals. Imagine, on top of that, doing all this less than 18 months after suffering a broken back in a race fall.

Those were precisely the circumstances in which Tabitha Worsley won the Randox Health Foxhunters' Chase at Aintree in April when she produced a rousing ride on Top Wood to outpoint the better-fancied Burning Ambition, the mount of leading Irish amateur Derek O'Connor.

Top Wood led over the final fence of the 2m5f contest but Burning Ambition swept into the lead at the Elbow on the punishing run-in. O'Connor's mount looked all set for victory at that stage but, with the mud flying and the crowd cheering, Worsley somehow conjured a renewed effort from Top Wood to wrest back the advantage and score by two lengths.

Worsley, the fifth woman to win one of the most prestigious jumps races for amateur riders, said: "It's amazing. Top Wood is such a tough horse. The other horse came flying past us, but Top Wood is not one who wants the stick too much, so I tried hands and heels as much as I could and he just stuck his neck out for me. He's a hero."

Victory crowned an incredible comeback for Worsley, 24, who had broken her back in November 2017 in a crashing fall over hurdles at Ludlow. Having suffered displaced and fractured T11 and T12 vertebrae, she was told to expect a minimum of six months before she could return to normal activity. Yet she was back riding in point-to-points in barely half that time and had a racecourse winner over hurdles just four months after the fall. Shortly after that, she broke her collarbone and spent another period on the sidelines.

Worsley, who still has rods in her back and shoulder, was celebrating her 14th racecourse success. "I've lost count of how many point-to-point winners I've ridden but I rode my 13th track winner at Market Rasen [the day before] and wanted to get off that number as soon as possible. To do it over the National fences is unbelievable."

Top Wood's trainer Kelly Morgan revealed after the race she had been up all night bathing Top Wood's foot in ice after he had trodden on a stone.

"He's incredibly tough," she said. "He's been branded a monkey but I've never believed it because all he's ever done for us is try. When he got headed he stuck his neck out. He's just so brave."

Pictures: JOHN GROSSICK (RACINGPOST.COM/PHOTOS)

#FeelTheExcitement
HEALTH
R LIFE
ANDOX
RANDOX

Final Furlong

Stories of the year – from the serious to the quirky

Doctor makes riding history

RACECOURSE doctor Guy Mitchell made a piece of sporting history in July when he became the first person with one eye to take part in a British horserace.

The 45-year-old, son of former trainer and champion amateur rider Philip Mitchell and half-brother of jockeys Jack and Freddie Mitchell, finished last of eight in an amateur riders' handicap at Newbury but it was the taking part that counted most. A fortnight later, on his second ride, he finished a close fifth in a blanket finish at Windsor.

Those rides fulfilled a long-held ambition for Mitchell, who had his right eye removed at the age of six following the development of a tumour but rode out for his father as a young boy and applied for a jockeys' licence aged 16 and again while at university. He was never given a full explanation as to why his application was not approved and gave up before deciding in his forties to try again, this time supported by BHA chief medical adviser Dr Jerry Hill.

▾ Guy Mitchell makes his racecourse debut at Newbury in July

Mitchell, who works regularly at Ascot and Goodwood, said: "I had to go through more stringent tests because of my eye but I passed everything, including all the fitness tests. The only person who beat me on those is aged 17."

On the reaction of others, he said: "My dad is very happy, my mum thinks I'm mad and my wife reckons I'm having a mid-life crisis, although the truth is that not being allowed to ride in races has, for me, been a full-life crisis.

"It's too easy to be angry about the past. I have to look forward, not backward. I need to seize this opportunity. The rules say you can ride until at least 55, and I'm only 45, so I still have plenty of time."

Bet without leaving our *fastest* ever app.

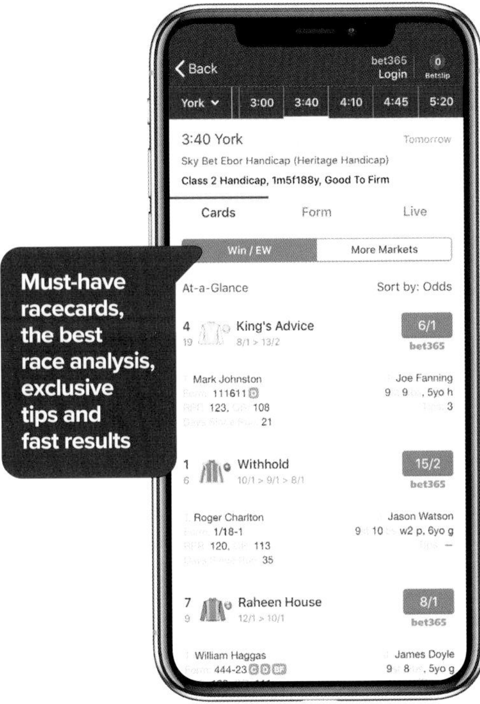

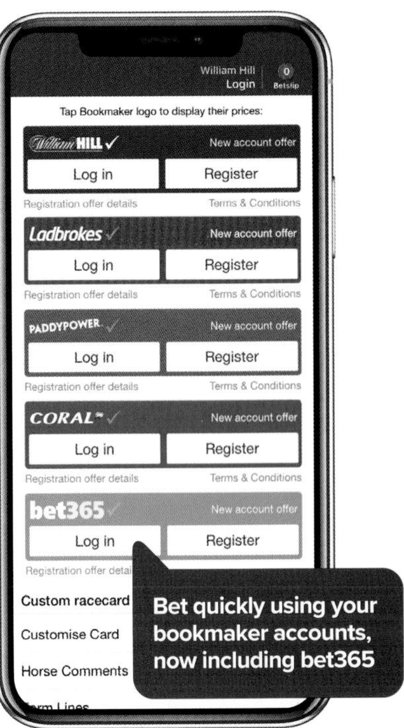

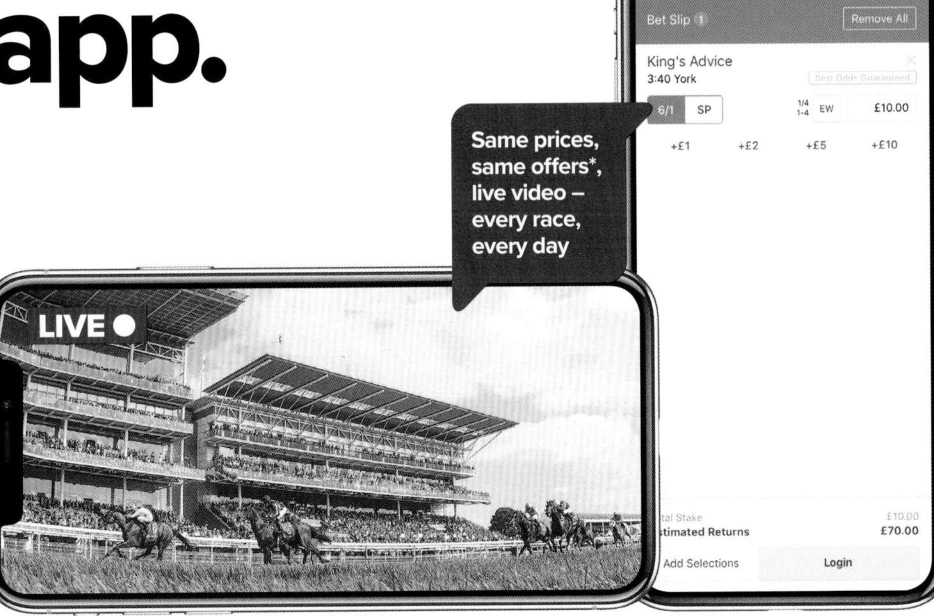

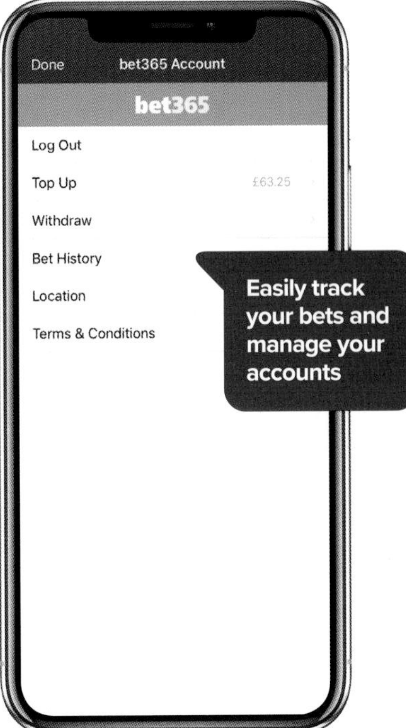

Download or update the free app

The Must-Have App For The Must-Have Info

RACING POST

Racing Post backs responsible gambling. 18+ begambleaware.org 0808 8020 133
*Best odds guaranteed, money back offers, Risk free bets. Price promise. Extra places.

RACING POST ANNUAL AWARDS

Our pick of the best of 2019

From top right, Bryony Frost on Frodon, Crystal Ocean, RSA Chase, Tiger Roll, Cieren Fallon, King's Advice and Defi Du Seuil v Lostintranslation

HORSE OF THE YEAR (FLAT)
Enable
Brilliant and brave, she gave her all and we loved her more even after Arc defeat

HORSE OF THE YEAR (JUMPS)
Tiger Roll
Aintree legend or Cheltenham legend, take your pick. Quite simply a legend

RACE OF THE YEAR (FLAT)
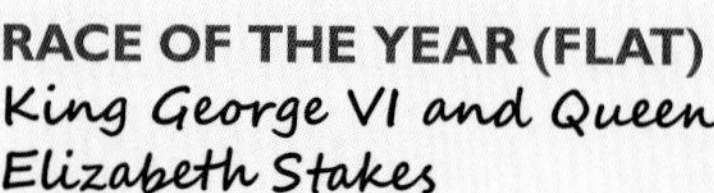
King George VI and Queen Elizabeth Stakes
Grundy v Bustino in 1975 is still revered; Enable v Crystal Ocean in 2019 will be too

RACE OF THE YEAR (JUMPS)
RSA Novices' Chase
Topofthegame was the aptly named winner in a thriller of the highest class

RIDE OF THE YEAR (FLAT)
Frankie Dettori, Enable, King George VI and Queen Elizabeth Stakes
Later he told us in detail what he did, and what he did that day was utterly breathtaking

RIDE OF THE YEAR (JUMPS)
Bryony Frost, Frodon, Ryanair Chase
Horse and rider were never more as one than on this unforgettable afternoon of high emotion

RISING STAR
Cieren Fallon
The name is slightly different from the famous father's; the son's latent talent is the same

COMEBACK OF THE YEAR
Billesdon Brook
Finally proved her 2018 1,000 Guineas was no fluke with a return to Group 1 success on the same course in the Sun Chariot

SURPRISE OF THE YEAR
Sovereign winning the Irish Derby
The Epsom also-ran ran away at the Curragh in a 33-1 stunner under Padraig Beggy

UNLUCKIEST HORSE
Crystal Ocean
Finally won his Group 1 but met Enable in irresistible form and then injury intervened

MOST IMPROVED HORSE
King's Advice
Started on a mark of 71 and eight wins later took a Glorious Goodwood handicap off 108

DISAPPOINTMENT OF THE YEAR
Masar
Once again a sporting decision to keep a Derby winner in training came to a sorry end

BEST 'I WAS THERE' MOMENT
Thursday of the Cheltenham Festival
Ryanair Chase/Stayers' Hurdle day is not usually the hottest ticket of the festival but it was this time

BEST RIVALRY
Defi Du Seuil and Lostintranslation
The score was 2-1 to Defi after three tough battles in a highly competitive novice chase division but it's still hard to say which one is best

HERE'S SOME GOOD NEWS . . .

IJF's Peter O'Sullevan House opens

Cieren Fallon tries out the equipment; inset, Sir Anthony McCoy at the official opening

PETER O'SULLEVAN HOUSE, the Injured Jockeys Fund's third rehabilitation and fitness centre, was officially opened by IJF president Sir Anthony McCoy in Newmarket on October 11.

Located next to the British Racing School, the £6m development complements the two existing IJF centres at Oaksey House in Lambourn and Jack Berry House in Malton.

The Newmarket centre, named in honour of the legendary racing commentator who died in 2015, has state-of-the-art rehabilitation and fitness facilities including physio treatment rooms, a hydrotherapy pool and a gym.

McCoy said: "With the opening of Peter O'Sullevan House, we have three rehabilitation and fitness centres around the country that help and support jockeys both during and after their careers. I can't tell you how lucky racing is to have this and how proud I am to be here. If facilities like these had existed when I started riding, I might still be going today!"

Brough Scott, chairman of the IJF, said: "It is entirely fitting that this remarkable centre is named after Peter O'Sullevan, one of racing's greatest supporters and friends. He would have been extremely proud of what we, in racing and at the IJF, have achieved in completing our third centre."

Sweet sixteen for Ireland's oldest winner in 32 years

SEE DOUBLE YOU became the oldest winner in Ireland for 32 years with victory at the age of 16 in a 3m1f handicap hurdle at Roscommon in July.

Trainer Ronan McNally was close to tears as his veteran star rolled back the years to record the 11th success of his career. "It's unbelievable," he said. "He did it at 15 but it's hard to believe he'd do it at 16. I bought this horse the day after my dad was buried, so he means a lot to me. The whole family loves him."

See Double You was ridden by talented conditional Darragh O'Keeffe, who was born just three years, one month and 26 days before his mount.

He was the oldest horse to win on the track in Ireland since The Ladys Master landed a Tipperary handicap chase for Matthew Duggan and Frank Berry in 1987.

AND HERE'S SOME BAD NEWS . . .

Towcester closes

Any hopes that racing might return to Towcester were extinguished in October with the news that the owners of the course had sold its ten fixtures for 2020 to Arena Racing Company.

Towcester, which had a racing tradition going back to 1876, had gone into administration in August 2018 citing "trading difficulties" and was subsequently sold to Fermor Land LLP, a company linked to owner and racecourse chairman Lord Hesketh. A search for an operator to run the Northamptonshire jumps track was unsuccessful.

The news was greeted with dismay by leading figures in jump racing. "It's tragic we're losing these types of places," said Nicky Henderson, the most successful trainer at Towcester over its last five years. "Towcester was unique and lovely. It was a proper National Hunt course with a friendly atmosphere."

Sir Anthony McCoy, who had a memorable day at Towcester in 2013 when he rode his 4,000th winner, said: "It's sad for racing when something like this happens and you have to worry about the business model of the sport when a track like Towcester is closed."

Gary Moore, who trained what proved to be the final winner at Towcester when Atalanta's Gold landed a mares' handicap hurdle on May 21, 2018, said the decision to close the track was "disgusting".

Towcester became the fourth British course to face closure in the past decade. Great Leighs shut in 2009 before reopening in 2015 as Chelmsford City, while Folkestone and Hereford closed in 2012, although jump racing returned to Hereford in 2016.

Miraculous recovery of abandoned racehorse

ONE of the year's most heartwarming stories centred on a former racehorse who once cost 240,000gns being nursed back to full health by an Irish rescue charity after she was found abandoned and in a desperate state.

War Celeste, a daughter of War Front who was bought by the China Horse Club as a yearling, had been in training with David Wachman but never raced and was sold to be a broodmare in 2015. She was found three years later locked in an abandoned yard in County Cork, along with ten other horses, as well as dogs and ponies.

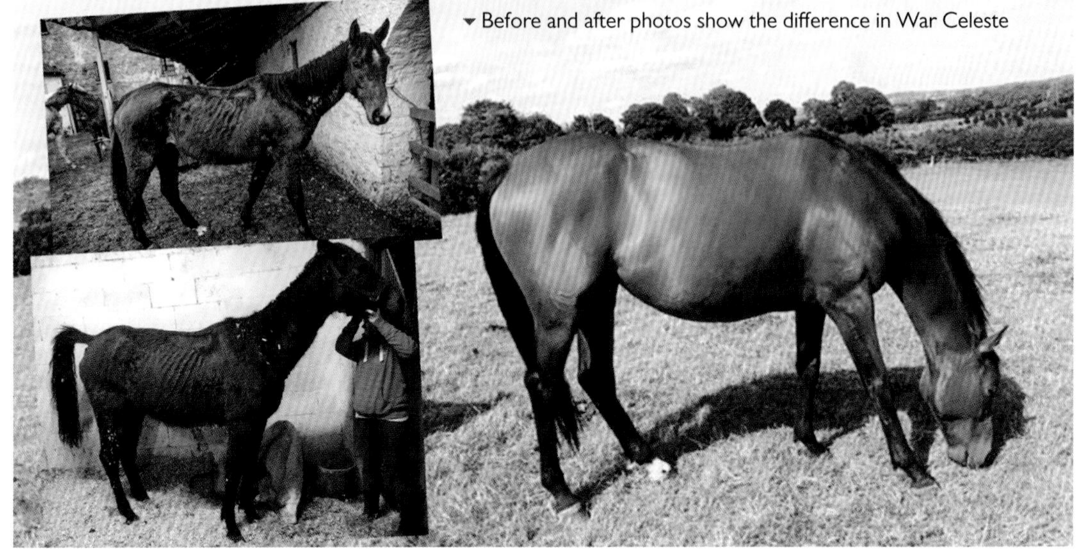

▾ Before and after photos show the difference in War Celeste

Some of the animals could not be saved and the outlook for War Celeste was not good after she was taken in by the My Lovely Horse Rescue charity.

Maddie Doyle, a volunteer for the organisation, said: "We have seen this [neglect] before but never on this scale. War Celeste had two rugs on her, but no bedding, so she was lying in manure, urine and there was no sign of feeding. She was a bag of bones underneath the rug."

She added: "Thoroughbreds aren't easy animals to bring back from the brink. When they get to that level you just think, 'We've lost them'. You look on the outside and think they need feeding, but there can be so much wrong on the inside with damage from starvation."

Thankfully, after months of hard work, the charity released photos showing the miraculous turnaround in War Celeste's health.

"We don't give up too easily," Doyle said. "We put in a lot of time and we have a team for weekly assessments, feeding and farriery work and she did it, she recovered. It's in the name 'War' – she's a fighter and came through it.

"It's a huge pleasure seeing her. Thoroughbreds are sensitive creatures, she's a very kind, gentle and good-natured mare, and it gives us a great feeling seeing her how she is now."

● The horse who was zero, not hero

CHICAGO SOCKS achieved a certain notoriety in September when he made his debut at the age of nine and was retired after being beaten so comprehensively that he was given a Racing Post Rating of zero.

The gelding finished last of ten in a 1m3½f novice stakes at Windsor and was estimated by the Racing Post racereader to have been beaten around half a mile – too far for the judge to measure it by conventional means and even further than the 223 lengths shown in the result.

William de Best-Turner, a part-time trainer who has had three winners from around 350 runners since 1999, said: "The only reason I ran him was to see if I could get any spark as he doesn't want to go unless he's surrounded by other horses.

"I was hoping other horses would carry him along, but unfortunately that didn't work. He's not a racehorse. He's going to go and be a dressage horse now."

Racing Post handicapper Sam Walker said: "He earned an RPR of zero for his dismal performance – and he only got that because we don't give negative numbers.

"Generally speaking horses rated in the 40s and low 50s struggle to win a race. Those rated in the 20s and 30s are effectively not even competitive racehorses in Britain. Then there's Chicago Socks."

● Britain's oldest racing fan dies at 110

RALPH HOARE, featured in last year's Racing Post Annual as Britain's oldest racegoer, sadly died at home in Gloucester in January at the age of 110.

Hoare, who remembered 1945 Derby winner Dante and being at Cheltenham for Arkle's three Gold Cups, made a memorable return to the festival in 2018 as a guest of the racecourse.

Recalling his grand day out to see Native River's Gold Cup triumph, his daughter Kate Hughes said: "I would say it was the most exciting and eventful day of his year. He was up at 8am and didn't flag all day. He enjoyed the sound of the Cheltenham roar once again and backed three winners and two second places.

"Throughout the day he was asked to pose for photos and the most memorable one was with Jack Kennedy, the youngest jockey on the course – their handshake spanned the 91 years between them."

She added: "My father died peacefully in his sleep. He was compos mentis and interested in sport until the end.

"His last words to my brother were: 'What was the Plymouth Argyle score on Saturday?'"

Classic milestone for father and son

JOHN and David Egan became the first father-and-son combination to take part in a British Classic since Victorian times when they lined up alongside each other in the 1,000 Guineas at Newmarket in May. David, 19, was third behind Hermosa on 7-2 favourite Qabala, while father John, 51, rode outsider Garrel Glen to finish 12th.

The last father and son to ride against each other in a Classic were Tom Cannon snr and jnr in the 1888 1,000 Guineas and St Leger.

"Even though she was favourite, I was surprised as I had no nerves and I treated it as just another race. You can't allow yourself to get carried away with all the fuss," said David, who had made his Classic debut the previous day when he came second last on outsider Emaraaty Ana in the 2,000 Guineas.

His proud father said: "I've always told David to treat the big races like any other and he rode a cool race. This is just the start and hopefully there will be other days for him."

▲ John and David Egan before their rides in the 1,000 Guineas

Another big day was not far away for David, who had his first Royal Ascot winner the following month when he rode 4-1 favourite Daahyeh to victory in the Group 3 Albany Stakes.

"I'm sorry, I'm getting a bit emotional, but I'd like to thank everyone who has helped me get to this point," said the 2017 champion apprentice, who had turned 20 two days earlier. "For someone young like myself coming to ride a favourite in a fancy race at Royal Ascot, it's a big deal. Everyone has worked hard for me through my whole life and it's great to thank them on these big days. I followed in my dad's footsteps and he's been a huge influence on my career."

● Uttoxeter runner gets pizza the action

NOT many horses live up to their name as well as Reckless Behavior, who in March managed to run out of Uttoxeter racecourse and get all the way to the town square before being caught near a Domino's Pizza shop.

The bizarre episode began when the tapes went up for a 2m4f handicap chase. The seven-year-old whipped round, leaving rider Sean Bowen on the floor, then crashed through the rails and escaped from the track. He made his way across several roundabouts on the streets of Uttoxeter before being caught.

Clerk of the course Eloise Quayle said: "Thankfully a woman came out of a pub as he was cantering down the high street. He slid to a halt and she got hold of his rein and he just stood there."

Reckless Behavior was pulled up on his next start but trainer Caroline Bailey then decided to fit him with a hood and that seemed to do the trick as he won a 3m handicap hurdle at Southwell in May. He was on his best behaviour that day.

● Trainer and horse celebrate win in pub

DID you hear the one about the horse walking into a bar? Of course you did, but it really happened in May when Irish owner-trainer Tom Shanahan took Charle Brune into his local for a few pints.

Shanahan had something worth celebrating. At the age of 53 he had his first winner when Charle Brune landed a 2m handicap hurdle at Wexford, having been backed from 33-1 to 10-1, and quickly made it two when the six-year-old defied a 6lb penalty to win another 2m handicap hurdle at Tipperary the following day. No winner in 30 years as a trainer and then two in the space of 26 hours.

Having won "a right few quid" backing Charle Brune, Shanahan made sure to mark the occasion. "It's a once-in-a-lifetime thing for me," he said.

"I was on my way home from Tipperary and I told Maggie Ryan in the Horse and Hound pub in Dualla that I was coming in for a few pints and I wouldn't be on my own.

"I told her the horse was coming in with me and that I wasn't taking no for an answer. It was tricky getting him in through the doors but the horse trusts me inside out. We had some craic, it was mighty!"

Shanahan, who runs a drain cleaning company in his day job, added: "It's been some week. An unforgettable one. It will never happen to me again but, I'll tell you, I enjoyed every second of it.

"We had to make the most of it. I just had to bring the horse into the pub."

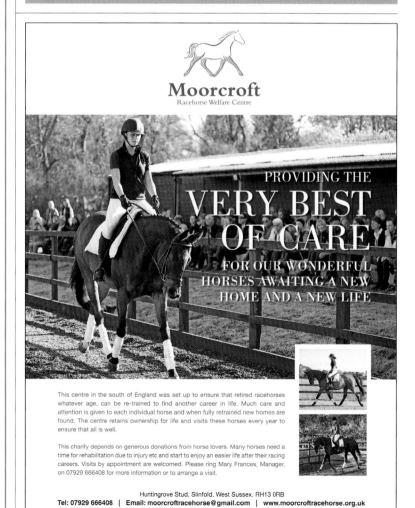

A-Z of 2019

The year digested into 26 bite-size chunks

B

M

A is for all-weather. Once the poor relation to turf racing, artificial surfaces have come into their own and juvenile champion Pinatubo followed Enable and Stradivarius, two more stars of 2019, in making his debut on the sand.

B is for bombshell. Gigginstown House Stud shocked the jump racing world in May with the announcement that it would wind down the operation and no longer buy new stock.

C is for the Curragh, whose €81 million redevelopment endured a difficult first year, with long queues, disappointing attendances, claims of elitism and a grandstand that makes a screeching noise when the wind blows in the wrong direction.

D is for demotion. Maximum Security went from first to 17th in the Kentucky Derby, with victory handed to Country House, after a controversial stewards' ruling on interference around the home turn.

C

E is for extremely able. Enable took centre stage again with wins in the Eclipse, an epic King George and the Yorkshire Oaks before going down fighting in her bid for a historic Arc hat-trick. And she'll be back to do it all again in 2020.

F is for FOBTs and funding. A new maximum stake of £2 for the controversial betting shop terminals led to numerous shop closures. That, in turn, was responsible for actual and threatened reductions in prize-money and a winter boycott of some Arena Racing Company fixtures.

G is for gone. Towcester was closed for racing in October after the jumps course's ten fixtures were sold to Arena Racing Company.

H is for hijab. Khadijah Mellah took racing to the front pages and the evening news with her groundbreaking victory in the Magnolia Cup at Goodwood in traditional Muslim headwear.

I is for internationalism. The racing world became a little smaller as Japan watched Deirdre land the Nassau Stakes at Goodwood and a global audience saw Australian wondermare Winx make a triumphant farewell at Randwick with her 33rd straight victory.

J is for jiggers. A notorious addition to the racing lexicon after Melbourne Cup-winning trainer Darren Weir was banned for four years by Racing Victoria in February following the discovery on his premises of three of these illegal devices used to give electric shocks to horses during training.

K is for kin. Pinatubo, Earthlight and Victor Ludorum, three top-class two-year-old sons of Shamardal, all won Group 1 races for Godolphin to set up an exciting Classics campaign in 2020.

L is for legend. Tiger Roll kept on rolling as he became the first since Red Rum to win back-to-back Grand Nationals, as well as scoring at the Cheltenham Festival for the fourth time.

M is for marathon but one that from 2020 will be slightly shorter, with a review into the National Hunt Chase leading to the Cheltenham Festival's 'four-miler' being reduced in trip to 3m5f 201yds following a controversial 2019 renewal in which only four of the 18 runners finished.

N is for numerical dominance. They just kept on adding up for Altior, Mark Johnston, Winx and Aidan O'Brien in a year packed with record-breaking feats.

O is for OBE. British champion jump jockey Richard Johnson went to London to visit the Queen after his inclusion in the New Year's Honours list.

P is for party pooper. Waldgeist spoiled the expected celebration of an Enable hat-trick with his late swoop to Arc victory, giving Andre Fabre an amazing eighth win in France's biggest race.

Q is for quadruple (again). The remarkable Stradivarius took all four legs of the stayers' £1m bonus for the second year in a row and is another of John Gosden's stars who will be in search of more riches in 2020.

R is for redemption. Paul Townend bounced back from his Punchestown low the previous spring with Al Boum Photo to hit the biggest high in the Cheltenham Gold Cup.

S is for shutdown. British racing was dramatically halted for six days in February to control an outbreak of equine flu.

T is for top. Where Ruby Walsh and Noel Fehily finished when they announced their retirements after Grade 1 wins at Punchestown and Cheltenham respectively.

U is for understudies. Seamie Heffernan and Padraig Beggy stepped up from supporting roles at Ballydoyle with their respective triumphs for Aidan O'Brien on Anthony Van Dyck in the Derby and Sovereign in the Irish Derby.

V is for value. Mustajeer, bought by owner David Spratt for 50,000gns in 2017, won approximately 12 times that amount for first prize in the £1m Ebor.

W is for the whip, the subject that just won't go away. In Ireland new directives limited riders to a maximum of eight strikes per race, leading to a spate of suspensions, while in Britain Charlie Fellowes got tongues wagging when he said his first Royal Ascot winner, Thanks Be, should have been disqualified because jockey Hayley Turner broke the whip rules.

X is for X-traordinary. Racing enjoyed a series of magical festival Thursdays from Cheltenham with Frodon and Paisley Park to Royal Ascot with Frankie Dettori and Goodwood with Khadijah Mellah.

Y is for young at heart. The 16-year-old See Double You became the oldest winner in Ireland for 32 years with victory in a handicap hurdle at Roscommon in July.

Z is for zoom. Battaash rocketed down the York straight in the Nunthorpe Stakes to break the mighty Dayjur's long-standing five-furlong record.

W

Racing in Britain was suspended for six days in February after an outbreak of equine influenza. This is the inside story of how the drama unfolded

HOW BRITISH RACING CAUGHT THE FLU

By Lee Mottershead

IT WAS on the 4.48pm to London Waterloo that British racing first discovered it had caught the flu. David Sykes was one of the passengers on that train, heading away from Kempton Park station, when he heard the news. Brant Dunshea was on a platform at Clapham Junction, Nick Rust was in his car and Donald McCain, a figure unluckily central to this story, was in a petrol station on the A49.

That Wednesday afternoon McCain had been travelling back from Ludlow, where Dry Lightening contested the track's maiden hurdle. Prior to being declared on Tuesday morning the horse was scoped, in line with McCain's recent policy. A clean bill of health was given. All was not right, however, with three other members of the team. "We've been dealing with bits and bobs of bugs all winter," says McCain, who, like so many trainers, has been seeing countless dirty noses.

Frustratingly, the troubled trio were not getting better. The discharge from their noses was not yellow but grey. Antibiotics were failing to ignite a recovery. McCain wanted to know more, so on Wednesday morning vet Alasdair Topp was called into action. "I asked him to take swabs of the three horses," says McCain. "I wanted to make sure we were hitting the bug with the right medicine."

Topp dispatched the swabs to the Animal Health Trust in Newmarket, from where Dr Richard Newton, the organisation's director of epidemiology and disease surveillance, was soon to pass on bad news to the BHA.

RACING POST

Friday, February 8, 2019 — racingpost.com — £2.90

LOCKDOWN

Equine flu forces British racing into shutdown for at least six days

. . . but the show goes on

Best bets for Dundalk and Jebel Ali

BONANZA BOY

Martin Pipe and Peter Scudamore on a famous win in the Racing Post Chase 30 years on

12 PAGES OF TOP FOOTBALL CONTENT FOR THE WEEKEND'S MATCHES

ASSIST

Senior members of the BHA had been at Kempton for an executive team meeting, after which chief executive Rust, chief regulatory officer Dunshea and Sykes, the director of equine health and welfare, stayed on for a meeting with RSPCA chief executive Chris Sherwood and advisers David Muir and Mark Kennedy.

Rust left Kempton in a car he was due to sell that evening. He was driving first to see jockeys' agent Dave Roberts at his home near Guildford, and then on to Herne Bay, the Kent seaside home of the woman set to be the car's new owner. Sykes and Dunshea left Kempton by train but not together. It was to Sykes that Newton delivered the bad news. The swabs from the three McCain horses had produced positive tests for equine influenza.

Sykes then tried to contact the colleagues he had recently left. They were not answering. Rust had his phone switched off for his meeting with Roberts. To his fellow Australian Dunshea, Sykes sent a text message. It contained just two words, both written in capitals. 'CALL ME.' "I was on a busy train and knew from the tone of the text it would be important, so I waited until I got off at Clapham and then called David from the platform," says Dunshea. They set about telling everyone who needed to know, including the BHA's racing department, which began researching the movements of McCain's latest runners.

McCain learned the news from Topp, who messaged him to say they needed to speak immediately. McCain pulled off the A49 and dialled Topp's number. "He told me there and then we had three cases of equine influenza," says McCain. "Those two words sounded terrible. I was shell-shocked. Not in a million years did I think it was going to be equine flu.

"Alasdair told me he would pass on my number to David Sykes, who rang me and talked me through the whole situation. He explained what would happen with immediate effect. He told me I would definitely be shut for at least two weeks and that Alasdair would come in on Thursday to blood test and swab every horse in the place."

McCain resumed his journey home. Rust was a long way from home and a long way from finishing his day. After saying goodbye to Roberts and switching on his phone he was confronted with 11 messages. While driving to Kent, Rust spoke with Dunshea and Sykes, discussing options and the best way forward.

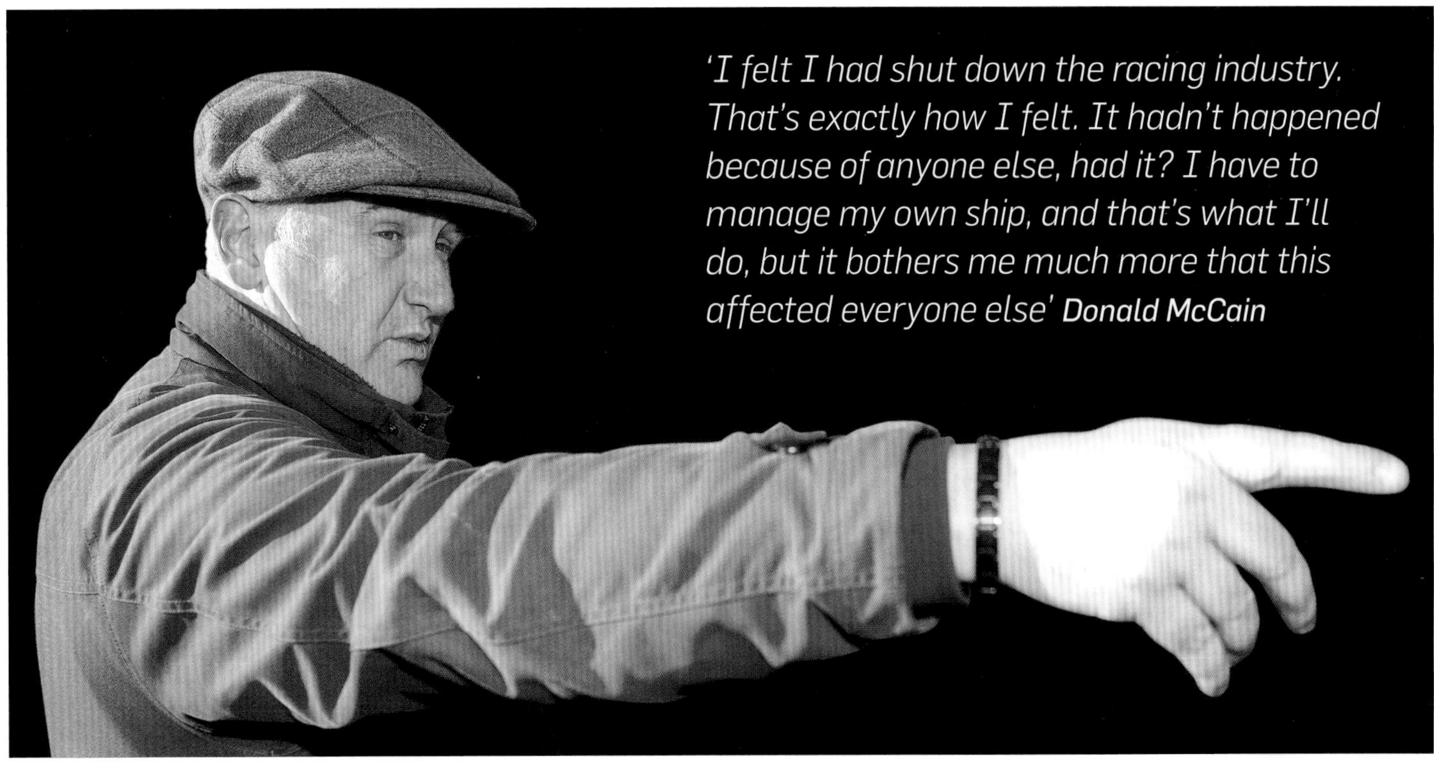
'I felt I had shut down the racing industry. That's exactly how I felt. It hadn't happened because of anyone else, had it? I have to manage my own ship, and that's what I'll do, but it bothers me much more that this affected everyone else' Donald McCain

★★★★

BACK in London chief operating officer Richard Wayman and head of racing Paul Johnson set about creating a list of all the trainers who had been represented that day at Ludlow and Ayr, where McCain had also fielded a runner, and Wolverhampton, which on Monday welcomed one of the trainer's rare Flat performers. If, as seemed likely, a yard would need to be isolated if one of its horses had been in contact with potentially infected McCain horses, that yard could surely not have runners in the immediate future. The Thursday fields were going to be badly affected. Time was not on the BHA's side but crucial decisions had to be made.

"To be frank, we wanted to make sure we had a bit of air cover for what we were planning to propose," says Rust. "Although it was clear to me we had two very experienced people in Brant and David leading the response, I wanted us to consult with more experts."

It was decided those consultations would be with the BHA's industry veterinary committee. A conference call was arranged for 9.30pm. Before that took place it was obvious a communications plan was needed rapidly. That job was handed to Robin Mounsey, the BHA's head of media.

The veterinary committee met, as arranged, at 9.30pm. Dunshea and Sykes presented their view that Thursday's racing had to be called off. "I explained to them the decision we made was going to be very important because we couldn't undo what happened tomorrow if we didn't do it right," says Sykes. "We normally meet twice a year and have some pretty frank and vigorous discussions, but there was nobody in that conference call who felt we should be racing on Thursday. The decision we made that night was absolutely the right one."

Rust was now on a train to St Pancras, after handing over the car and being taken by its new owner's son to Herne Bay station. "My own view was we shouldn't take any chances and we should show good leadership," he says.

He made a series of calls, including one to Newbury supremo Julian Thick, whose showpiece Saturday fixture was plainly in doubt. Also busy on the phone was Mounsey, who received the help of Nick Craven, Weatherbys' communications director. Craven accessed the company's text service to inform trainers that racing on Thursday had been cancelled, while Izzy Desailly at the Professional Jockeys Association informed members of the news. At the same time Mounsey began writing a press release and tweet that informed the world of the equine influenza outbreak at 11.23pm.

★★★★

AS THE world found out British racing had been halted, so did McCain. "It flashed up on my phone," he says. "That was heartbreaking. I felt I had shut down the racing industry. That's exactly how I felt. It hadn't happened because of anyone else, had it? I have to manage my own ship, and that's what I'll do, but it bothers me much more that this affected everyone else."

The following day, one from which fixtures at Doncaster, Ffos Las, Huntingdon and Chelmsford had been expunged, McCain set about informing his owners that Bankhouse Stables was home to the horses with flu, although most already knew.

The BHA had not named him but instead stated horses from the infected stables raced at Ayr and Ludlow. McCain was the only trainer to have had runners at the two meetings. "Every single one of my owners was great," he says.

McCain began making the calls at 6.30am. The West Sussex-based Dunshea, who worked until after 1am on Thursday morning, was out of bed at 4.30am and on the first train to London. Rust was already in the capital having spent the night at The Caledonian Club, where numerous further calls and emails were completed. He had eaten nothing since the Kempton RSPCA lunch. "By Thursday morning I was starving," he recalls. "I confess I went to a dreadful McDonald's just along from the BHA's High Holborn office. I manage to avoid it most mornings, but given I hadn't eaten since the Kempton lunch I decided I needed breakfast."

Dunshea was in High Holborn soon after the door of the BHA's office building was unlocked at 7.30am. "I realised we needed to set up a control centre and coordinate everything from there," he says.

A meeting room named Frankel was chosen to be that control centre. Senior executives gathered for a 9am update, while all trainers with horses who might have come into contact with McCain's were advised of biosecurity measures and asked not to move horses. As

▸▸ *Continues page 224*

the BHA began to organise a new veterinary committee meeting, corporate affairs manager Ross Hamilton briefed government and parliamentarians.

For McCain, it was all somewhat surreal. Topp and a colleague had begun testing every horse, while grooms were working in a racing yard now closed to outsiders. A television cameraman ensconced himself outside the main entrance.

For Dunshea, who was working for Harness Racing Victoria when equine influenza struck his homeland in 2007, the experience was eerily familiar. "It felt like I was living an identical day to one I lived 12 years ago," he says.

"The most important thing you have to focus on at a time like that is doing everything you possibly can for the sport you love. Everything else comes second. From that past experience I knew it was all about containing and controlling horse movement. That was critical."

Also critical was keeping stakeholders informed of what was happening and what was likely to happen. A message had previously been put out saying a verdict on whether racing could take place from Friday onwards would be announced on Thursday evening. Conversations conducted through a WhatsApp group of key BHA personnel, in the Frankel room and elsewhere, made it obvious the sport needed to know sooner.

Another meeting of the veterinary committee was brought forward. Based on the available science it was proposed racing should be stopped until Wednesday at the earliest. Again there was unanimity. "We came to the view we had to lock this down and get control of it," says Rust.

Sykes and Dunshea agreed. It was clear horses from stables across the breadth of the country would have to be tested for a disease whose symptoms can take three days to become visible. With the swabs then needing to be processed at the Animal Health Trust's Newmarket headquarters, there was no way an operation of such scale could be completed quickly.

An unrelated meeting of the BHA's industry-wide Racing Group had begun at 2pm. At 3.45pm Wayman brought Dunshea into the room. Those inside it, including trainers, administrators, racecourse representatives and members of the media, were told of the suspension by Dunshea, who bore the face of a man lacking sleep. The tie was still on but the top button of his pink shirt was undone.

"I have no doubt we did the right thing," says Sykes. "Things like streptococcus [strangles] and rhinopneumonitis [herpes] are contagious but nowhere near as contagious as equine influenza. It is super contagious. It's a bushfire."

This is an edited version of an article that appeared in the Racing Post on February 11

▲ Extra care: Precautionary measures are taken at Daniel Kubler's yard in Upper Lambourn in February with disinfectant spraying, checking of vaccination information in horse passports and attention to cleanliness around the stables

What happened next

The equine influenza outbreak did not spread widely and the majority view was that the BHA had been wise to act prudently in ordering the shutdown, which was to last for six days from Thursday, February 7.

With racehorse swabs being transported nationwide, the Animal Health Trust was required to carry out more tests in five days than it would in a normal year.

On shutdown Sunday it was revealed four horses in the care of Simon Crisford had tested positive. That news was unwelcome. Much better received was the BHA's announcement the following day that racing would resume on the Wednesday, albeit in a risk-managed way, one stipulation being eligibility to race was dependent on a horse having had a flu vaccination in the previous six months, rather than the standard 12 months.

The BBC's evening news programmes carried an upbeat report from the comeback fixture at Plumpton, whose bosses were happy to have survived the flu. Even happier was the Jockey Club, which had understandably been deeply concerned the Cheltenham Festival might be lost.

It was not lost but plenty of money was forfeited elsewhere. In total, it was estimated that the brief shutdown had cost the racing and bookmaking industry in the region of £15m.

One of the main victims was Arena Racing Company, whose financial hit was thought to be roughly £2m. Even so, chief executive Martin Cruddace spoke for many when he said: "Notwithstanding we are the racecourse group that has suffered the most, we think the BHA excelled, acting completely and entirely properly. If it has been perceived as an overreaction, then maybe overreaction was the right reaction."